C000170820

A WOMAN AT WAR

U.S.

A WOMAN AT WAR

MARLENE DIETRICH REMEMBERED

Edited by J. DAVID RIVA GUY STERN, ADVISORY EDITOR

A Painted Turtle book
Detroit, Michigan

© 2006 by Wayne State University Press, Detroit, Michigan 48201. All rights reserved. No part of this book may be reproduced without formal permission. Manufactured in China.

10 09 08 07 06 5 4 3 2 1

Library of Congress Cataloging-in-Publication Data

Riva, J. David, 1961–
A woman at war : Marlene Dietrich remembered / J. David Riva ;
Guy Stern, advisory editor.
p. cm. — (A painted turtle book)
ISBN 0-8143-3249-8 (cloth : alk. paper)
1. Dietrich, Marlene. 2. Entertainers—Germany—Biography.
3. Dietrich, Marlene—Friends and associates. I. Stern, Guy, 1922–
II. Title. III. Series.
PN2658.D5R57 2006
791.4302'8092—dc22
2005034962

All photos courtesy of the Riva family's private collection, the Landesarchiv Berlin, and the Marlene Dietrich Collection of Filmmuseum Berlin.

∞ The paper used in this publication meets the minimum requirements of the American National Standard for Information Sciences—Permanence of Paper for Printed Library Materials, ANSI Z39.48-1984.

Design by Michele Myatt Quinn
Typeset by Maya Rhodes
Composed in Minion and Gill Sans

CONTENTS

FOREWORD

The first time my mother was to appear at the famous Café de Paris in London, the inevitable question of who would or could serve to present her became a delicate as well as diplomatic problem. This wasn't Vegas, nor was the Café de Paris, although technically a nightclub, anything but the most exclusive venue second only to command performances of royal stature.

After many meetings, a rather brilliant concept was suggested—instead of one man proclaiming, "And here, ladies and gentlemen, lords and ladies—Miss Marlene Dietrich," there should be a whole slew of famous men, a different one each night of her engagement. The term "famous men" was not meant lightly. Any category of artistic fame was eligible, and to top it off, these gentlemen would also be required to write their own personal introduction. Terrific idea! But two solid weeks worth of famous men all willing to write, proclaim their written adoration in person—*and* in white tie and tails? Impossible, was my first reaction. Oh, there were certainly enough famous males in England, there always are—but not all might be willing, even if persuaded that their talents extended to putting down their own thoughts on paper.

For some incalculable reason, none of these potential hurdles bothered my mother. She simply telephoned Noël Coward, Ernest Hemingway, Jean Cocteau, Kenneth Tynan, and any of the other world-famous men that were a part of her circle of intimate friends. She asked them to compose a suitable piece, appear or choose someone equally illustrious to say it for them, and that was that. And in the end, that was Dietrich. Not only were her professional instincts always correct, but, like a general, her assurance and execution of a concept were perfection.

Some of the best and most genuine words ever written by those many talented men were not for a Hollywood movie star—a glamor queen about to warble a few banal songs in a rococo night club—but for one they considered one their own—a human being they had chosen to admire. This, too, is what made Dietrich "Dietrich."

The next time my mother appeared at the Café de Paris, the roster of men was replaced by one of women. While this, too, was theatrically successful, somehow the ladies never quite reached the heights of lyrical prose of their counterparts. My mother forgave them, which in Dietrich's world meant that she forgot them and framed the glowing tributes of Coward, Hemingway, and all those that deserved such an honor.

What *was* it that made Dietrich so unique, regardless of her justifiable fame and beauty? Many have and have had the same, and yet without achieving that special timelessness of international intrinsic acceptance that that sheer name, Marlene Dietrich, engenders. Even I, who knew her best, who sat in judgment of so many faults, never once could fault her innate intelligence nor her soldier's courage to act upon her hatred of Hitler that began long before it became fashionable. Long before the burning of books, the shattering of glass, Chamberlain's appraisement, or the orchestration of death, my mother seemed to actually feel the evil about to destroy the land of her birth, the same evil that would forever change the concept of humanity. In this, her hatred was never private, never silent. Her loathing was vocal, passionate, and influential. She handed it on for others to acknowledge and join; fame carries with it the duty to use it beyond its origin.

This book, this work of words spoken by so many with such genuine admiration, is astounding. It is this longevity of homage that impresses me, that proves once again that Dietrich did her duty—which she and she alone chose to do. For that she truly deserves to be remembered.

MARIA RIVA

ACKNOWLEDGMENTS

This work is dedicated to many people, not the least of which are represented in these pages, including my mother, Maria. Beyond that I have to remember my father, William Riva, who graduated from Wayne State University and remained, throughout my life, my best friend. Finally, I could not have done any of this without the love and support of Darren Davis and his family; I will always appreciate their friendship.

I would like to extend additional thanks to Dr. Christine Fischer-Defoy, the senior researcher for this project; to Werner Sudendorf, curator of the Filmmuseum Berlin; and to Silke Ronneberg of the Filmmuseum's Marlene Dietrich Collection.

I am told that in the world of publishing it is beyond rare to find a publisher or editor one can actually work with and remain friends with after a project is put to rest. If that is true, then I have been blessed by the participation of the director of Wayne State University Press, Jane Hoehner, and my editor, Carrie Downes. I would also like to thank Mr. Lindsay Scott for his help on a tight deadline.

INTRODUCTION

J. DAVID RIVA

One morning in the early 1980s, I found myself alone with my grandmother—Mass, as we used to call her—while she made breakfast. She was an accomplished cook who could cope with a single potato and a few leeks as well as a grocery list fit for a fine hotel and in both cases create a meal fit for a king. She was a talented woman at what her generation may have referred to as "survival" but we might better describe as "life." I was already in my twenties and had spent a good deal of time with her growing up. She was a force in our family, as well as the world, and she had no compunctions about it. What people thought of her or felt about her was, of course, important, but at the same time, these exterior opinions did little to influence her actions. She treated an informed dislike of her with respect, indeed as much as she discounted mindless adoration. Stupidity, as she called it, was worse than any disease. She spent a lifetime being as real as reality made her, and while this was not the most grandmotherly of deportments, she was for all intents and purposes a symbol of truth. It was, of course, *her* truth, but anyone who knows anything about Marlene knows that to her there was no distinction. During her life, when these two definitions came together—the real truth and her own truth—things happened, and happened in ways that only magicians could understand. The very walls of Jericho would have collapsed under this kind of force—and, in many ways, structures just as solid did.

As we sat there, eating her now famous scrambled eggs, I asked her about lots of things that I thought were important to her. I was a fairly inquisitive person back then. I asked her about my grandfather, Papi, about her singing, and finally the conversation came around to what my school chums thought of her, how they "didn't get it," but that their mothers and fathers did. "And just who are *they?*" was the response. I didn't know it then but it was a symptom of just being too tired to explain the world to yet another generation. The old world had gone, and I have no doubt that even she saw little value in dredging it up over a couple of eggs. Changing the subject, I asked her what her favorite part of performing was. I was interested at the time because I had just become an assistant talent agent at International Creative Management (ICM) in New York, and I felt, rather naively, that understanding the performer's psyche was important. Her answer was not immediate. In fact I had unwittingly caught her off-guard somehow—which was rare for her. She sighed and told me about how she constructed the order of songs, and how hard it was to find a "Burt Bacharach"—"only one of Bacharach," she would say. But halfway through her answer the conversation began to shift to performing, not in theaters but in the Ardennes forest and in USO camps during World War II. Slowly but completely, the entire discussion of performing was distilled into a reminiscence of what one would think was hardly a fond subject—her performing and serving in World War II. We spoke for an hour or so, which was a lot for Mass, and she told me things about the war and in effect about the world that I never knew—and more to the point never knew *she* contemplated. The work she did then was clearly the most important thing she had ever done for *herself*—this was *her* passion, not the celebrated show business passion created to sell tickets and the Dietrich image. *This* was personal, and in that instant I saw a window into a woman that few, including her family, ever had the chance to see. She was German after all, but as long as she was just an "actress," any inner conflict of nationality or political activism was hardly on the public agenda. But she wasn't what she appeared to be. She never was. And I, like so many before me and since, fell victim to her incredible ability as a manipulator of image. It was only when that window opened for an instant that her truth became evident. It was her key. All people have a key to their soul and their motivations in life, and despite the outward appearance, it may not be what is obvious. Most are hidden, practiced privately, and combined with the outward image to further enjoy but not reveal inner passion. Marlene was a consummate professional singer, actress, and personality, but she was so much more.

Many years later I was able to research and discover more about my illustrious grandmother and get to know the woman behind what the world and I knew of her. To my surprise there were many who knew this woman whom I had only glimpsed. Many of their accounts are contained in these pages. If nothing else I hope that these impressions will be combined with the better-known Dietrich and complete, as best as possible, the picture of my Grandmother Mass, Marlene Dietrich.

All those years ago, as she bused our breakfast dishes and began washing them, I told her that I would love to tell my school friends that she was in the war and that she had won the Medal of Freedom. With a small satirical smile she said, "Be sure to tell them what side I was on."

I suddenly realized
That I'm
An IMMIGRANT!
I never used that
Word before
(For *myself*
I mean!)
I read so much
About IMMIGRANTS
How they must
Adjust
To customs
And the words
Of foreign lands
Maybe because
I was never
Treated
Like an
Immigrant!
Nobody made
Excuses
For me.
Not then—
Not now.
Nobody cares
About my roots
Just as well!!!

Marlene Dietrich
April 15, 1985

VOLKER KUEHN

VOLKER KUEHN is an author, cabaret artist, and a director of film, television, and theater, as well as a specialist in cabaret history in Germany. From 1959 to 1963 he did one-night stands as an entertainer across America. He began his professional career in 1963 with a monthly satiric radio show on the Hessian radio station. Since 1970 he has been living as a freelance author and director in the western part of Berlin. He has written a number of books and produced television documentaries about the German cabaret and is renowned as an expert on German cabaret author and composer Friedrich Hollaender. Volker also wrote and directed a play titled *Marlene,* which starred Judy Winter and ran for more than five hundred performances.

Marlene Dietrich in old Berlin. For many who were with her then, she was a kind of prototype. The young Marlene's experiences mirrored what was going on in Berlin at the time. Things were happening for young people, and she took her piece of the action. She was very young, emancipated, undaunted by authority. She had exactly what they said Berlin had after World War I: a zest for life, being crazy, doing new things, doing things you normally wouldn't do, having no respect for narrow-minded people. In this great conglomerate where the arts had their first big renaissance, here in the Renaissance Theater, Marlene was in the thick of it. She was everywhere that something was happening. They were having fun at parties, and they knew how to draw on life's essence by celebrating. And Marlene played a big role in that. She impressed herself on people, who were enthusiastic about her, because she gave her opinions without any reservations. This was the message of the young people who had broken rank with the kaiser's [emperor's] era and said, now something brand new is going to begin.

I have to say that for the generation that I belong to, the '20s was not just a model, but a yearning. If someone would ask you, if you were born again, when would you like to live? In the '20s, of course. Why? Whether this was true in all cases I don't know, but for my generation, the '20s had everything that was worth living for. Not too limited, not too petty, but high class instead, liberal, somewhat expansive, which a young man wants. You find the boundaries drawn too narrow, with all the little gardens fenced in and always somebody there saying, "Forbidden, forbidden, forbidden." And all of that, according to our notion the '20s, was completely different then. Certainly that is connected to an enormous historical change. You've got to imagine in 1918 this insane first world war was at an end. This was a deep slump for the people, such that we can't imagine. It was the first great battle of materials. It was no longer a case of people. Machines were fighting each other, and there was sacrifice of life that had never happened on such a scale in history. Battles with materials—these tank battles in France, these battlefields. As a young person, I saw Verdun, where the French and the Germans had decided to be archenemies. For two and a half years they battled for five hundred meters. And it went back and forth over a period of years. And there were unimaginable numbers, hundreds of thousands, who bled to death. I don't know the numbers or have exact statistics on how many people died per square meter, I think it was two and a half. On a flatland which is huge. This insanity, which the Germans at home scarcely noticed because there was such hunger. 1917 must have been a terrible year of hunger. It was called the "turnip winter." Ten thousand died of starvation. All these things, this holy world of the Hollenzollerns. They were all monarchists and loved their emperor. At some point that all stopped, when the people noticed that the man was crazy, if he said, "We will accept further proclamations of war." You've got to imagine it. He broke a world war out of its boundaries, because he had his own problems. And the English—they were all related to each other. Then one would only have had to look at a globe, and should have with Hitler, and said, "Look how little Germany is, and look at the rest of the world." And then they said, "Who still wants to? Who wants to declare war against us? No problem." It was a form of complete insanity, where one would say later, you can only have that on drugs. Usually something like that wouldn't occur to an average lunatic.

This situation fell completely apart in 1918. The world concept was destroyed, the good old turn of the century that people remembered as being relatively good to them. At the beginning of the Industrial Revolution, people started to see the sun on the horizon. Then there was the military surrender, which for some people was terrible, especially the ones who were oriented toward Prussia. It was clear, something new had to come. The new thing was, if you want to call it that, an anarchy in business, politics, culture. It was good for culture, because there wasn't anything there. Klabund, a well-known poet who I think ought to be rediscovered, wrote a poem entitled "Berlin 1918." He describes only red flags, blood everywhere, and so on, and then at the end of every line he writes, "We want to have fun again" [Wir wollen uns wieder amüsieren]. And that exactly describes the mood. And you have to imagine that suddenly everything was possible that had not been before. The moral barriers fell away. Artistically everything was completely new in concept. Cabaret and theater reached back to the attempts by Dadaists in Zurich in the Cabaret Voltaire to put the world into question. That was related to the world war. Many of the people had been soldiers and had seen that it was insanity that had made them delusional. And then they said that the concept of art had to be rethought. Art is "shit" was their attitude. "Meaning is only found in nonsense." All this was no grammar school prank. Behind this there was unbelievable suffering, a lot of personal emotion. The cabaret had the same basis. That was the fantastic part, it was like giving blood to a child born nearly dead; it was barely a living corpse. Everything was caught up in censorship, the usual way of hearing and seeing for people who just plodded along. You had to say, "Well nothing much is going to happen here." When a thought occurred, it was censored, was forbidden. They had to have permission to do anything. All this suddenly ruptured. It was like a pressure cooker, and everything escapes through the pressure valve. The painting scene, music scene—they were all young people, who, don't forget, were in their twenties. A very young Brecht who came from the countryside to Berlin and caused a sensation by being different from the others. He dressed differently, was abusive, had no respect for authority. He'd go to important people, tell a director, "You ass, go away, we'll do it ourselves, you don't know anything." Just being young was valued, like today, but nowadays, being an old man, I'd describe them as too "lazy assed." There's nothing in them that says, "We're going to make this happen." They adapt to the situation and look at where the trend is going. The painter Franz Marc had a nice phrase for it back then, "Tradition, yes, but only where it's a case of *creating* tradition." They didn't want to pull out the old ones. They said, "*We* are the tradition, we are building it now, we're incorporating it. We're not going to sanctify everything from twenty years ago." This was the situation. Cabaret played a big role in this. Everyone did everything. German thinking had put things into little boxes for a long time, "This is type 'a' and this is type 'b.' This is serious music and this is popular music, and one has nothing to do with the other." If somebody made music type "b" like Marlene, then there had been the view, "We cannot appreciate it, it is somehow 'yucky.'"

As far as I can judge, Marlene was a real child of these "roaring '20s." In Germany we call it the Golden '20s, which is nonsense. Walter Mehring said, "I don't know what is supposed to have been 'golden' about it." It was terrible but fantastic, because there has never been a time since in which people were spurring each other on and were curious about everything, about *everything*—social, political, and above all cultural stories. Marlene was actually a Prussian to the end; that always fascinated me, because those two things didn't usually go together. She was living out the Prussian part, that discipline, and its very opposite, which weren't compatible at all. It fascinated me that Marlene was an independent person who was so emancipated that she didn't care a fig about what people thought of her. She lived whatever she wanted to, and that was at a time when she was not yet the big star, when it was not so easy to live that way. For example, the way she got along with colleagues, right at the beginning. There was her friendship with Cleo Waldorf, for example, who was a great role model to her. She was another person who said, "I'll live the way I want, and whoever doesn't like it, can leave. And if I have any troubles, I'll plough on through." That was the wonderful thing about this type of woman. They didn't want to be the little homemaker at the stove. They didn't want to just mix in, they wanted to set the accents. Marlene did just that. I've spoken with many who witnessed that cabaret period, especially where they set very clear accents, and said, "I want that; I don't want that." They weren't to be bought, although it is always difficult for actors to be hired for a job, if you want to see it that way. She always said early on what she wanted. Inside of Berlin's artist colony she was a prototype. But that didn't happen in western Germany, because the emperor's influence was still felt. Authority played a big role. We weren't able to shake that off until the '60s. You've got to imagine that in this country. It took a long time for us, because we had questions for our parents, our parents' generation, that never were answered. One day we finally said, "Fuck off" [in English]. That's the way it was. But in the '20s in the cultural scene it was quite different. It was a huge interchange. There was the way the people interacted. The most disparate people knew each other. They also had an amazing amount to do. They put together a cabaret revue sometimes in a week, day, or night. They still had the time to sit down with each other, to fight, to yell at each other on the street, and so on. The film people, the cabaret players, and so on were in lively interaction with one another, in a lively discussion. That also defines this period and, of course, the poor economy. Maybe they are interlinked. I'm not sure, and I wish it would be different. But always where the economic situation is precarious, where there is high unemployment, when people are insecure, that is always fertile soil for a cultural scene that can really spread out, that can really get a head start.

The National Socialists came very early. They were already there by 1922–23, which one always forgets, but nobody took them seriously. That was especially the case in Berlin, which had always been liberal. They thought, that's something for the

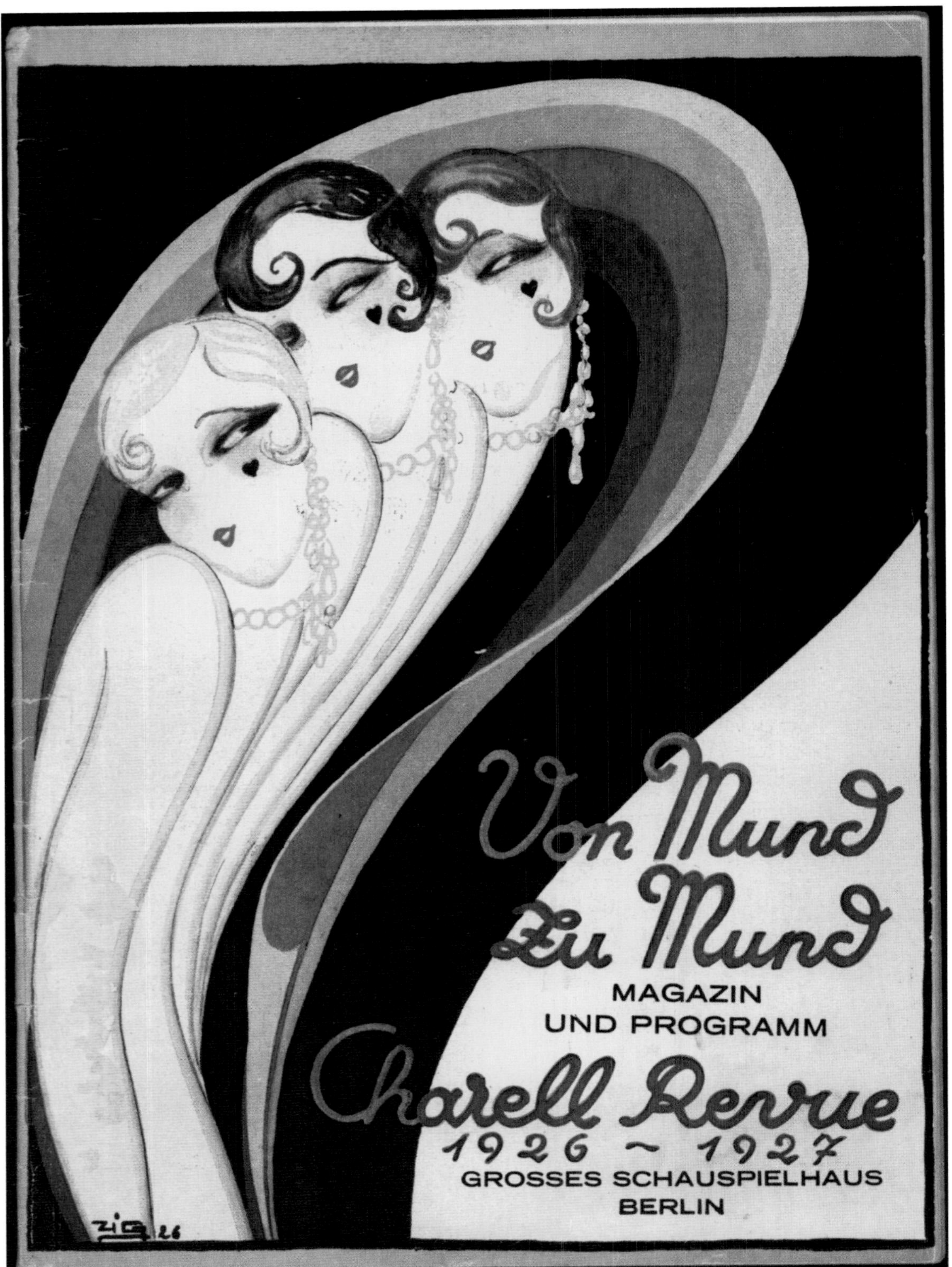

One of Marlene's many revues of the 1926–27 season.

provinces, they've all got a screw loose anyway, nuts. Then in 1923 there was the march to the Feldherrnhalle [Generals' Memorial Hall]. Then people thought that had to do with all the coups, the right-wingers. Those are the Reich army people, the soldiers who still can't give up, who haven't accepted that they really have lost the war. In any case the first traces were already in the culture. Not so much in the theater, and not so much in Berlin, above all. I think you have to differentiate between the provinces and Berlin. Berlin was always an international city, especially in the '20s. You shouldn't forget. People came from everywhere. Nowadays we are having this debate again. People forget what it meant in the '20s. Berlin got fresh blood. The people came from Galicia [eastern Europe] and here and there. There were so many Russians who came after the Russian Revolution, for example, who populated the Ku-Damm [Kurfürstendamm], so much so, that I'm told they had signs in the stores that said, "German spoken here, too." That was supposed to say in a joking way that all the nationalities were represented. Not only was the city enhanced culturally by this, but was fed by it. Komedien Harmonitz, if you read the biographies of these people, they came from all corners of Europe and came together here and did something brand new. That set the climate of the '20s, in Berlin, too. To make it short, this didn't affect the artists much, except where money was involved. For example, the UFA speaks another language. Why? Because early on there, Mr. Hugenberg, who was a German nationalist, had the final word. There were also already leanings toward the right. That always existed in Germany, and it was perhaps also a countermovement against this unbelievably open society that was developing there. For example, homosexuality was not a topic in the '20s. They were further along in the picture, like with homosexual marriage, than they are now. Things are being discussed now by the party on the right, the CSU, where you have to put your head in your hands and say, "We already took care of that in the '20s. It was only repealed and destroyed by the Nazis." I'm only pointing things out. Like [Magnus] Hirschfeld, the sexual philosopher. These were people who in that time made an enormous impression. In film, however, UFA got its start with the weekly newsreels in the first world war, which we always keep forgetting. But all its themes, this admiration of Friedrich the Great, movies about the Hohenzollerns, that was a little like what the illustrateds did in later years, what's happening in the king's court for example. It was always connected to an ultraconservative position. That started early on. In 1929, with the introduction of sound films, these topics were taken up. Maybe I ought to mention that in 1930, the year in which *The Blue Angel* was

Marlene with Margo Lion and Oskar Karlweis. Margo and Marlene sang "We're the Best of Friends" while both wore a lesbian symbol, a bouquet of violets.

filmed, no, *shown,* it was filmed in 1929 and 1930. You find out pretty quickly that *The Blue Angel* was an exception. Not like the other films, like *Dawning* [Morgenrot], which was a box-office hit. It portrays the soul-searching of a German woman, because she has to take leave of her husband, because he was on a U-boat in the first world war, when this was set, and the U-boat went under. Then these awful words are spoken, "We Germans do not know perhaps, how to live. But how to die, that we know." The main role was played by Camilla Spira. In March 1933 at the film premiere, with Mr. Goering and Mr. Goebbels in attendance, she received a big wreath from the UFA. She looked so "German," with blond hair and blue eyes, like a little Gretel, and the wreath said, "The representative of the German woman." And fourteen days later, they realized, "You have a Jewish father, we're so sorry," and she was shipped off to the concentration camp, to Westerborg. By good fortune she survived. She told me this story, and she told me that naturally she hadn't grasped the meaning of it. But she asked herself later if that was because artists didn't concern themselves much with political things. They said, "This Hitler, he's an Austrian, what do we have to do with that, he wouldn't dare to go to Berlin. We don't have to take it so seriously." The artists were more involved with themselves. Camilla Spira told me she was sitting with an attorney, and he said, "Did you hear? Hitler became the Reich's chancellor." She said, "That doesn't interest me much. I've got to play the White Horse, Baccherelle, and they're doing a new project, and I've got the tryout tomorrow at eleven. I'm still playing the evening appearance. I don't have time to worry about this stuff. In four weeks they'll have a new chancellor, it changes all the time." That was pretty much the mood.

There is a bitter moral to this that I should perhaps mention. Kurt Robicek was the head of Comedians' Cabaret [Kabaret der Komiker], which was the biggest cabaret in Berlin, on the Kurfürstendam. He had a comedian who was in the play whose name was Kurt Lilien. Both of them were Jews. In 1932 Robicek said, "Hey, Kurt, don't you think we ought to look around for a country where we could go if things continue the way they are?" And Lilien said, "I don't know, what you mean. Why?" "Well, don't you think there could be a situation here in Berlin, in Germany, where we'd have to leave?" And Lilien said, "How do you get that idea? No, I don't believe it." And Robicek said, "Haven't you read *Mein Kampf,* that book by Hitler?" Kurt Lilien said, "I don't read bad books." This story is true and in short it has a bitter moral. Kurt Robicek, who was at least aware enough that he had read *Mein Kampf,* he was forewarned. In early 1933 he left quickly for Vienna and to America. He went to New York and tried to reopen the Kabarett der Komiker, but it was a total flop. Kurt Lilien, who could not imagine it, who stayed in Germany, said, "I was in the first world war, I was an officer, I have the Iron Cross. Nothing will happen to me." He did not want to accept that suddenly there were destructive [atavistic] conditions in Germany that were unimaginable for a civilized people. He stayed here and ended up in the gas furnaces of Auschwitz.

In this mix of cultural "aliveness," Marlene was somebody who thought not too much would happen in serious theater, but instead when one was a cabaret player, because the cabaret was always the springboard for a theater career. She was in films more than she admitted later on. She was not entirely naive when she made *The Blue Angel,* but she looked around like the others here and was at every audition. I know that one of her first appearances in the cabaret field was for Spoliansky. Mischa Spoliansky was a very big, popular composer who wrote revues with a heavy jazz influence, played Gershwin, and Cole Porter. Gershwin visited him here in Berlin and was enthusiastic about his playing. He was a piano virtuoso. Around the corner here on the Kurfürstendamm he did a revue that exactly captured the feel of the times [zeitgeist]. They brought this entire debauched society onto the stage. There was an audition, and Marlene sang there like twenty or thirty others. The director pulled her out right away, saying, "Her voice. She's scratchy. Bring on the next one." Spoliansky didn't know her at all, but found something in her voice. He said, "Leave it . . . I'll set the key a little lower. I think the voice will sound better when it's lower." And then he played, and it was still not enough. He made it lower again, and then they found something in it and said, "Okay, we'll take her." And that was this revue, that Spoliansky did at the theater in the Kurfürstendamm with Margo Lion. That was her first big appearance, when the best friend sings with the best friend. Everybody knew everybody. Spoliansky was a composer that everybody admired, including me. Friedrich Hollaender followed. He was the son of an operetta composer who was well known at the turn of the century because he had written the Metropole revues. And this Friedrich Hollaender was doing cabaret early on, in 1919 when the war was over, with Max Reinhardt, by the way. Then suddenly it was all young people that they didn't know, who were unknowns, who were making names for themselves there—Walter Mehring, Kurt Tucholsky, then, as I said, Friedrich Hollaender, who then brought Mischa Spoliansky along as a musical director. And then Werner Richard Heimann, by the way, who wrote melodies for UFA, like "The Congress Dances": "It's only once, it'll never come again" [Das gibt's nur einmal, das kommt nie wieder]. He was also in *Die Wilde Bühne* [Wild Stage], which is around the corner, too. It was in the cellar of the Theater of the West. It was a cabaret that a woman had, Trude Hesterberg. She was a little like Marlene—they all knew everybody—because she was also a self-assured woman. They had never before known a twenty-three-year-old woman to suddenly say, "I'm going to open a cabaret." And she pulled together all the important authors, who fifty years later not only sounded good but had also mastered the concept of good cabaret. She had the certainty that Tucholsky should do the text, and Walter Mehring, and they had fun. Every evening we had something different. And they were cutting-edge and political and unique. Bert Brecht tried his hand, and the people booed him. And then Walter Mehring got onto the stage and said, "You are going to remember this evening. You will certainly not describe it the way it was. You will boast that you were here on this evening. It was a failure, but not for Bert Brecht [who brought *Death of a Soldier* to the stage]. . . . It was a failure for the public."

When the Nazis grabbed the power in Germany in 1933, hardly any of the artists could imagine that this entire culture that defined the '20s, which was unusual and new and revolutionary and anarchist, that all that could be extinguished overnight and over twelve years. Don't forget that in May ten thousand artists, the last ones, left this land in the dead of night, and most of these wonderful artists died in the concentration camps in Auschwitz, in Treblinka, and more. For me, as a young man, I've got to say, I had to learn about all that in 1945, that an entire culture was broken off, especially this winking, joking, creative Jewish culture that was in the cabaret in the '20s, that we young people had only read about. All that was gone. The theater had bled to death, and music, too, and painting was gone. You can hardly imagine what kind of effect that had. In the German arts you had to slowly start to put it—into our awareness—how much the culture was in deficit. I think in the fifty years that we have behind us, that separate us from the end of fascism, that we still haven't been able to accomplish a restoration of this culture. We have lost not only the Jewish segment but also the element of politically wide-awake artists, who all had to leave Germany back then.

My admiration for Marlene, I'll say that without any bathos, is such that I imagine if I were in the same situation as her, that I would hope to have the strength to act as she did. There are many people in Germany to this day, two generations now, who don't know anything about it. They said, "Where was Marlene, when things were going so badly for us Germans? She was in the land of milk and honey." I am quite proud of Marlene, after the fact, because she was one of the few people who left this country, even when she didn't have to, because she had that feeling that as a decent German during this period she could not be part of the culture that was terribly ingrained after 1933, that she did not want to participate in that. I think she rose above this question. It is a combination of decency and solidarity for other people who *had* to leave, who had the wrong grandmother, so after the fact I say, I tip my hat to Marlene.

The German premiere of Marlene's piece by Pam Gams was here in this theater. But we didn't do the original. We looked at it and thought it was too general. We thought we have to bring Marlene back to Berlin, where she came from, and where she wanted to be at the end. I rewrote into this piece by Pam Gams a brand-new part about the concert in May 1960, when Marlene returned to Germany. She wanted to go to Berlin—it was her Berlin—and then suddenly there were these old unteachable people in the streets saying, "Marlene go home, we don't love you, we don't want to see you." That is the plot for our German premiere here, to show how she is torn internally. On the one side, she really was rejected. They let her know, "We don't like you because you were against us in the war," which is crazy. The others loved her and what she was. I thought, we have to bring this conflict back to Berlin. That's why, in the Marlene piece that I wrote, Marlene plays the big role in Berlin because I thought that was a point where she was especially involved. It was not just one of her many appearances, but rather, for this one she was afraid. But she wanted to win over the Berliners and she succeeded.

I don't think that art is the most important of all things. My generation, and I'm saying this very personally, had to learn that moral concerns actually make the difference in whether art succeeds or not. That's it. Just a few days ago in this theater, I produced and wrote a play about Gustav Gründgens, that is, the man about whom Klaus Mann wrote *Mephisto*. In there it is said he adapted himself so well that he said, "I speak only German, I'm a German artist, so I'll stay here, no matter what. And I'll work out a deal with those people." And he did that. Artists have a tendency to think that way, whether I play under Stalin or Roosevelt or Hitler or Chiang Kai-sheck, what the heck, the important thing is that I can play my roles, that *I* can be *me* on the stage, that I can show my art. I think Marlene Dietrich is an example that there are other considerations, not only for living, but also for art, because art always has to do with truth. Marlene Dietrich could have continued her career in Germany in the '30s—Goebbels was clamoring for her, Goebbels wanted her back. There were offers. When Marlene left, UFA Studios didn't have a star anymore. There was scarcely anyone in the second or third place that could have substituted for her. I've got to say, against that background, for my generation, Marlene was a motivation. It can't be just about money, art can't be merely pretty. You need this foundation based on truth, otherwise you can throw yourself onto the garbage heap right away.

THOMAS LANGHOFF

Zurich-born theater director and manager **THOMAS LANGHOFF** was the son of actor, director, and theater manager Wolfgang Langhoff. His parents had fled to Switzerland in 1934 during the Nazi reign, and they returned to East Berlin after the war. After attending the College for Theater Art in Leipzig, he was engaged from 1963 until 1971 by the City Theater of Potsdam (then part of the German Democratic Republic). He was later a guest director at the Maxim-Gorki-Theater in East Berlin, worked for the television network of the German Democratic Republic, and also worked as a guest director in the Federal Republic. In 1991, he became the theater manager of the famed location where Marlene began her career—the Deutsches Theater in Berlin.

I've always said that this is the most beautiful theater in the world. It's the theater of Berlin and of Max Reinhardt, a theater with a great tradition. Almost all the German actors of the last century have played here. And it is still a prestigious theater. The actor and the dramatist are the center of things here, and I hope for a long time to come. Jewish merchants took the Royal Wilhelmstadt Theater and turned it into the German Theater [Deutsches Theater]. They financed it, and had the chance here to create a new kind of theater. They produced the works of Strindberg, Ibsen, and Gerhard Hauptmann. It was the first theater in Germany, and Max Reinhardt turned it into the German equivalent of Comédie Française. Among others, in this actor's studio of the German Theater, there was Marlene Dietrich. She started her career in this theater, was an unknown little beginner, a pupil, who was selected because of her looks. No one could have imagined that she would become what she did.

People talk about the Golden '20s and especially about Berlin as a city of theater and culture. From what my parents said and from what I've read, that was true. The city was blessed to have Jewishness colliding with absurdity, and that was very, very productive. There were the Jewish artists in Berlin, and the whole revue tradition that started so much, and the meeting up of western European and eastern Jews. All these things made it into a melting pot, where interesting, crazy, and unique things happened. Not that it was always the way it was portrayed in films. The Golden '20s absolutely had a dark side, and I don't believe that everything in the past is that lovely. But it was a very creative time there. There were countless theaters, so many theaters had plays every night, and they were all full. There were amusement places—you have to

The Deutsches Theater in Berlin in the 1920s, where Marlene began her career.

be into this time period culturally, then you have an idea.

Of course this girl from the middle class, Marlene Dietrich, was a symbol for a certain kind of liberation in a certain time. It's interesting that this liberation is in Prussia, where the limitations on behavior were notably strict. This was where the taboos fell away, but this happened because of this city's explosive mixture. Where you noticed that the corsets were being loosened and the shackles were falling away. There were always certain people where that was concentrated. People like Marlene Dietrich. My God, dancing naked in Berlin was created by Josephine Baker! So much was happening that people could not have imagined. For us nowadays it would have been ludicrous, not at all shocking. But back then it happened with such an impact that the influence is still felt today. I also believe that in our world culture, not only in Europe but also in Europe especially, we still talk about and experience what was begun in the '20s. And yes film began then also.

It's an interesting question, the relationship between the theater and film. Film was considered second class in the beginning. It was variety-show-like and sensational, and real art was the theater. Film actors who worked in film up until the '20s had no access to a higher calling. They were un-

Marlene talks with her fellow performers and the passing public in front of the theater, 1920s.

A production still of one of Marlene's many plays at the Deutsches Theater.

knowns, more burlesque player types. In the '20s, Berlin's development was very much influenced of course by Hollywood and Russia, where film was created by Griffith and Eisenstein. It culminated here in Berlin, and the art of film, especially with the very young Marlene Dietrich, suddenly became valued. Suddenly it was its own art form, and the first ones were the ones who went to Hollywood: Marlene Dietrich, Jannings, who was in America for awhile—they were the big film actors in Germany. The influence from Hollywood got bigger and bigger. You can call it good or bad, but it *is* so. Nothing happens anymore without the American film industry. There is something to be gained even from the friction and the disagreements. But there is no sense in denying it. The entire world is Hollywood.

It must have been hard in the beginning. The actors had to fight for continuity between the various branches of art. And we know from Marlene and from others that, at first, the theater people and the directors did not want it at all. And an actor who wanted a career in film had to fight the battle himself. It only came later. It is still a problem today. We still haven't quite solved it. Somebody will say, but he's only a film actor. Or film people will say, ooh, he's only a theater player. And actors who are equally strong on both sides, I don't know an example—Dustin Hoffman, perhaps? No, they are rare. Of course there are specialists, and it's a pity. We did not get to experience Marlene Dietrich's theater presence later. Chansons and songs, yes, of course, but whether she would have been as good on the stage as in film, we don't know, and we won't know. In any case I believe there are two different occupations that have this same basis and that actors can switch back and forth between the genres. It actually started in Berlin. They said, "Oh, I'd like to try that out." It's not a disgrace to appear once in a revue. That is no disgrace for a good actor. This separation into "serious" and "entertainment"—that had loosened up and such grand people as Dietrich were part of that.

Berlin was a multicultural city. Influences from many lands met here, especially Jewish culture, which played an important role here in all branches of the arts, like music, theater, painting, and so on. Young new artists arose, like Marlene Dietrich, but others, too, whose names appeared like stars in the sky. It was quite a starry sky; there were a lot of them. And all at once it was over. Clouds moved in front of the stars, and the individual stars became paler and paler, or they disappeared. I am always saddened that this potential in the arts and culture—and I ponder it a lot—was not able to curb the rise of Adolf Hitler. Those are two painful developments. I was born as an émigré, but this place is mine. I am from here. People like Marlene Dietrich, well, she probably had various reasons to go. Some left just for being Jews, a few artists left because they were Communists, artists like Tucholsky who didn't want to stay here at all, didn't want to live here. There were some who understood that they were accomplices in its development, or who suffered under the fact that it was not stopped, that they didn't understand. So this beautiful, wonderful, starry sky faded and went dark. But it still carried on in America, in Russia, in Switzerland. That's where I was born. I had a Jewish grandmother and a Communist grandfather. My parents did theater in Switzerland, and I was born there. And like Bertolt Brecht and *all* the others, Marlene Dietrich, too, this lives on, while it withered in the other cultures. Nowadays it is a treasure for all of us. It doesn't belong to the Germans, not to the Americans. It belongs to all the people of the world, and that is quite wonderful.

In 1960 when Marlene came back here to Berlin, I was still a young man and found that quite exciting and good. I was raised anti-fascist, as an émigré. I knew about Marlene Dietrich, as an artist. Of course I liked her a lot in a sexual way, and I admired her for her political views. I don't know what was more important to me; I believe that her legs were more important than the political views. But I myself grew up an émigré, convinced that the people would be thrilled to have her back. I was completely surprised and dumbfounded about these reactions at opposite extremes. It was neither rejection nor support. It was split, and there were very many people, older ones, too, who said, "She should stay away now, she didn't want to come back anyway, she had the high life with the Yankees, we don't want to have her anymore, we don't ever want to see her again." There were demonstrations, too. I was completely floored. I would have grabbed a sword and run in front of her to clear the way. It astonished me. I only later understood that this city was, maybe not at a later date, but for sure back in 1960, too small for Marlene perhaps. The path was just too far to go for this small-minded shrunken-up city. Maybe that will be different in Berlin some day. But you've got to say it, all the tributes, the back and forth, should a street be built there, or should we do that, or the like, it shows a little of the pettiness that we had. And it shows the greatness that this person had attained. Of course Marlene Dietrich has become a symbol, a person that you cannot recognize anymore, but rather a picture of herself. It is a good picture. The picture stands for personal freedom. It stands for internationality. What is very important for me personally, it stands for anti-fascism. The picture stands for personal artistic egoism. It doesn't matter whether she was a completely normal person who used a bathroom. We cannot value that greatness highly enough, what she means to us, and for every new generation. Maybe the phrase "a little goddess-like" is not entirely wrong. I think of her often, and I think it is good that she was once here.

We thought that this German theater is the right place for an honor for Marlene Dietrich. We prepared a revue, which showed biographical segments. Our actresses sang the best-known songs. It was a wonderful show, which had an honored guest. That was Billy Wilder, who sat in the first row. We were happy about it, and I believe he was, too. The difference compared to 1960 is tremendous. There is no more aversion, no more reservations. Nowadays we are proud that one of this city's greatest daughters is Marlene Dietrich. Anything sad or unpleasant has been forgotten. And that's good.

NICHOLAS VON STERNBERG

Besides being the son of Joseph von Sternberg, Marlene's notable director and mentor, **NICHOLAS VON STERNBERG** is an accomplished cinematographer in his own right. Having studied the art of lighting from the world's best, he made his own mark on films such as *Crime and Punishment* and *Texasville.* His knowledge of his father's technique and his methods of crafting a scene made his understanding of Marlene's early training and deportment on the set possible for a layperson to grasp. Much like Michelangelo sculpting marble, the elder von Sternberg revealed his image from the raw material that was Marlene. Nicholas continues to write and shoot films, and he remains an artist with a unique perspective on one of the most important collaborations in the business.

My father, Joseph von Sternberg, had an idea in his mind, and an image in his mind, of a person that he wanted to see in *The Blue Angel* who didn't exist. And he was not happy with the choices that he was offered when he was in Berlin for the leading lady.

And he had created this image, based on his own knowledge of painting, of post-impressionism and expressionism. And he had this image of someone that he couldn't find, that didn't exist.

And he looked at a lot of photos, and he auditioned someone else, whom Erich Pommer and Emil Jannings wanted to star in the film, and he just wasn't satisfied with her. And then he went to a play that Hans Albers was in, who is another actor that had been cast in the film. And leaning against the wings of the theater was Marlene.

And she wasn't even onstage yet, and he just saw someone who was immediately unlike all the other actors who were aware that he was there in the audience. Marlene wasn't trying real hard to impress him.

She was distant and disinterested, and she just showed complete disdain for what was going on in front of her. And I think that interested him because he saw in her disinterest something different, something that was very appealing, a distance that he wanted in that character, in the character of "Lola."

And then when she got onstage to do a song, she was wearing a costume that was kind of two-dimensional. It had a kind of a front that seemed normal, and then at some point in the song, she turned around to reveal her underwear. And I think he liked what he saw there, too. That's what he was looking for. He liked that she took her time moving across the stage. He liked the way she moved. Marlene had the body, she had the expression, and she could sing.

And so he called her in to meet him. And then when she came in to talk to him, she thought it was for a bit part. She didn't think that she was going to be a leading lady, or that he was interested in finding a leading lady.

So, she was quite distant during their first interview. And that interested him, too, that this actor wasn't trying real hard. And that reinforced her attitude, this distance and this isolation.

And at that point, Pommer and Jannings came in, and they didn't like her at all. They both knew her well. She'd been in quite a few films already. And plays.

As a matter of fact, I think everybody at UFA knew who she was, but nobody wanted her to be in

Marlene and her director, Joseph von Sternberg, on the set of *The Blue Angel,* 1929

the movie. They all felt that anything that she was in would flop.

But my dad just wasn't interested in their opinion at all. He had his own vision as an artist. And he really wasn't exactly interested in what he saw in front of him anyway. He was interested in what was in his mind, making everything fit into his vision.

So, she kind of tried to talk him out of using her. She said, "Well, I didn't know I was being called in for this part," and that kind of thing. And she had to walk back and forth across the room, and it looked like she was going to bump into something.

My dad looked at the films that she'd been in previously. And it was like taking a cold shower. He didn't like what he saw on film at all. But he still persisted, and decided to test her. But in the end it was he who had to convince her that he could handle her. She said, "You know, I've seen your films. I like the way you handle men, but I don't know if you can really handle a woman." And he said, "I'll show you that I can handle you." Nobody really liked the test at UFA. As a matter of fact the other directors at UFA were watching the test, and one of them stood up and said, "Look, anybody can see that the other actress is better. There's no question." And my dad just said, "Well, thank you for confirming my judgment." And at that point, Erich Pommer stood up and he said, "Well, if it's your decision, Joe, to use this actress, I'm behind you a hundred percent," which is, I think, a wonderful attribute for a producer, to be that much of a believer in a director's work, despite all other advice, and even your own opinion.

And, my dad was delighted with the test, and later went on to show it to Bud Schulberg. And on the basis of that test Schulberg invited Marlene to come to America, to Paramount, to do *Morocco.*

Morocco opened at Graumann's Chinese Theater and it was a big hit. It was one of the top films of 1930. And I think Paramount wanted to introduce Dietrich as an American star. They really didn't necessarily want to emphasize the fact that she was a German star. They wanted her to come in and start fresh here, especially since she was basically a new face. The American audience had no familiarity with her at all prior to her coming here. But *Morocco* was a tremendous hit because the American audience saw many things in her that they had never seen before. Not the least of which was seeing Marlene, a woman, wearing pants in one scene, in a tuxedo. It was a tremendous thing for Americans to see any woman wearing pants. She kissed another woman full on the lips, and did all sorts of things that were very risqué and probably very stimulating for an American audience to see.

But there was a lot more to her relationship with my father than that. Beyond the vision that my dad had of her, and the way he was able to build a story around her visually, the thing that was really unique about their relationship was their artistic relationship. And that's a very special thing that has to be dealt with and dwelt upon because it isn't something that you find every day. You don't find two people who can work together and have chemistry together in any field, who can really add to each other and stimulate each other creatively. That's a rare thing to find, no matter where you look.

And to find that in an actress is an extraordinary thing for a director. It's not a thing to be taken lightly. And that was the way it was. They did have a great artistic relationship, and that is proven onscreen. There can be no doubt of that. And that's the important thing about their relationship. She responded to him in a way that no other actress had ever responded. And he found the ideal performer in her. He found someone who listened to every word, and built upon every word, built upon his ideas, someone who understood his vision.

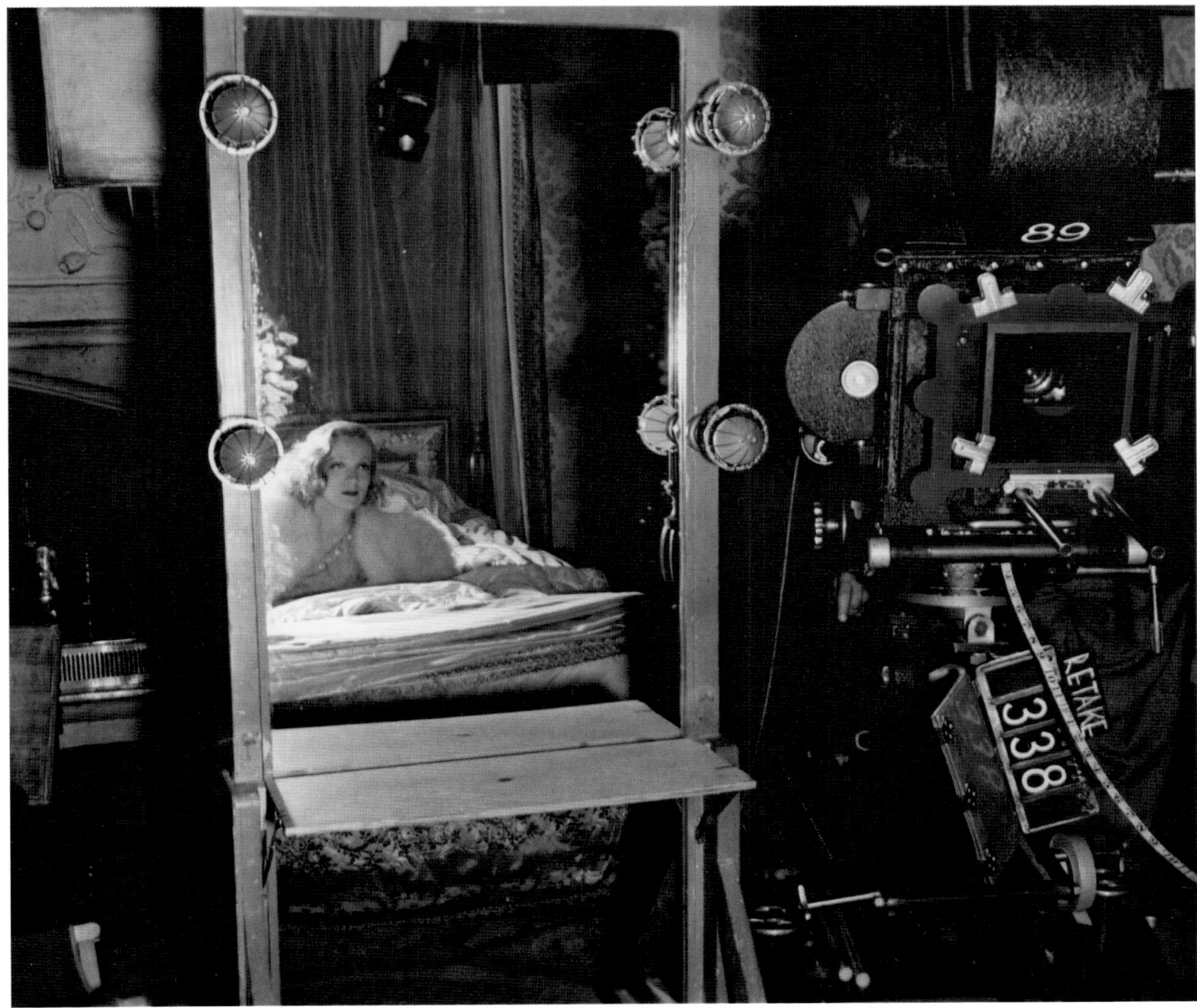

Later, Marlene used a mirror to check her own lighting, as taught by von Sternberg.

And [*he sighs*], I'm sure he found that tremendously exciting day after day, far more exciting than anything you could imagine even beyond what is seen onscreen. I think my father [*he sighs*] was probably one of the most controlling directors that ever worked in Hollywood. I think that his favorite way of making a film was the opposite of a documentary, if you can imagine. It was the opposite of walking into a real place and photographing it. He wanted to create his own reality. And that included the light—he was a painter, from the time he was a boy. He saw everything in terms of light. He expressed himself in terms of light.

And he would light a set differently than anyone ever lit a set. My father would place a light, and then build the scene around it, not just light a scene. And then he'd hang a net and create shadows, and burn holes in the nets with a cigarette to make individual rays of light shine down.

And then he'd place Marlene into that light, light that had been built just for her. She'd be the brightest object in the set, with everything appearing modeled and modulated around her.

And she was able to understand my dad's unique way of working. I mean, no one else worked like that, and I don't believe that very many people have ever worked like that, even to this day. It's very expensive. It's time consuming.

My father would only do maybe two hundred shots in a film so he could spend a lot of time on each scene, make it really individual in the way that a master craftsman would chisel a statue, for instance, or carve a piece of furniture.

My father would craft a scene in a unique way, which made that scene unique. And working with him, Marlene could see that.

I mean, that must have been stimulating to her. It must have also created an image for her of a director that other directors couldn't match.

Hal Moore, who worked with her on two films after she broke with my dad, told me that before the shot, she would say, "Where are you, Joe?" because nothing was like working with him.

It must have been tremendously stimulating to see him express himself through his lighting, and through these strange sets that he had built by artists, very talented sculptors and painters. Most were refugees from the war, or escaping from something, and he'd bring them into Paramount and have them work with him and create these wonderful expressionistic and impressionistic works of art to surround the actors with.

It must have been a tremendously exciting and stimulating experience for Marlene as well to be there. And she must have learned a great deal from that, and been influenced by that. But looked at from the other side, no one else was able to create this image, this goddess onscreen, the way that he did. And so, to be that goddess, to be created, to be molded, and perhaps to bring something out that's already there, to reveal something that's inside you, that no one else on earth could reveal—that, too, must have been a wonderful, great feeling for her every day on the set.

And to go to dailies or to go to the theater afterward, or to be recognized the way she was, to achieve the fame that she did, and to express herself artistically the way she did all would have been a great experience for her.

And as far as their friendship goes, it's hard to say. Like I said, we don't really know everything there is to know about two people's personal lives, and it doesn't matter. But what we see onscreen, that is what's important.

For my father, finding Marlene was like Michelangelo finding the ideal marble, the ideal stone to work with, or like Caravaggio discovering the perfect color that he could express his emotions in.

My father saw filmmaking the same way he saw painting.

He loved to paint. He loved to sculpt. And to him making a film was just as unique a way of expressing himself. That's all he was interested in—expressing himself emotionally through his work.

And he wasn't very popular, really. He had such strong convictions on the set. He didn't really allow people freedom. He didn't allow the other actors freedom; they felt like they were confined in a straitjacket often on a set, and described him as dictatorial.

And that was fine with him. He didn't care whether he was popular with anyone. All he wanted to do was make his own film, with his own vision, with no one interfering with him.

And, eventually, that probably caused resentment among other directors and other people he was involved with, and so it did effect his career negatively in the long run. But I don't think he cared.

He wasn't interested in selling himself. He wasn't interested in being popular. He wasn't interested in—in making money. All he wanted to do was express himself. That's all he cared about. The way my father felt is proven by the work. And in Marlene, in her, he found the ideal medium for his emotional expression. And that's what comes out in the movies. They're very emotional. Every moment spent with her was emotional. And I believe he was able to carry that along to the other actors who were working with her as well. It's not easy to be an individual in Hollywood, and even harder to have the courage to express yourself as an individual outwardly, to do something that other people aren't doing, and not worry about how the movie's going to do, or how it's going to sell, but just how you're going to express yourself as an artist. Marlene had this quality, learned or born but really the same.

PARAMOUNT PUBLIX CORPORATION
5451 MARATHON STREET HOLLYWOOD, CALIFORNIA
WEST COAST STUDIOS
HOLLYWOOD 2400 CABLE ADDRESS "FAMFILM"

4. Juni 31

Geliebter,

ich höre eben von Forst, dass er Dich im Eden getroffen hat, ich bin verzweifelt, dass Du so einen seltenen Berliner Abend ausgerechnet mit Mutti verbringst. Was, zum Teufel kann Dich dazu verleiten. Ich hoffte durch das Wohnen im Eden Dir die zwei Tage unbeschwert au machen.--Du bist doch ein Affe. Was macht denn Tami?????????

Mutti schickt mir heute diesen Bankbrief, bitte schicke Du ihn weiter, ich habe keine Aufstellung bekommen, nur grade dieses Papier.--

Die Dicke schickt hunderttausend Küsschen.--Sie betet doch seit einiger Zeit auf den Knieen vor dem Bett, und gestern machte sie zum Schluss ein halbes Kreuz, (also, sie zeigte sich an die Stirn und dann auf den Magen) und sagte dann: das ist irgend etwas Heiliges:-------

Sie wird jetzt Maschine schreiben, ich arbeite fast täglich mit ihr.--

Heidede----das hat sie ganz allein und ganz schnell geschrieben.--

Sie ist so herrlich, dass es mich unglücklich macht, weil Du nicht da bist, Liebster. Manchmal sieht sie mich in ihrer unbeschreiblichen Weise an und sagt: der Pappa fehlt Dir wohl---:

Sie denkt ununterbrochen an Deine Augen; als ich ein Augenwasser holen liess, weil meine Augen oft tränen in der Sonne, wollte sie Dir unbedingt die Flasche schicken, Du musst ihr mal schreiben wie es Deinen Augen geht.

Sie malt jetzt für Dich ein Bild. Wir denken immer an Dich Liebster, und wenn sie sich

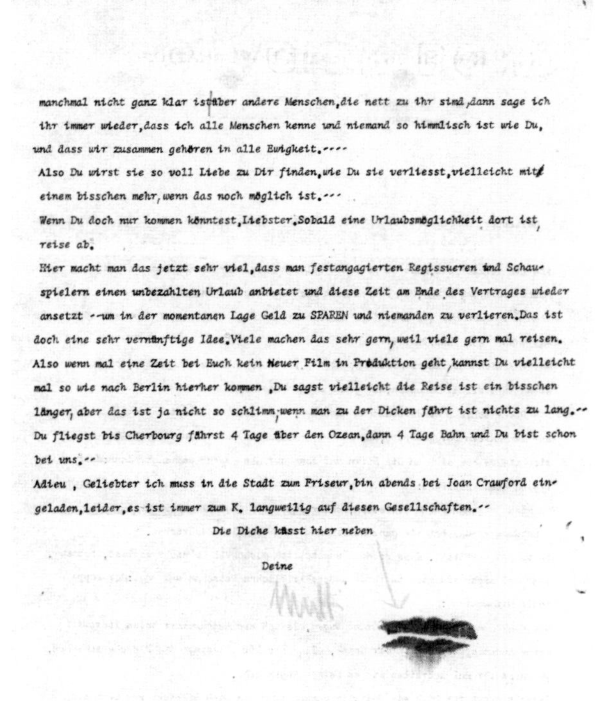
manchmal nicht ganz klar ist, über andere Menschen, die nett zu ihr sind, dann sage ich ihr immer wieder, dass ich alle Menschen kenne und niemand so himmlisch ist wie Du, und dass wir zusammen gehören in alle Ewigkeit.----

Also Du wirst sie so voll Liebe zu Dir finden, wie Du sie verliesst, vielleicht mit einem bisschen mehr, wenn das noch möglich ist.---

Wenn Du doch nur kommen könntest, Liebster. Sobald eine Urlaubsmöglichkeit dort ist, reise ab.

Hier macht man das jetzt sehr viel, dass man festangagierten Regissueren und Schauspielern einen unbezahlten Urlaub anbietet und diese Zeit am Ende des Vertrages wieder ansetzt --um in der momentanen Lage Geld zu SPAREN und niemanden zu verlieren. Das ist doch eine sehr vernünftige Idee. Viele machen das sehr gern, weil viele gern mal reisen. Also wenn mal eine Zeit bei Euch kein Neuer Film in Produktion geht, kannst Du vielleicht mal so wie nach Berlin hierher kommen, Du sagst vielleicht die Reise ist ein bisschen länger, aber das ist ja nicht so schlimm, wenn man zu der Dicken fährt ist nichts zu lang.--

Du fliegst bis Cherbourg fährst 4 Tage über den Ozean, dann 4 Tage Bahn und Du bist schon bei uns.--

Adieu, Geliebter ich muss in die Stadt zum Friseur, bin abends bei Joan Crawford eingeladen, leider, es ist immer zum K. langweilig auf diesen Gesellschaften.--

Die Diche küsst hier neben

Deine

Mutti

A heartfelt letter from Marlene to Rudy while she was working at Paramount. She writes of Maria, "She's so adorable that it makes me unhappy that you aren't here, my love. Sometimes she looks at me in her indescribable way and says: 'I guess you miss Papa.' . . . She is painting a picture for you right now. We always think of you, darling, and when she isn't completely sure about other people who are nice to her, then I tell her again and again that I know all human beings and that nobody is so wonderful as you, and that we belong together for all eternity. In short, you will find her as filled with love for you as when you left her, perhaps even a bit more, if that is possible." She closes the letter with a jab at the Hollywood lifestyle: "I have to go into the city to the hairdresser. I've been invited to the house of Joan Crawford. Unfortunately. These parties are nauseatingly boring."

And of course they both came from the same geographical place, Germany. That can make a huge difference.

It's hard to know exactly how much contact they had in 1938, but just before Hitler invaded Austria my father had been in England making *I, Claudius* with Charles Laughton. After the film was cancelled, he went to Vienna and after a while returned to England to write. When he heard that Hitler invaded Austria soon after he had left it was devastating to him because my father's family was there, family that he later lost during the war.

My father had a romantic vision of Austria as a beautiful place of the Old World, of music and art—not the way that one would necessarily think of it automatically. And he really detested the idea that Hitler came in and took it over.

I would imagine [*he sighs*] that Marlene did know about that and was sensitive to that. And many Germans were sensitive to events, and didn't feel positive about Hitler in any way. There were many Germans who did leave Germany just because Hitler came to power. And although it's hard to say exactly what was in her mind, Marlene seemed to have a sense of my father's feelings, his devastation, his personal loss. She may have done everything she could do, for the American war effort, partially because of that—it's hard to say—or partially because she had just as strong feelings about having someone come to power and crush your home, art, and other nations, and roll over them the way that Hitler did.

But no matter why, one of the things that really was extraordinary about Marlene was her effort during the war.

She wasn't just there entertaining the troops. She also helped demoralize the German troops through her songs, and by those Germans knowing that she was over there with the Americans. I mean, the word filtered through somehow, and it did help us overcome Hitler and help us win the war.

It must have taken tremendous courage for her as a German to go that close to her native country during a time of war—put herself at this tremendous personal risk.

We don't think of things that way. We don't put ourselves at risk that way, the way she did. She didn't have to do that. As a performer, she could have done anything she wanted to do. She could have stayed in Hollywood and been perfectly comfortable.

She didn't do that. She went out there and put herself on the line, and that's a tremendous thing. That's a kind of conviction you don't find every day.

She didn't just sally through the wartime years. She took the time to make the greatest contribution she could possibly make as an individual in the war effort. There's nothing that she could have done that would have been more powerful.

She couldn't have picked up a rifle and made that much difference, even if women were allowed to fight. She used her artistic ability. Her nostalgic songs came through to the German troops when they heard her voice and felt demoralized, and her performances close to the front built up the American soldiers and made them feel good about what they were doing. In the end, she influenced tens of thousands of people.

It was a tremendous effort and contribution that she made.

VOLKER SCHLÖENDORFF

Award-winning film director and producer **VOLKER SCHLÖENDORFF** founded the production company Bioskop Film in 1973, along with Reinhard Hauff and Eberhard Junkersdorf. He is well known for his film adaptations of literary works, including *Death of a Salesman* and *The Handmaid's Tale,* and most notably *The Tin Drum,* which proved to be a milestone when it was awarded the Palme d'Or at the Cannes Film Festival—the first ever awarded to a German-directed film. *The Tin Drum* went on in 1980 to become the first German film to win an Academy Award for Best Foreign Language Film. After the collapse of the German Democratic Republic, Schlöendorff assumed the position of CEO of the UFA Studios in Potsdam-Babelsberg (now Studio Babelsberg GmbH). Also a professor at the European Graduate School in Saas-Fe, he continues to direct and was awarded the Blue Angel award at the 2000 Berlin International Film Festival for *The Legend of Rita.* We spoke in the cavernous sound stage named after Marlene where they originally shot *The Blue Angel* in 1929.

This is the sound stage where *The Blue Angel* was filmed. Back then, in 1930, Fritz Lang was shooting *M* next door in the "Tonkreuz," I think. Other films were shot on this stage before: *The Blue Angel, Metropolis, The Nibelungen,* Murnau's *The Last Laugh, Asphalt,*—in other words, the great silent films of the day. But before *The Blue Angel,* Marlene herself had rather small roles, in *Tragedy of Love* and—I don't even know the titles. She really needed Sternberg, to come here from Hollywood to discover her in Berlin and to entrust her with this role. Before then she was an unknown, and eighty years later Marlene Dietrich is the most famous star to ever have worked here, and that's why in the UFA Studio advertising it says that this is the studio in which Marlene Dietrich "crossed her legs." [*Laughs.*] We named this sound stage the Marlene Dietrich Stage, just as we renamed the squares and streets all around here: we have the Billy Wilder Plaza; there are streets named after Joseph von Sternberg, Fritz Lang, Murnau, Pabst, and Lubitsch, and right behind here, there's one for Friedrich Hollaender, the composer of *The Blue Angel* and of *A Foreign Affair.*

Marlene did not only make it big before the war, but after the war she made one of the most exciting films, *A Foreign Affair,* which plays in Berlin, in which she sang the famous "Black Market." Most of the names that I mentioned already immigrated to Hollywood of course because of the Nazis in 1933. Billy Wilder said there had already been an emigration before that, of the "gifted ones," not those who had to flee the Nazis, but those who were bought up by Hollywood because of their talent. And thus, Lubitsch went over in 1927, Friedrich Wilhelm Murnau went over for *Sunrise,* and Emil Jannings of course went over with Lubitsch in 1927. I think Jannings got the first Oscar for a male leading role. Then he returned with all the clout of his American Oscar, as the most well-known German actor, and he was the star of *The Blue Angel.* He had planned his costar part, this role of Lola, for someone else. So had the studio. It took all of Sternberg's influence to get Marlene into the role.

During the silent film era, the competition between Hollywood and the European studios, especially UFA, was very lively, since there were no language barriers—the films were silent. They say

Marlene and Billy Wilder on the set of *A Foreign Affair,* 1948.

that when Fritz Lang came to New York to show *The Nibelungen,* he saw the skyscrapers for the first time and came back here to copy that in *Metropolis.* Paramount had its own production office in Berlin. During the period of inflation when a dollar was worth a billion marks, there was a plan in Hollywood to buy this studio. Then the German nationalist powers that be intervened.

Hugenberg, who was kind of a German Hearst, a press tsar, gave the UFA Studio support in order to keep it in German hands. The whole history of this studio is an up and down one, in films and in manpower. It is a people's business, that is, the studios are here, but the people come and go. Erich Pommer was the big producer for the UFA here in Berlin and then worked in Hollywood. Of course he took all the talented people that he knew with him. Not only the big directors like Fritz Lang, Murnau, and Lubitsch, but also the film cutters, the scenery builders, the stage crew. Whatever talent he knew of, he took with him to Hollywood. I don't know how they carried on here in 1933 after the creative people, the Jews, were gone. But they did work. We know the results, and we know the films. But only after 1945 did the studio have a short period of unfettered production.

Hildegard Knef's first film, *The Murderers Are Among Us,* was here. Then shortly after that, 1948–49, socialism came and the DEFA. The wall wasn't up yet, but there was an Iron Curtain, and so the studio was once again cut off from the rest of the world, for the next forty years. Actually, it was only after the fall of the wall in 1989 that we became a modern studio again, and films are being made by

The film studio soundstage in Babelsberg—where *The Blue Angel* was shot—was renamed the Marlene Dietrich Hall.

Polanski, Jean-Jacques Arneau, and myself.

Marlene was one of the few positive German role models. She turned her back on the Nazis of her own free will. She sang and was at the front more than Eisenhower, as Billy Wilder says. She really got involved, and right after the war she came back here. Marlene was one of the first civilians who came to Germany with the American troops and who saw the horror of the camps. What few people know is that Billy Wilder was there, too, and made a film, *The Death Mills,* about Bergen-Belsen. In spite of this, these two wanted to come back to Berlin in 1948 to make a film, *A Foreign Affair,* in the destroyed city. The only problem was that Marlene's role was that of a Nazi woman, a real Nazi who was a real fighter and who was married to a Nazi, and then "redeems herself," so to speak, at the end when the Americans come. But this role that she played went against everything she believed in. Billy told me that on the last day of filming she wrote him a note that said, "Only you, Billy, could make me play a part like that." That shows how close their friendship was.

In spite of everything, she still felt she was a German. And that is a first-rate role model. Someone comes along, who sells "glamor," but at the same time she remains the "Prussian officer's daughter." So she embodies great qualities. On the one hand, if you can take Billy Wilder's word for it, she was the perfect German housemother who fried potatoes with eggs sunny-side up. If she heard someone up in the stage lights sneezing, she not only said, "Gesundheit," but she also sent some aspirin up there and said, "You've got to eat some chicken soup," and "Did you eat your chicken soup yet?" On the other hand, she had this mania. Since she had such a good relationship with the lighting crew, she'd say, "But this one here, this spotlight is not good at all, could you put it over there, and this key light here, I don't like it either." Then the people didn't do it, and then she'd say, "Billy, tell the lighting crew they should change the lights." Billy said, "That's why I have a DP [director of photography]. You relight after him, but keep me out of it."

Marlene Dietrich and Billy Wilder were surely very, very close friends. Marlene lived for years in his garden bungalow, and he lived in the main house with Audrey. That was in Malibu. Even before that, Billy had always looked to reconnect with Berlin. He remained a Berlin fanatic until the day he died. Of course Marlene was "Berlin incarnate." You couldn't ask for better. I also think that while the two of them created glamor, they were both very incisive and political people, and that's pretty rare. So they understood each other very well. The third thing is that they liked to receive friends, together at Billy's house and with Audrey, and then they did all kinds of practical jokes with the guests. They'd act as if he was having an affair with her, or that she was having an affair with Garbo—anything that would create some amusing gossip for them.

So after the wall came down, this old state studio, formerly the UFA Studio, the Socialist studio, was on the market so to speak, and a French group took it over. By a stroke of fate, I became the studio head charged with making this studio state of the art. Its legends were so far in the past, *Metropolis* and the like, and the only one who was still a living legend for me was Marlene Dietrich. We still had huge photos of Marlene. We had hung them up in the hallways. Every morning, when I went to this difficult job, this drudgery, and went up the stairs, there was this picture of Marlene. It was my encouragement. Now I knew why I was doing this. It was for my postwar generation. And she helped me see that, because I think it was what she was trying to do also.

A. C. LYLES

From his humble beginnings as a theater usher in Florida to his inauguration on the Hollywood Walk of Fame, **A. C. LYLES** is that most rare of species. He is a producer who has managed not only to be a success but to also call the same studio home for seventy-six years. That studio, Paramount Pictures, is where he and Marlene met, and they worked together while she made her first American films with Joseph von Sternberg. A. C. remembers his early days with Zukor, the founder of the studio, and the "sassy" Marlene. Producer of over a hundred films and endless television series, he remains the voice of the golden age of Hollywood that Marlene was destined to embody yet subsequently resented.

I probably have the shortest résumé in Hollywood history: 1928 to 2004, seventy-six years with Paramount. But although I may have a short résumé, I have a very long memory, and along with that long memory come the wonderful people that have made Paramount possible over the years, and the unique qualities they brought to the studio here. Of these, none was more important than Marlene Dietrich.

I was born in Jacksonville, Florida, in 1919, and on my tenth birthday in 1929, I saw a picture called *Wings,* the first picture to win the Academy Award, with Charles "Buddy" Rogers, Claire Bow, Richard Arlen, and a small part played by Gary Cooper. And I went right to the manager of the Paramount Theater—studios owned the theaters at that time—and I got a job handing out bills on the corner—"Now Showing," and things like that—and putting bumper stickers on cars. Then they made me a page, put me in a uniform under the spotlight. It was a big, major theater that seated about two thousand people, and my job was to greet the people when they came in. I was ten years old; I said, "Good evening, welcome to Paramount Theaters. I hope you enjoy the show; we'll see you next week," and things like that. A short time after that Adolph Zukor came to town. He was the president of Paramount and he stopped over and visited the Paramount Theater. I went right up and asked him if he would bring me to Hollywood and teach me to make movies. And, I don't know, maybe he did what he did to get rid of me (he laughs), but he said, "Kid, you know, if you continue going to school and keep in touch with me, I'll see what can I do." So keeping in touch with Mr. Zukor meant doing well in school and that every Sunday I would write him a letter. Nothing else meant anything to me, except working at the Paramount Theater, and what was I going to write Mr. Zukor this week. And I never heard from him. It didn't bother me, because I knew Mr. Zukor was expecting me to come get a job. And then Gary Cooper came to town. When I heard he was coming, I got to the airport and went right up to where the plane stopped off. I told him that I was going to be here with him at the studio in a short while, and he said, "Well, how do you know that?" And I said, "Mr. Zukor's expecting me," I said. "I'm keeping in touch, I'm writing him a letter every Sunday," and he said, "What have you heard from him?" I said, "I haven't heard from him, but he's just waiting for me to get out there." So Gary Cooper said, "Give me a piece of paper," and I handed him a pencil and he said, "Dear Mr. Zukor, I'm looking forward to seeing. . . . What's your name, kid?" I said,

With Maurice Chevalier on the set of *Shanghai Express*, Paramount 1931.

"A. C. Lyles; A, period, C, period, L-y-l-e-s." He wrote down, "Dear Mr. Zukor, I'm looking forward to A. C. Lyles being with us at the studio, Gary Cooper." So the next letter I wrote on Sunday, of course, was about Gary Cooper and me. Then for the first time I heard from Mr. Zukor. Not really, I heard from his secretary, Sydney Brecker. She said, "Mr. Zukor's been getting your letters every week, and he just wanted you to know that you don't have to write every week, you can write every two or three months, and that would be fine." To hell with that, I continued writing Mr. Zukor every Sunday. But then I had another person, his secretary, Sydney Brecker, so I wrote her every Sunday, too!

When I was about fifteen, I think it was 1935 or '36, I got a one-way ticket to Los Angeles on the day coach. The day coach meant that you sit up all the way, and it was not air conditioned then; you had to lower a window and you got filthy, because smoke was coming in, and other things. They had what they called a butcher that went around with a tray slung around him and he sold sandwiches and things. I had $28 pinned in my coat, two loaves of bread, two jars of peanut butter, and a sack of apples for my food. I think then it was four days and four nights you sat up. There was a men's room, and in the morning you'd go there and there'd be six guys shaving in front of the mirror, and everything. So it wasn't deluxe travel, and you sat up, you know, all the way from Florida to here. I'd made arrangements to stay with a couple originally from my hometown. When I got here, to Los Angeles, I naturally took a streetcar and went right to the Paramount studio with my suitcase. I went to the gateman and I told him, "Mr. Zukor was expecting me for a job," and he said, "Yeah, we hear that all the time." I said, "No, it's really true." I said, "If you just go around and tell Sydney Brecker I'm here." Well, that was the key, that I knew the secretary, so he called Sydney. She said, "Oh, yes, send him down," and I met Mr. Zukor and he gave me a job.

So I became an office boy. And that's how it all came about. They say those were the golden years, and it's true. And at that time, we had 125, 130 actors and actresses under contract. People on the lot were so good to me, all the players and stars and things. And Marlene Dietrich, she couldn't have been nicer to me, all through the years. She was just wonderful to me. She knew my story, how I got here, and things. A lot of times she'd alter the story a little. I remember that she would tell some people sometimes, "This was my biggest fan. He was in Florida and saw my pictures and wanted to meet me, so he came to Hollywood to meet me." She sort of personalized my adventure coming out here, saying that I was one of the fans, and that I came to meet *her*, and then *she* saw to it that I got a job on the lot, and things. And then she'd add more personal things about the letters that I'd sent her, instead of Mr. Zukor. So we had a running gag about how I got on the lot with her.

I remember having a story told to me, and Mr. Zukor was present. I think he saw that *The Blue Angel* was made in Germany, and they did two versions of it, German and English. He fell in love with Marlene Dietrich and brought her to America, and he had also brought the director over, Joseph von Sternberg. As I understand it, he was a little apprehensive about releasing this picture with an unknown personality in America. But in the meantime, Gary Cooper had made *Wings*. He's on the screen maybe two minutes, but that two minutes was so important, it made him a big star, and a big star at Paramount. And Adolph Zukor, having the eye for talent that he did, put Coop right into four or five big pictures, and he became really like an overnight success, and one of the biggest stars at Paramount. In the meantime, Zukor had *The Blue Angel.* So he didn't release that right away, but instead he made a picture, *Morocco,* with Gary Cooper and this new personality, Marlene Dietrich. And that was a way of introducing her to America with a big star, and she became an equally big star. Then he released *The Blue Angel,* and that's how smart he was, and that's a great advantage she had, to be at a studio where somebody thought that highly of her that he orchestrated that kind of an introduction for her. And the picture, when it came out, she made a tremendous success out of *Morocco,* because she was a very daring, daring person. I happened to see the picture rerun the other night, and it is still shocking in a way, but this stuff was unheard of then. The outfit that she wore in that one scene, for instance, where she has the top hat and everything, which was completely unknown at that time. And then, of course, the scene at the table where she looks down at this beautiful girl . . . and then she looks at Cooper . . . then she looks at the girl, and leans over and kisses her on the mouth. My God, that was explosive. That was really something. But the whole picture made her a tremendous star: the songs, the costumes, the wardrobe, the lighting of the picture, the way she looked. And she was the most individual actress of her time. Every scene, she added something to it. She could do more with just her looks, and looking left and right—she was just magnificent. And at the end where she follows Gary Cooper out in the desert and takes off her shoes and she just fades off to that. She faded off in that picture, but she faded in to every movie fan in America, and became the biggest star that we had at Paramount. She became the queen of the lot in six months and in all the theaters around the world almost immediately after. And that was interesting because people didn't think of her as a German actress. She immediately became a part of Hollywood. She immediately became almost like an American icon. I don't think I've ever seen anyone come and do one picture, and explode on the American public and the worldwide public as much as Marlene Dietrich did. You look back over what she contributed to our business and to Paramount, and I don't know of anyone who contributed more than Marlene Dietrich.

Adolph Zukor had a tremendous influence on Marlene Dietrich. He knew that she would be a big star here, the same way he knew from two months of filming that Gary Cooper could be one of our biggest stars here; or how he brought Shirley Temple here for a part, her first important role. Betty Grable started here. A young fellow of nineteen years old came on the lot, William Beedle, and Zukor saw a screen test on him and said that he's going to be big. He became William Holden. Zukor had a great sense of talent and how it could be used to its best advantage. I remember he brought a young actress up from Broadway, and she had a scene or just a few scenes in this picture. In the scene she walks into a nightclub and takes off her fur coat and puts it down for the hat check girl. The hat check girl looks at the fur coat, looks at all her diamonds, and says, "Oh, my goodness." And this unknown Broadway gal says, "Goodness had nothing to do with it." And from that *one* scene Mae West became one of our biggest stars.

Mae West was one of our big stars, and she did a picture here called *It Ain't No Sin.* As a publicity stunt, we put fifty parrots in a room and played a looped tape, twenty-four hours a day, screaming out, "It ain't no sin, it ain't no sin, it ain't no sin." And after a few months those parrots were screaming, "It ain't no sin, it ain't no sin." We had beautiful, expensive traveling crates made for them, and playpens made for them, and we were going to send them all over the world, these fifty parrots, caroling, "It ain't no sin, it ain't no sin, it ain't no sin."

At a studio dinner with Mae West, December 3, 1935.

And it was going to be a great publicity stunt. They were going to be in the lobbies of Paramount theaters and advertise this film. Just when everything was ready for them to be shipped, two weeks before we were going to ship them, the New York office changed the name of the picture from *It Ain't No Sin* to *She Done Him Wrong.* So we got stuck with fifty screaming parrots yelling out, "It ain't no sin," and the picture was called *She Done Him Wrong.* Now, parrots have a long life—so if you ever run across a parrot that is screaming, "It ain't no sin, it ain't no sin," you can say, "Oh, my God, that's a Mae West parrot." I think Mae got kick out of that, although we were a little annoyed!

But Marlene and Mae were so close. They were always on the lot together. They were both, well, saucy and sassy. Saucy and sassy. A lot like what they were in the movies they made.

I remember that the furniture in Marlene's dressing room was covered in white furry material. Everything was very shaggy, and Mae [*he laughs*]—Mae West would come in to visit her, and sit there and compliment her on this furniture. And Marlene said, "Why do you like my furniture so much?" And Mae West said, "Because it tickles my ass." [*He laughs.*] And Marlene thought that this was wonderful!

And, you know, they were great friends. Marlene Dietrich was [he laughs] the sauciest, sassiest gal I think I ever knew—she and Mae. And, you know, she would do things—she was very provocative in her dress and everything that she did. I don't think any audience, the men in that audience, looked up and saw Marlene and didn't say, "Ooh, I—I wish I were her lover." And yet she didn't intimidate the women who were with them and, knowing Marlene, to all the men who said, "I wish I were her lover," I wouldn't be too surprised if [he laughs] Marlene would have said, "Hey, here's my number," you know!?

I think the sexiness in Marlene was just, had to be natural, because what you saw on the screen was almost like she was here, with her looks and her studying of people, and the way she delivered her lines and things. You know, Marlene had so many talents that've never been shown on the screen. She played the violin. She played the piano. [*He laughs.*] And she loved to play the musical saw. She'd put it between her legs and play the saw, and I said, "Why do you do that?" She said, "It gives me a chance to show off my legs." She was a very saucy, sassy lady.

Marlene's personality on the screen was also that of her private life, because she was such an individual when she came here. She had a white tuxedo that she wore, and I don't remember if it was from a picture or not, but I remember her walking around a lot in that. She was a very individual lady. She became such an important part of our lives here. The thing that I think was interesting about her, as we talk, and I reminisce now about her: everybody loved Marlene on the lot. They saw her at 6:30 in the morning when she came in for hair and makeup, to report on the set at 8:00, or 8:30, whatever; then they saw her on the set and she was all beautifully gowned and beautifully made up. They saw her at all different stages and all different stages of her life. This is the truth. Normally people say someone was a great gal, a wonderful actress, but then they add a "but something." Or they say, "She was a great actress, a wonderful person; however . . ." something. I never heard anybody say anything about Marlene and then add a "but" or a "however" with it. She was a greatly sought-after star for pictures. At the height of her career, she could have done anything that she wanted to do. She had the complete selection of directors, writers, and even studios; she could select anything that she wanted to do.

But Zukor knew about Marlene's past, where she had come from. And like Sternberg, he knew what she could do, what she should do. I had heard stories, of course, about the life in Germany before the Nazi period, and the different things that were accepted—the sexual freedom between men and women, and men and men, and everything else. And she was part of that and brought it with her. You know, you always hear that America's made up of every nationality you can certainly think of, and they all helped build this nation, didn't they? Hollywood's the same way. Just think of all the different nationalities and different personalities that came from all over the world; Marlene Dietrich and Hedy Lamarr, the Billy Wilders who came here and contributed so greatly, not only to Paramount but also to the building of the motion picture industry. This industry, I think, is the most influential media ever made. Pictures are being filmed today that will be shown all over the world, in perpetuity. Pictures that you see on television now. I saw a picture the other night that I produced forty-seven years ago, and at the time we were doing it I certainly didn't realize I'd be seeing it forty-seven years later in my home, sitting there, watching it. And the pictures that Marlene made in Germany and then the pictures that Marlene made here are being shown. Just like the other night they showed *Morocco,* and all the other pictures that she did. So the pictures will be shown in perpetuity and for generations. And there are people who can tell you her dialogue from *Judgment at Nuremberg,* between Marlene and Spencer Tracy. They can quote you the same way that you can. And many are young people. It's a powerful thing. In Detroit they make automobiles; here, at Paramount and in Hollywood, we make dreams. This is a dream factory. We put it on paper, we put it on film, and it goes out to the public.

When Hitler cancelled people's dreams in Germany, many of them came here to make them. A lot of German artists came to Hollywood after the Hitler regime. They came here and became very influential in our business, and contributed greatly. We owe them a hell of a lot because of their addition to the process. Even if only one person had come over, and it had been Marlene Dietrich, it would have been a tremendous contribution. See, being so close to her, you may not realize what her influence was on American film, and the American audience. It was tremendous. It was absolutely tremendous. And when she came to America, I think that was a way of life, where she was from, and maybe she reproduced a lot of that here, obliquely, by the way she dressed, by kissing a woman in a scene, on her lips, which was very shocking. I was very interested, because in the picture, when she does that, well, I saw, even felt the shock, too! But she introduced a lot of her way of life from Berlin to America. And, of course, there were countless stories about her personal life that were rather racy for the business and she was very political. But no one was shocked, no one said, "Oh, my God." Her pictures weren't banned or anything like that here. She just had the ability to make it all look light. It was just normal; it was just a natural European thing, a European mystique perhaps. And what I think is the most important point, she didn't try to *hide it.* She said and did it out in the open. I never heard anyone say anything unkind about her way of life that some people could have said was so risqué and things like that. At the same time there were some actresses, American actresses, who also did things, but *their* pictures would be shelved or delayed forever, basically banned, and it was the end of a career. But Marlene got away with it because she was up front about everything.

It's not as if she didn't have competition, at least in business. Her biggest business rival was Garbo, and Paramount wanted to compete with MGM on this. They were both very smoldering European types. And she was an icon also. One difference between Greta Garbo and Marlene was that Garbo became somewhat of a recluse. No one knew her well, whereas Marlene was private, but private in a very public way. I met Ms. Garbo once. It was an interesting conversation, because she knew Jimmy Cagney was my good friend, and we had lunches together here, and she wanted to know about him, and that was interesting. She was a gal. Even I just referred to her as Garbo, just the last name, like Dietrich. And there are people that all you have to do is say that one name. Duke, you know that's John Wayne, Garbo, you know it's Greta Garbo. Bogie, you know is Humphrey Bogart. And all you have to say is . . . you don't have to say, "Marlene Dietrich," just say, "Dietrich." And a lot of people on the lot referred to her as Dietrich because she had that instant recognition, that instant recognition of *name*. And somehow, or perhaps not by surprise, there has only been one Marlene also. We've had our Marilyns on the screen, there have been a lot of different people, but there's never been anyone who took Marlene's first name on the screen, let alone her last. I don't think they would dare, of course, because they would be instantly compared to the original, and I don't know if anybody could live up to that. It would be very unwise for a studio to name someone after her.

The thing that's also interesting is that we have pictures of everybody, the stars and people of the Paramount family, everywhere, but the really big stars, the ones that became part of our "bricks and mortar" of the studio—we had buildings named for them. The one that we chose for Marlene Dietrich is right across from the commissary, and there was a purpose in having that across from the commissary. The buildings named for others—Gary Cooper, Bing Crosby, Bob Hope, and myself— were scattered around the lot. But there's only one central point in the lot, where everybody goes almost every day, and that's the commissary. Her building was right across from the commissary, the *only one* near the commissary, so that everybody who comes to the commissary, even today, sees the big building plaque with her name on it. That building was purposely selected for her, because it was the center of the lot; the social center of the lot, where we had parties every night and everything. And also interesting, right across the street from hers is the Gary Cooper building, and we put those two together, because they together, too, started Hollywood history here. So she enjoys, by having a building here, she enjoys all that convergence of humanity. . . . And also, of course, you have to think she might like the location because she was a good cook, and loved to cook, too—she fed everybody.

Marlene had that mysterious quality that the camera seems to pick up. The camera fell in love with her, and the audience fell in love with what the camera saw. And that was a beautiful, beautiful association with the camera and the audience. She had a way that was very distinct. You know, if you look back, the big stars, there was something very unique about each of them. Cary Grant had polish, Fred Astaire was such an elegant person, Bob Hope was such a unique actor, and John Wayne was *the* all-American hero. She had a very distinct personality herself that no one has ever tried to capture or tried to imitate with any success since. Probably because they couldn't do it without that person that Marlene was underneath; it wasn't the roles alone. In all the pictures that she did and then later when she went to Vegas, she just brought that inner being with her. I've never seen so much publicity about a gown, in my life, as that gown that she wore on the stage in Las Vegas. Everything she did, she created. She created. She continued to create herself all the time, and to renew herself all the time. And she was never out of the public eye. She was never out of public film. She always had something going for her; from the picture she did for Sternberg to Hitchcock, I mean look at the personality that she brought to that. All the pictures are so different, and so appealing. She had something that very few people have, and very few people can have, because you can't create what she had. She was just so natural.

Also, for me, a very interesting point is that she was not only popular with the public. Everybody on this lot—the security people, the waitresses, the grips, electricians, the art directors, producers, directors, writers—they all loved her, and she loved them. When we named the building for her, I had them take a picture of it, and I sent it to her with a note that said, "I just want you to know that you may be in Europe, but you're here with us." She was very appreciative. Today, her building is the headquarters for our television publicity department. When they tell somebody where they are located on the Paramount lot, they always say it with great honor that they're in the Marlene Dietrich building, which is true. But everybody on the lot loved her. Van Johnson adored her, and they used to correspond a lot. Wally Westmore was head of makeup department and liked her, and Nellie Manley, who was in our hairdressing department, they were great friends. So her close friends were not only fellow stars and writers and directors and producers, but they were people on the lot, heads of departments like Wally and Nelly and, of course, Edith Head. That was a legendary combination; together they created some of the most amazing costumes and gowns. Even later when Marlene did some films away from Paramount she had it written in her contract that Edith would do her wardrobe and we, Paramount, would lend Edith out to do it, because Marlene would do anything for her, and we'd be happy to give her the services of Edith and help Marlene any way we could.

After 1945, life changed for everyone. I enlisted as private in the air force. They sent me down to Officer Candidate School until they commissioned me, and I became a public relations officer. I wasn't a flying officer. And I wound up being a public relations man in various fields, when finally I was assigned to Admiral Nimitz's personal staff. Admiral Nimitz had charge of the Pacific, while Eisenhower had charge of Europe. We were stationed in Pearl Harbor just after the attack. My office was right above his office there, at CINCPAO, which was Commander in Chief, Pacific Area of Operations. I can't say I did anything great, because I stayed there in Hawaii. But as part of Paramount, we did what we could as a studio back home. During the war, one of the things that Hollywood stressed greatly was the entertainment of the troops, and everyone, most of the stars, went overseas. Of these Marlene and Bob Hope, of course, were well known. Martha Rae, Bing Crosby, Jimmy Cagney; a lot of the guys went over, and a lot of the women went over. They were very popular, of course, with the troops in going over. It was just perfect for that. And it is the anniversary day of Pearl Harbor, and in Hollywood one of the big attractions, the biggest attraction here was the Hollywood Canteen, which was a U.S. club. . . . All the stars went out there: Dorothy Moore, Hedy Lamarr, and Bette Davis. And also the men went out: Bogart and Cagney, and every night the place was crowded. And Marlene was there; she'd serve the food and everything. . . . The problem was everybody wanted to dance with her, and everybody wanted to say hi and dance with Marlene Dietrich. And there was a big line standing in front of her, and the poor guys who wanted to dance with her just would do a minute, and there'd be a tap on the shoulder to cut in. And she thoroughly enjoyed it, going down, and she spent a lot of time with the troops; as much as anybody. She never, never. . . . I don't remember any incident where she capitalized on being a personality, and entertaining, and things. A lot of the stars, you know, it was just natural with them, but no, she never did a television special where she addressed the troops and things like that. It was very personal to her, and very touching, and very sincere. I think she was a very loyal, loyal person. She was very loyal to this country, and very loyal to Paramount, and Adolph Zukor had always been very open about how Paramount brought her here, and things like this. And I think of all the studios where she worked, this probably was her favorite, because it was her home here. But we all thought about the fact that she was going out selling war bonds to raise money to fight her home country, where her mother still lived. And I never heard her say, I never heard her make any reference to the fact that she grieved over being in that position. I think the people who saw her were more concerned about it than she was. She was so concentrated on American soldiers. And then she went to camps and eventually overseas, even though it probably killed her career at the time. You can only imagine what all this meant to those guys fighting. Listen: can you imagine being at a military camp in Tallahassee, Florida, somewhere waiting to be shipped out and getting to see this gal? Or being over there, preparing to fight some guy you don't even know who is trying to get you, but there you are waiting to do this and Marlene Dietrich arrives, someone that you've seen on the screen, someone you've been a fan of, and here you are watching her in person? I would think that would be overwhelming. Well, look at where she was appearing, or Bing was appearing, or Bob Hope was appearing, look at the audience's faces. The jubilance that they had, that someone like that came over to join them, to be with them in this time, and entertain them. If they couldn't perform, they just talked, told them stories and things. You didn't have to be a Bob Hope or Marlene, who could sing. Martha Rae would just tell jokes and things. But Marlene also misbehaved. She went pretty far out there, really close to the actual front lines. She went to places . . . listen, as a matter of fact, I would think the War Department and the studios were certainly worried about where she was, because she went to places where it was . . . I mean, really dangerous. I mean, my God, she almost got caught in the Battle of the Bulge. There was even this one newspaper article that said she was captured. Then that was retracted and in its place they published a picture of Marlene with a soldier and a puppy he had found in the rubble somewhere. And I thought, isn't that interesting, that this soldier had found this little homeless puppy and was taking care of it, and now he's there with Marlene Dietrich with this homeless puppy, and she was talking to him and petting it; petting his puppy that he's rescued. That was a wonderful picture, but I think probably a big relief too, to see that she was okay.

Here at Paramount, we, too, were at war in a way. During that time, most if not all of our films were either glorifications of war or escapist fare. Whenever and wherever they could, they certainly injected a feeling of patriotism, Americanism, proud to be an American, and tried to instill patriotism into the country. They also tried to glorify the workers who were building all the military equipment, and helped with recruitment. A lot of the pictures were on target. I really think the studios did a magnificent job at that time. Directors like George Stevens, who did *Shane* for us, did a lot of those pictures then. William Wyler did a great movie. They went over and did *The Memphis Belle* and things, later. And a lot of that film is being used in films today with war scenes and things, almost like stock footage.

Isn't it interesting that Marlene Dietrich has been off the screen a long time, but she still has her impact? I think people will remember her early pictures, but maybe not as well as her later pictures, like *Judgment at Nuremberg.* She was marvelous in *Judgment at Nuremberg.* You know, I knew Spencer Tracy very well, and I knew some of the other people in the picture, like Judy Garland. It was interesting to see Marlene Dietrich playing a person, a German, saying that the German people were not the brightest people in the world, or they didn't know as much as people thought they did. It was an interesting twist to the story, and for the woman. But when she said it you absolutely believed her. Spencer Tracy's best line comes after hers and he, like her, knew that if she didn't sell hers right, his would fall flat. In a way, for those who knew her, *his* line fit her feelings far better. But, it was delivered by an *actress,* with conviction and beauty, too. The dialogue she had was just great in that picture, romantic *and* combative dialogue with Spencer Tracy.

You know, it's funny, when I see a picture, and I've seen thousands of pictures made and produced, I just get so caught up in the picture that I forget that they are people I know. Like with Dietrich and Spencer Tracy, who was one of my closest buddies, I just seem to lose myself in the film. And then after the picture, when I think about it, I realize ooh, my God, Spence was doing this and that, and Marlene was doing things, it's really just because they are so good, and it happened with other close friends, too, like Jimmy Cagney and Duke. And I'd lose myself in that picture so much, and I don't think of them as my friends. Because they're such good actors. Then I realized, hey, I know her, and that's completely different than I know her to be. But it's just the same thing as watching Jimmy Cagney murder somebody. He wasn't a murderer, but at that time when I saw it, goddamn it, he was a murderer. He killed that person. And later on, I said, "Oh, Jimmy's the sweetest, nicest guy in the world. He wouldn't kill somebody." Or a woman plays a bitchy role, and I know her. At that time, she is a bitch on the screen, but then I say, "Oh, she's a good gal." That's when they're good actors and good actresses, when they can do that wonderful part with the play of truth. And no one was more in the moment than Marlene Dietrich.

My good pal Van Johnson kept in touch with her after she left Hollywood for good. I remember one time Van telling me, I think I remember right, that he went to a restaurant or something, right across from where she was living in Paris. And he called her, and they were *close* friends, and said, "I'm across the street, can I see you?" But she

Marlene at the gates of Paramount Pictures, Hollywood, 1933.

didn't see him, and then the documentary she did with Maximilian Schell came out, where she just spoke, but you didn't see her. I thought that was interesting, and I also thought she was right to stay off camera. Her voice was great, and just hearing her; you could use your imagination as to how she looked. And I think that was smart of her. Her philosophy was that she felt that people would remember her the way they saw her last, and I think that that's absolutely true. There are lots of examples of that—Marilyn Monroe, James Dean. It's true, and I'm so happy she didn't do it. What I don't know is if she really was a recluse like many people said she was. I like to say she was private. See, I never saw a picture of her that was uncomplimentary. I think because she became very private at the right time, and I never saw a picture of her on the front page of these tabloids that you get at shopping centers, you know the ones that run very uncomplimentary pictures of, particularly, actresses. I don't remember ever seeing one of those of her. She was just always a private person, and not only in retirement. Jimmy Cagney was that way. He was just private. Steve McQueen was that way. But she was right in the end; people do remember her, at worst seventy-five, not the ninety-one she lived to. And her personality is still the same in the minds of everybody.

One of the things that I've talked about over the years is our logo, the Paramount Pictures logo. Our logo is very popular, one of the most popular, well-known logos. It's the mountain, the blue sky, and the twenty-two stars. And when I was his office boy, I once asked Mr. Zukor why there were twenty-two stars. I was always curious about those twenty-two stars. At the time the logo was made, did we have twenty-two actors under contract, or were there just twenty-two states, I didn't know. So I said, "Mr. Zukor, why do we have twenty-two stars in our logo?" He said, "A. C., we have twenty-two stars because they fit the space." So this is a great thing; it is like most things, it's about business. But the twenty-two stars, I think, really do represent more than that. They represent the stars, writers, directors, producers, art directors, cameramen, waitresses, security people, and all the others that keep a dream factory running. But I think the stars, the apex; there are names there that helped make the studio. And in helping make Paramount, they helped make Hollywood itself. And Marlene Dietrich's name is right there, I think, in the apex up there, with Mr. Zukor and the other great people who have made Paramount and Hollywood what they were and have become. And when I see our logo, particularly the original logo, which I like better than any of them, and I look at that, as it flashes on the screen, I think of so many people whose names are invisibly engraved on those stars there. Her name is certainly there. But it's funny how you look at things. You never get blasé about things on the Paramount lot. Every day I walk by her building here. I walk by there, and I always, always look to see if her name plaque is kept well polished. And when we have tourists on our lot we have these young pages to take them around, to point out the different buildings and that is always a prime stop. Sometimes I go out and talk to the visitors. And when they pass her building and her name's mentioned, somebody always, in the group of tourists, has a story to tell about her. It's interesting how even the young people have a story to tell. They remember reading about "this," or they saw something on television, where she did this or that, or whatever, and they have something to say, they have their own personal reflection on her, and she still means something to them. Just as she will always mean a lot to Paramount and everyone who knew her.

ANDRÉ G. BRUNELIN

ANDRÉ G. BRUNELIN was a close friend of the French actor Jean Gabin, dating from the early 1950s. His acclaimed Gabin biography includes details of the long and serious affair between Gabin and Marlene, particularly their turbulent experiences just before, during, and after World War II. When Gabin came to America, fleeing the Nazis that had overrun France, Marlene helped him settle in and prevented the FBI from classifying him as "an alien enemy," assuring them that he was not a sympathizer of the Vichy government. During this time of war in Europe, but neutrality in the United States, Gabin and Marlene both felt it was necessary to fight in any way they could. Eventually this led to Gabin's joining the Free French forces under de Gaulle, and probably influenced Marlene's decision to join the USO and perform for the Allied forces overseas. They met several times throughout Europe during Gabin's tour of duty, Marlene organizing the times and places, an amazing feat given the security at the time. After France was liberated they lived together at the George V Hotel in Paris. In the end, their affair ended sadly for both, but their relationship was responsible for much of what Marlene did during that time and what she became later.

Marlene Dietrich and Jean Gabin met in New York, in a French cabaret called La Vie Parisienne. Jean used to go there because there was a French singer who sang there. Marlene went there, too. They had met before the war but they met again there before going to Hollywood. This encounter between Marlene and Jean was fated. At the time, Marlene was taking care of a lot of different people, emigrants from Paris and all over Europe, so I think she was very attracted to Gabin, he being a recent transplant from France. She took care of Gabin before falling in love with him. She helped him get his first contract to make his first movie in the United States. But I think that they got together very soon after. They rented a house in Brentwood that belonged to Greta Garbo and Garbo had the house next door. I think that Garbo was a little bit surprised by this couple, this association of Marlene, who was also her biggest competition, and this French guy, he a little bit vulgar and rude. Garbo was fascinated with them and she had a tendency, at the end of the day, to go to the end of her garden and step on top of her trash bins to look at what was going on next door at Gabin and Dietrich's house. Gabin was so amused by that, that he made everyone who would come and visit them wait for that moment when Garbo, with a large hat and sunglasses, would climb on top of her trash bins to check out what was going on in Gabin and Dietrich's house.

But, to talk more seriously about this couple, it was an antonymic couple in the sense that they both represented in their professional lives two opposing myths: Marlene, her feminine eroticism and fantasy, etc., and Gabin, more the worker kind, laborer, Parisian, etc. This relationship could only make fireworks. It was an encounter that really shocked many in the United States. It shocked them because of what Marlene was doing, the way she was living anyway, but with the addition of this Frenchman, who had done some very hard and violent movies, who was well known in the United States. It shocked the American Puritanism a lot back then. You must remember that Gabin was a star. He was treated like a star when he arrived in Hollywood. So they were both famous, but my feeling is that if Marlene had been in private life what she represented outside, to the public, Gabin would not have fallen in love with this woman. In private life, Marlene was a very different person, in a way pretty close to him. She was incredibly generous, not complicated. I think she loved him passionately. She has said and written that, for her, he was an ideal man, that he was one of the men she loved the most. But I think that if Marlene had been in private the way she was in the exterior world, Gabin would simply not have put up with her. He was a man too simple to put up with that. Marlene, in her everyday life, was someone who would wait for Gabin at their doorstep exactly like a bourgeois woman would have done it; she would get his slippers and his supper. Friends have told me that they saw her on her knees in front of Gabin to take off his shoes! She learned how to cook the kind of cuisine that Gabin loved. Gabin loved a kind of French cuisine that was very nutritious. She learned to do that, to please him. Their big distraction at home was when they would receive people and get Gabin to play the accordion he had brought to the United States and sing. Gabin loved to sing. She put a scarf around his neck and a cap while he was kind of playing the accordion and it would, of course, remind him of Paris where they would sing that kind of song.

I think that without Marlene, Gabin's life in Hollywood would have been unbearable. He hated Hollywood. He hated Hollywood because he didn't feel at home. He learned English rather quickly because he had an incredible ear, so he spoke English but with a remarkable accent.

I think that without Marlene, or at least without the life Marlene had created for them, Gabin would have suffered a lot more than he did during his stay in the United States. Even then, he still felt like a stranger toward the American way of life. Marlene and Gabin lived most of the time in their little world, without going out. But Marlene loved to go out. She loved to bring him to the theater, the concert, and the opera. Gabin hated it. He would fall asleep while listening to music. She would take him to parties where they met other actors and show-business people. Gabin followed, but he was not happy with all that. Most of all he had this strong determination to go back to France as soon as possible. He felt that the Allies had to win the war and he thought that he had to do something himself for that. He didn't see himself coming back to France after it was all over and then shake people's hands saying, "Here I am, I am back, I was living the good life in the States while you were suffering." So he got the idea to enlist in the French Liberation Forces under De Gaulle, and in the end, I think it was one of the major reasons that Marlene decided to enlist herself. Marlene did a lot for the propaganda services in the United States. She did a lot of radio shows and war bond drives. She went anywhere they would send her to promote the war effort. Let's not forget that she was German. In spite of that she performed for the GIs and she would inaugurate war ships. Early on, she was involved with war bonds and things and she dragged Gabin to those kinds of events, but for Gabin that wasn't enough. I think that without Gabin, Marlene might have spent the war exactly the same way. She might not have thought about getting more involved directly. It's Gabin who inspired her to enlist.

Well, we know what happened. Gabin didn't enlist right away because they didn't want him. He was already about forty years old at the time and anyway, where would they put him? He was an international star. So finally he was asked to be in a propaganda movie, *The French Liberation Forces.* He made the movie and then, obstinate, he went back to New York where he finally got permission to enlist in the Free French Navy. He only asked for

Dietrich and Gabin, New York, 1944.

one thing when he enlisted as a sailor. At the time, French sailors had to wear this collar that looked a little ridiculous and, worse, a cap with a large red pompom. Gabin said, "I am forty years old. I would look ridiculous with this collar and the red pompom, so give me a position in the navy where I wouldn't have to wear that." So he was given the position where he could wear a cap without the red pompom or collar. "It suits me better," he said.

Marlene was upset that Jean was going to go. When he finally got his orders, she joined him in New York and they spent two or three days together. She accompanied him to Norfolk, Virginia, the port where he was going to embark. They spent the evening together—they went to the movies and she took him all the way to the ramp of the boat and he waved and she said bye just like that but it was a gut-wrenching separation. They didn't know if they would see each other again. After all, it was war.

Gabin arrived in Algiers in March 1943. He was asked to be an instructor for the Free French sailors in an instruction center called the "Sirocco center." He was there stuck in Algiers, and a few weeks later, Marlene arrived and she enlisted. She had received the approval to enlist. She was in Algiers for a short time with the USO before joining the front line somewhere in Italy, around Monte Cassino. The reunion of Gabin and Marlene in Algiers was, of course, amazing in this city where so much was happening. Gabin was just an officer in the Free French Navy while Marlene was wearing a beautiful uniform of an American Army captain. She was invited to all the dinner parties and the receptions. People knew who he was; they knew that he was Jean Gabin. Everywhere, she would drag Gabin, who wasn't comfortable because, again, it wasn't really his crowd. But they were together. Soon, Marlene left for the Italian front line where she actually was involved in the battle. You know, at the end of the war, she wore three stripes on her uniform. It means that she was on the front line for ten months. Ten months of involvement in battle. After all, it's not nothing! And actually, on the Italian front line, she was, strangely enough, under the command of another French actor who had enlisted, Jean-Pierre Aumont. They fell in a trap where they almost were taken prisoners by the Germans. They managed to get away. And that was said to have happened a second time to Marlene, at the end of '44 in Bastogne, in the French Ardennes, where the Germans attacked a group of French soldiers she was part of, and this time she was taken prisoner. Don't forget that the Germans had sworn to shoot her if they ever took her prisoner. And when it was known that she had been trapped by the Germans, there is a young American general, very handsome, named Gavin . . . I think that Marlene thanked him her own way later. . . . He decided to rescue her. He was in command of a parachutist troop and with his troop they "jumped" on the location where she had been kept as a prisoner and they took her from the Germans' hands like that. . . . I think she became good friends with Mr. Gavin later. Later she told us that she had not been captured but was about to be, but either way it was very dramatic. No, in the end, Marlene fought a beautiful war, what we call a beautiful war, and the proof is that, you know, Americans don't grant honors that easily, and she got a medal and of course those three stripes that meant that she had spent ten months on the battlefield, even before her work in Germany for the troops right after.

During the war, now and then, she would meet with Gabin, sometimes in Algiers. She arrived in France at the very end of the war for her last tour. Gabin arrived a little bit later in October. They met in Paris, both on army leave, but Gabin soon left with the Second Battalion for the Voges, for the battle of the Voges. But at least they spent a few days together. Gabin had enlisted for the duration of the war, and so when the war ended, May 8, 1945, he thought naively that he would go home the next day. Of course, that's not how it happens. He had to wait a few weeks before being released from the army. Now attached to a tank unit, they were stationed at what had been an airport near Munich. One day, there was a gathering of tanks from the Second Battalion and Allied forces in honor of De Gaulle and Montgomery, who were reviewing the troops. There were hundreds of tanks and Gabin was at the front of his tank because he was commander of a tank, and in the midst of all those tanks he sees a small silhouette that was running, and screaming, "Jean, Jean, Jean!" It was Marlene, walking in the mud, who was looking for him. She knew that he was there. It's the other soldiers who told her that he was farther down. So she finally arrived at his tank. "What are you doing here?" he asked. "I want to kiss you," she said. He said, "There are too many people." But someone helped her climb up on the tank and she kissed him passionately. All the soldiers started applauding. . . . After all it was Marlene and they knew that it was Gabin. . . . So, this is how their war service ended. Before long, they went back to Paris.

Nineteen forty-five. It's the end of the war. Jean has been released from the army, Marlene also. They find themselves back in Paris; they live together at the hotel. It is not the Paris either of them knew. They're surprised to find out something that they were not expecting, that means the depuration period, all French were not in the resistance, contrary to what they had been told. Some of Gabin's friends were marginalized for their behavior during the war, an atmosphere in which Gabin felt very uneasy. He felt that he was not welcome. Despite the facts, he is seen as a star freshly returning from Hollywood where he had hidden during the war. Nobody knows that he fought the war, that he had enlisted. Much of that misunderstanding may have come from him, since he didn't talk about his military service. He didn't want to talk about it. Naturally, to make things worse, Marlene is German-born and they didn't know what she really did during the war either. So there is an underlying hostility that is manifested against them. This couple that was scandalous in Hollywood is again a little bit scandalous in France. But, Gabin being Gabin, he decides to make a movie. Gabin asked Marlene to be part of it, because increasingly his new and very real problem was to ensure that Marlene stayed in France, which proves that, at that time, he was still very much in love with Marlene. He wanted to make her stay in France because he didn't want to go back to the United States. So they are going to make a movie together, a film project with Carné and Prévert called *The Doors of the Night.* But here again they become uncomfortable

Paris, January 1945. The war and their relationship are almost over.

with the topic of the film, which is based on harsh reality. The film talks about the resistance, as well as the people who collaborated with the Germans. It is a very hard film and very shocking to Gabin and Marlene, who don't want such things to be said about France or the war. As soldiers they took it very personally. So they decide not to make *The Doors of the Night,* which will accentuate a certain discomfort about them in the business. They then try to make another movie together in France called *Martin Roumagnac.* Although it is completed, it's a total flop, which marks the end of their relationship. Jean is over forty years old, wants to divorce his wife, and is obsessed with the idea of getting married and having children with Marlene. Marlene is also married but doesn't want to get a divorce, she can't have children anymore anyway, and her career is in the United States. Gabin refuses to go to the United States so it's the beginning of the breakup. It's going to last another two years like this. Off and on Marlene goes to the States, comes back, they try to get back together, but things don't go well. In the end, they were condemned to break up. I think personally that if Marlene could have stayed in France, if Marlene could have had a career in France, Gabin would have renounced the idea of getting married and having children. These were things he really wanted, but coupled with the thought of living in Hollywood . . . well, it was too much. So it's the breakup, a violent breakup from Gabin's side. He knows Marlene too well. He knows that she is going to try and hang on to him and that she will for years unless it is a strong break. For Marlene's part, she's not mad at him for being married and having children with another woman; she's too generous for that. She knows that it is Gabin's idea. What she is upset about is that Gabin broke their friendship; Gabin doesn't want to see her again. Gabin doesn't want to see her again because he is afraid that Marlene will invade his future family life. She would have liked to be friends with Dominique, Gabin's wife. She would have liked to take care of Gabin's children. Gabin always said that she was the good old German mommy. Gabin didn't want this, so he broke up in a way that really upset Marlene. But she still did crazy things.

Gabin didn't live very far from Marlene in Paris. There was a café at the bottom of Gabin's building and she asked friends like Jean Marais or Jean Cocteau to go with her and she would sit for hours in the café trying to catch a glimpse of Gabin. She'd drag friends to see Gabin's movies; she would see them three or four times. She would call him at home. Gabin refused to talk to her. His wife, to her credit, would try to calm Marlene down. They were very unhappy years for Marlene, for both of them. One day, Gabin and his wife went into an antique shop. Marlene had followed them. Gabin was furious. He ran toward her and forced her to leave the shop. It was a horrible scene. It was his wife who told me the story. He was very hard about it all from then on.

Marlene kept on loving Jean despite infidelities. She had other lovers, she had other relationships, but she kept for Gabin a sort of passion. You know, Jean died in 1976. Marlene's husband, Rudy Sieber, had died a few months earlier. When she learned of Jean's death she said, "I am a widow for the second time." So she had, until the end, a real passion for this man.

When Jean enlisted in the war, he was so convinced that he would not come back he gave everything to Marlene. He had bought in the States three magnificent paintings: a Renoir, a Sisley, and a Vlaminck and he gave them to her as a present. And when the war ended, he found himself living with Marlene in Paris. They lived at the hotel Claridge. Just before Jean's birthday, Marlene asked

Vendredi 15 Novembre 46

Je ne voulais plus t'écrire, mais un mot que tu as mis dans le télégramme de Paul m'oblige à une rectification. Je ne veux pas revenir sur toute notre vie passée, il y aurait trop à dire. Mais quand je relis tes premières lettres après ton départ de France avec tout ce qu'elles avaient d'amour et d'espoir, je dois dire que c'est toi qui es moche. Tout ce que je puis te dire : C'était donc ça ton grand Amour. Je ne suis plus dupe Marlène, je l'ai été des années. Tu aimes ton indépendance, tu aimes t'envoyer en l'air quand il te fait plaisir, après tout c'est ton droit. Amuse toi bien, c'est toi qui as raison. Je me retire. Je ne veux plus jamais te voir, jamais te rencontrer. Je ne veux même plus te voir dans le film que nous avons tourné ensemble et qui aura marqué la fin de notre histoire, car ça a été toute une histoire, maintenant autre chose. Bien que tu penses le contraire j'ai été d'une régularité absolue envers toi, et jusqu'à maintenant comme je te l'avais promis dans une de mes lettres je

n'avais vu aucune fille. Tu dois bien comprendre que cette stupidité a assez duré et qu'à mon tour je ne me gêne plus, je vais en baiser une belle.

J.

Gabin has decided to end their relationship and stay in France, November 15, 1946. He writes: "I am no longer a fool, Marlene; I have been one for years. You like your independence. . . . I do not want to ever see you again, ever meet you again. I even don't want to see you in the movies in which we performed and which marked the end of our history together, because it was quite a history."

him, "What do you want for your birthday?" And Jean, who had a hidden agenda, said, "What would make me happy is to see my paintings again." They were in a safe somewhere in New York in the bank. The next day, Marlene sends a message to New York and has the paintings brought to Paris. She hangs them on the wall in the hotel apartment—the three paintings: the Renoir, the Sisley, and the Vlaminck—and Gabin has tears in his eyes in front of his paintings. They spend a wonderful birthday evening and two days later Marlene leaves for New York and takes the paintings with her. Gabin was upset. He had asked to see them again and he had! But he really wanted them back. He told me, "Okay, it was a gift, but I did it because I thought I was going to die. She could have given me one, the Renoir for example." When I met with Gabin in 1952 and '53 he was still telling that story and adding, "Do you realize how much those paintings are worth? Two hundred million French francs." Since he would tell the story often, the price would go up every year. At the end the paintings cost one billion. He gave one billion to Marlene. In any case he never saw those paintings again!

The question remains as to what Marlene's importance is today. I'm not sure it's her movies, because most of her films have aged a lot. The characters she was playing, she was symbolizing, are also a little out of date. I think that what she represents the most for the new generation, if you get close to what she really was, is that she was a woman who was liberated before the time when women got liberated. I think that she was one of the first examples of a modern woman and who wanted her freedom above all.

Marlene on performing in Europe for the Allied forces:

"I wasn't hurt, but my hands and feet got frozen stiff in the Ardennes because we were always driving around in Jeeps. The Germans were more likely to fire at closed Jeeps. And since we drove pretty fast and I never wore gloves and it was always cold and rainy and our shoes were wet . . . it got very cold. But we couldn't [and] we didn't pay much attention to it.

"It was a hard time, it wasn't easy. But it was wonderful. I went first to Africa and Sicily, Italy, and then before we went into Rome, I went into Anzio. I played in Anzio quite awhile. We were stranded there—we couldn't get into Rome and then we finally went in.

"And then I went back to America because I had to get other people to play with me because not everyone wanted to stay out so long. And then I went to Greenland, Iceland, we went over to England, and then went from England to France, and the front was then near Namur—which the Americans used to call 'Namur toujours l'amour.'"

WILLIAM F. "BUCK" DAWSON

A World War II veteran of the Eighty-Second Airborne Division, **WILLIAM F. "BUCK" DAWSON** was one of the first Americans to enter Berlin, was in charge of the press corps for General James Gavin and the Eighty-Second Airborne, and was largely responsible for the rediscovery of Josephine von Losch, Marlene's mother, in Berlin. Marlene took an instant liking to him—partly because he was handsome and partly because he had the courage of a lion. His "chutzpah," as she called it, was on a par with her own, and they remained friends for over forty years. I can't thank Buck enough for what he did for our family during the war and what he's done since.

A year or two before the end of the war, General James Gavin called me to his command post, which was somewhere in the middle of the Dutch woods, and said he was having PR problems. He was having trouble getting word into the States about what the Eighty-Second Airborne Division was doing at the time because the British general Montgomery was censoring, or at least spinning, the news accounts to make this particular advance on the Germans look more like an all-British operation.

And technically it was at the time, but two-thirds of the troops involved were American Airborne. Nobody even knew the Eighty-Second was up there. So, Gavin decided to send me down to Paris to see what I could do about planting a few stories and getting the press interested, maybe even get them to come up or at least set them straight as to what was really going on.

It was a long, hard trip to get down to Paris because the British had the road all clogged with their tanks and things. I had this old command car, a tremendous Horst, which we had captured from the Germans. It was actually Hermann Goering's old staff car—he was the big heavyset guy who was head of the German air force. On the way down toward Paris I sort of knocked off all of one side, getting past the British tanks. When I finally got as far as Eindhoven, I bartered a very fine-looking dress uniform cap [probably from a Luftwaffe pilot] for a spot on a Paris-bound British plane.

So, I finally got down to Paris and I stayed at the Lafayette Hotel or something. But the press were down at the Scrib, so my mission was to go down there and interest as many correspondents as possible to come up to the front and see us in Holland, and get my stories on radio and so forth and so on.

I remember I'd just about finished my work with the press guys and done some good but not a lot when they made a suggestion. They were all talking about Marlene Dietrich, who'd just arrived in Paris for the first time since the liberation. So they said, "Why don't you go down and see Marlene Dietrich? She'd love to hear your story and she'd love to be involved, that will get a lot of attention," and so forth and so on. I said, "No, I'm not up to that. I'm just a . . . I'm just a . . . just a kid, hero—hero-worshiper of Marlene Dietrich, and I—I just couldn't do it." And they said, "Well, you got to do it if you want a story." So, I went home and I deliberately didn't shave that night. The next morning I got dressed in my dirtiest fatigues, the ones that I'd come down in. I got my helmet on, and with my parachute carbine in hand went down to the Ritz Hotel, where Marlene Dietrich was supposed to be staying. I went down on one of those charcoal-burning buses and got off about a block before the Ritz and tried to get up my nerve. When I got inside, I went straight up to the front desk guys, and asked for Marlene Dietrich. They looked at me like I was crazy or something, and then sent me over to an adjoining desk, where there was this pompous American major who was busy screening people. So, undaunted, I explained to this guy that I'd come down from the front up in Holland, and that General Gavin had sent me down to see Marlene Dietrich [which he hadn't, of course] and bring her back up to Holland.

Well, he thought I was an imposter, which, in a way, I was, kind of. So, he said, "No, you can't. You absolutely can't do it."

And I said, "Well, can I send her a message?" He said, "Yeah, but it won't do you any good." So, I scrawled out in pencil—on the back of a sheet of paper or something that I'd had stuffed in my pocket—this note to Marlene about me coming down to see her, and about my general up in Holland needing her, and stuff like that. I sent this boy up with my message, which he carried on a little platter. He looked like one of these "Johnny boys" we used to say, like an advertisement for Philip Morris or something.

Marlene uses her famous legs to identify herself, Aschaffenburg, Germany, April 1945.

I thought nothing would happen, and after a while I sort of had begun to wish that I hadn't come, given the looks I was getting. Well, anyhow, he goes up with the note, and then all of a sudden a couple of minutes later, a sort of hush came over the whole Ritz. I followed the gaze of the people to the end of the lobby where there was this long stairway, and sashaying down the stairway came this gorgeous creature. It was Marlene Dietrich. And I sort of said, "Oh, God, what's going to happen now?" I quickly stepped back and got behind the potted plants, and then she came into the lobby and said, "Lieutenant Dawson—where's Lieutenant Dawson?" She had my note in her hand. Scared to death, I stepped out and said, "I'm Lieutenant Dawson," and immediately started stammering my restatement about what the general wanted and God knows what else. Gently cutting me off she said, "Well, let's go where it's more comfortable and have a talk." So, she took me into the middle of the Ritz dining room. As we sat down I noticed that we were surrounded by brass—colonels in full dress, majors, and everything else—all of them glaring at me and wondering how this unkempt boor got to see Marlene Dietrich. I was still in my combat fatigues. I knew they were wondering, "Who is this filthy character and what is he doing in our dining room dressed like that?" So, I took off my helmet and put it down on the floor with my parachute carbine, all the time wondering when these guys are gonna get rid of me. Here they were at the Ritz with their girlfriends trying to tell them how great they are and all of a sudden wondering who this tramp is that Marlene is with. And so we sat there and Marlene ordered tea, all while the room stared at us—but I have to say that it really seemed like she was eating it up, too. She had a sort of impish grin on her face, like she enjoyed the whole thing. It was a lot of fun. So I went over my story, a bit more clearly this time about how we wanted to get her up to the front, and that General Gavin particularly wanted to have her up there because we had just captured land immediately adjoining Germany, a place called Bergindoff. And just over the hill from Bergindoff was Germany.

I had this concept for the press about her being the first German American, first native German, whatever, to get back to Germany. Headline: "World's Most Famous Legs Come Back to Germany." I was, I have to admit, sort of enamored by her legs anyway, so getting them back into Germany sounded good to me.

And she said, "Oh, my dear, I couldn't possibly do that, you know I'm a prisoner of the army, and they have me over here as a virtual prisoner to entertain the troops, and all that. I couldn't possibly get permission to go up there to the front, but I promise you I'll come up there as soon as I can and join you."

And then she asked me if I wanted an autographed picture, so I said, "Will you please autograph it to the Eighty-Second Division, instead of to me?" So, she autographed a big glam shot to the Eighty-Second Airborne, a gorgeous picture I still have. She then excused herself and said she had to go, so we were through with the visit, but she had taken down all the details that she needed to have, and while still promising to see what could be done, she shook my hand and went back upstairs. So I was left in the Ritz dining room with all the glaring colonels, although by this time I was gaining confidence, more confidence, by the moment. So, I'm kind of grinning back at them, you know? As if to say, "Well, what the—blank—are you staring at, you, you buggers, you rear-echelon bastards?" and stuff like that. So, grinning, I got up and left. As I walked into the press room at the Scrib, all the reporters asked me at once, "Well, how'd you make out?" and "Where were you?" and "Did you see Marlene Dietrich?" I said, "Yeah," and told them the story and what she said. So everybody was quite excited.

Things being as they were, she didn't make it into Holland before I saw her again in Paris.

After our campaign in Holland the military decided to relieve us of our worn-out parachute boots and replace them. Naturally General Patton's group got our new boots when they arrived. Patton had taken the shipment of boots and given them out to his tank crews. Naturally the paratroopers were all furious, so they were yanking the truckers out

Marlene takes her show on the road, unofficially, Regensburg, Germany, June 1945.

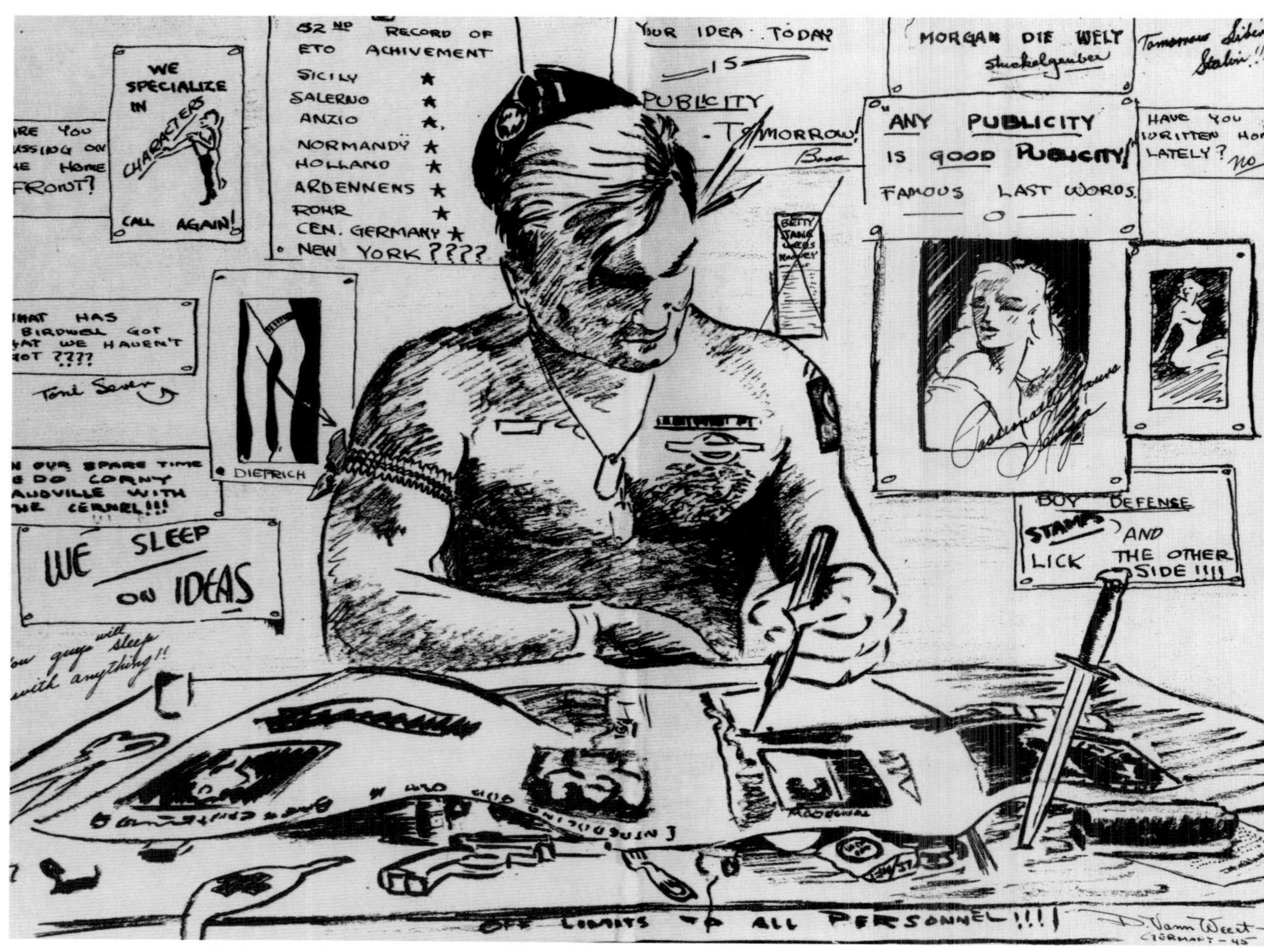

A 1945 cartoon by D. Van Weert of Buck Dawson, from *Stand Up and Hook Up*. On his right arm he wears the garter Marlene had given him as a prize for the war-bond drive.

of the tanks and out of the trucks along the Red Ball Highway and all, taking their boots and putting their other boots on by mistake. It was a mess. In the middle of this we were competing in a war-bond drive with other divisions.

So, they sent me back down to Paris with another guy to take this money that we collected, 'cause we were trying to make enough money for the drive. We had well over a million dollars to take back down to Paris. When we arrived down there, it was in the middle of the night and nothing was open till the next morning. Well, in the meantime, I went to see Marlene again. When I arrived, and, uh, here was a—almost a double of a guy with the same name, only it's "John Gabin" instead of "James Gavin" in the room. And, uh, he's smiling and thinks—getting a big kick out of the whole thing. I asked her, I said, "We've got this war-bond drive going on and we've got to have some kind of a prize, something from you to set the thing off. And we'd like to have, uh, I've got to have a set of your silk stockings." And she said, "I can't possibly get any of those for you. They're worth a fortune, and anyway, I can't get them." "But," she said, "Let me see what I have." So, she's rifling through the drawer trying to find something that would be appropriate for this Eighty-Second prize. And the Eighty-Second, they've already announced that the first prize is a free trip back to the States for, uh, a week's furlough or something, and stuff like that. But I needed something in a publicity way and all that would be attractive. Then she said, "Would these do?" and pulls out these beautiful, uh . . . garters out of her things and gives me two of those. So, what was better than Marlene Dietrich's garters? They were, pink, uh, silk with black lace hanging off the end so you could stretch it out. And I said, "Will you autograph them for me?" So, we stretched them out like that, and she writes "Marlene." When they were dry enough, I took them with me as a grand prize. She was great to do it. Later that day we finally got the money deposited, and we started our journey back.

When I arrived back to the division, it was again after midnight, about three, and I wondered what was going on because all the lights were on. And I thought, "What are the lights doing on at three o'clock in the morning?"

I woke up my roommate. I noticed that all his stuff was packed, and I said, "What's the matter?" He said, "We're pushing out tomorrow morning, the Germans have just counterattacked and broken through up near Bastogne, and we're leaving at seven in the morning." He was talking about the Battle of the Bulge, as we later knew it. None of us had time to get ready for this thing. We'd just had our stuff in the footlockers from Holland; I hadn't even cleaned my rifle. So, I got my stuff out and ready, and we got into these trucks and nearly froze on the way up. I put the garters in my pocket and forgot about them. When we got up there, a little later in the Battle of the Bulge, we went out on a night patrol. We were supposed to be replaced by the Eighty-Seventh Division, and the Eighty-Seventh Division hadn't shown up. They were stuck in the snow somewhere. And then there was some cavalry troop that was supposed to take over for them, and they didn't show up. So, my one platoon was out protecting the entire flank of the First Army.

So, I'm out on the night patrol for something like thirty-six hours in the deep snow. Our mission was to bring back prisoners and things like that, which we did. We got seven prisoners and we came back all charged up, but exhausted, too. Out of nowhere, I got this note—I got this notice to come on up to division headquarters, and I thought Colonel Winneke, the chief of staff, wanted me. I thought, well, they're gonna give me a decoration or something for this thing. All smiles, I went into the office, and here was the colonel with a copy of

Stars and Stripes. The story had just broken, and on the front page was this cartoon of me with a paratrooper cap on, leaning over Marlene handing me this garter. Inside was the story about getting the garters, the war-bond drive, and all that. I remembered the garters were still in my pocket. My wife, incidentally, used one of them when we got married.

Colonel Winneke was from my hometown, and he was mad as hell. He said, "By God, you're gonna exploit this division for the last time. I'm sending you down the line, and I hope you get killed." So, he sends me back down to the line company, which I'd originally been in before I was brought up to division headquarters to do the PR work and stuff like that. So, I went down, and sure enough, the next day, the very next day, my first day with the platoon, we were the lead platoon attacking into the Siegfried Line. We ended up with about fifteen people left that night, and thank God they didn't have, you know, real first-class troops left in the line at that time. The 325-E Company were then pulled back to regroup.

And it was then that Marlene Dietrich came up to visit the division for the first time. When she got off the plane, they brought her to division headquarters. Everybody was all excited and things like that, and she says, "Well, where's Lieutenant Dawson? I want to see Lieutenant Dawson. He's the guy that got me to come—that's why I'm here."

And General Gavin, with a smile on his face, turns to Colonel Winneke and he says, "Yes, Colonel, where is Lieutenant Dawson?" So, they send down [*he laughs*]—they send the general's car down the next day, with Marlene in it, to announce to my company commander and the battalion that she's there to get me. All my troops, my platoon, who kind of liked me anyway, are out there looking and watching Marlene Dietrich ask for me, and so the battalion commander sends me on back up. Later on he said, "Well, it's got to be either this or that. I can't have our combat exercises interrupted by these movie stars coming down to visit Dawson. He's got to either be up at division headquarters, or down here in the company: one thing or the other," and so he, and General Gavin, got me back up to headquarters. That's how Marlene saved me from the salt mines and got me back up to the division headquarters where I could roam around on the recons and do the things that I wanted to do. She befriended me automatically I guess and I her.

The next time I saw her after that was when we had moved on into Berlin. During the war Marlene's mother had stayed in Berlin and they had not been able to communicate at all. General Gavin had tracked her, but no one had seen her yet. When we knew we were gonna go into Berlin, I went down to Paris again to see Marlene at the George V Hotel, and again "John Gabin" was visiting. I figured he must be a regular because every time I went to see her, he seemed to be around her apartment or something. So, anyway, Marlene gave me all this stuff to take to her mother in Berlin, Josephine von Losch. I was all excited about that.

When I got back to the division we went on into Berlin. I came in on a C-47, and we looked out the window as we circled to land. All the houses didn't have any roofs on them. It was all just a roofless town that they lived in, as roofless as the regime now was, and, uh, it was just wonderful. Not "wonderful" that way, but in a "finished" way. It was actually really grim. When we got into Tempelhof airport we toured around and it was just rubble everywhere. There were statues with their heads on the ground. We got all sorts of joke pictures, snapshots, put the heads back on the statues, and things like that. You just can't imagine how bad the situation was. I didn't see how they were ever gonna repair or make anything of the place. In the middle of the destroyed city I found and met Marlene's mother, Josephine, who was a wonderful person. She said she'd run a jewelry store but, of course, everything had been bombed out and wrecked. When I ran into her, she had a very simple apartment, but she was a wonderful host. She wanted us to come in, have tea, and so she was entertaining us instead of our taking care of her. She seemed to be taking care of us. I told her that Marlene had asked me to come and get her some extra rations, and that General Gavin would be looking in on her and all these things. And she seemed delighted. She served tea and wanted to give me a gift. So she rummaged around, not through her lingerie drawer like Marlene had done, but she rummaged through her stuff and she found this bunch of watches, one that she'd held for a German Luftwaffe pilot. This was the kind of watch that went around the sleeve of a flight jacket worn by a Stukka dive-bomber pilot. These pilots have this big, heavy flight jacket, and this band went around the arm and looked almost like it was big enough to go around the fetlock of a horse, and it had this wonderful watch on it, where he'd time the bomb as he was on his way down, "Achtung," and so forth and so on, and then pull out. So Josephine gave me that watch, poured tea, and although we had a great time together, she was worried for her other daughter, Liesel, and her family but didn't have much information. I wrote Marlene to tell her.

Berlin, August 16th.
After the Riviera I came straight to Berlin as part of the advance party. In my first full day here I went to see your mother—your mother has very little information on your sister and her family. I'm sorry, I tried. If you find them, please write her through General Gavin or myself, and we'll deliver it—perhaps better, myself, as there are political implications if the general starts messing with mail from German civilians.

When I first came into Berlin, Marlene also asked me if I would find a lavender copy of *The Blue Angel* for her at the German UFA Studio. Well, we were getting ready for the Summit Conference in Potsdam with Harry Truman, Stalin, and Churchill. So I couldn't get anywhere near UFA Studio, but I did get to Telefunken, which is sort of a U.S. headquarters where they made all these recordings. And I got some. Pretty much all the recordings that I could find of Marlene singing. It seemed like the labels had all been changed on the American recordings, slightly different from the originals. But they were Decca Records that had been changed to Braunschweig, and all sorts of things. I got "Lili Marlene" and "See What the Boys in the Back Room Will Have," and several of these other things. And some of the more traditional songs that she'd done in the *Blue Angel* days, and things like that. And she liked them very much. I also got one whale of a record collection, which I took back and finally donated to the University of Michigan. Bruckner's Fifth and Seventh, and other things that we didn't even know existed at the time.

Marlene's mother, Josephine von Losch, is found in the summer of 1945.

Within a week or two, Marlene was back at the division again and she more or less stayed in Berlin and adopted the Eighty-Second at that point. It was real fun to go with Marlene when she went out to see the troops and things because they would just stand there adoring her, and I was just eating it up, too, because I was the guy who was bringing her out. She visited the guys in the field, too. We'd be riding around in the back of the general's car and she'd come up with a story like how she knew Alexander Fleming who discovered penicillin. Now we all new about penicillin, of course, 'cause that was a great savior, uh, for any kind of social life we might be having. So she said she ate moldy bread regularly! I didn't know how sound her medical theories were, but they sure looked good on her. I'd have to talk all night to tell you all the stories she told on those rides. But, anyhow, when she did a show or something for the guys, I'd sit there and I'd look out at their faces and be proud that I'd had something to do with getting her there. She had a way of performing to each individual soldier as if he were the only man in the world. That's the way I felt, and I think that's the way we all felt about her. When you think about it, how they all reacted to her was wonderful. She was an ex-German—well, she was still a German, but she was all-American, too, and yet she was back there and just had taken over these guys. When she performed, uh, it was just tremendous. The guys—they just were, you know, all smiles, and everybody was showing off and doing some little stunt to get her attention. And it was great. She just simply blended into this thing like she was one of the guys, although she sure didn't look like one of the guys.

She'd put on shows in the only theater that was left standing in Berlin, the Titania Palast. It was a very modern place, but the only one left, and not a grandiose opera house or anything like that. When I went back a few years later, it was a pants factory, a jeans factory, and I couldn't believe they didn't even have plaques up on the wall for the people who had been there and worked there. Anyway, at the time I was more or less involved backstage and everything, but I didn't actually participate in the show. We got all kinds of pictures, which I sent back to the States. We had some other wonderful shows, too, and they were huge shows. Performers would come over, like we had Jack Benny, and Martha Tilton, who was everybody's favorite singer at the time, Benny Goodman and Larry Adler on the harmonica, and all this stuff. That's the kind of big productions that were coming over from the States. But they'd only be there for a few days, and then they went back home again. Marlene stayed. She came in and she did essentially a one-woman show. When she came out on that stage, she wowed everybody, you know. Some of the real severe critics would say, "Well, she can't sing and she can't dance and she can't act." But, boy, let me tell you, she could stand up there and do nothing better than anybody in the world. And it was just wonderful. She'd play this thing on the saw, she'd put an old saw between her knees and whang away on it, and that was just glorious because it wasn't like anything any of us expected of her. She'd put it between her legs and we didn't know whether to look at the saw or the legs. I mean, the glamor girl of all glamor girls playing the saw! [*He laughs.*] She just had us in the palm of her hand. She'd growl out these wonderful songs and in this seductive voice, like "See What the Boys in the Backroom Will Have." Well, those "boys" were all there and they loved it to death! Marlene had a way of captivating all the guys. And, even though at that time she was getting along—she was, as I recall, about forty-seven years old. She was, well, quite a bit older than most of the gals that we were used to in the USO shows. But she had everybody captivated, and she already had this act down, the beaded dress and everything else. And when she came out, she just had the whole gang eating out of the palm of her hand. And, of course, I was getting prouder by the moment and regaining confidence in myself in all these things, too. Marlene Dietrich was the ultimate glamor girl, and we all had worshiped her from afar. But when she came to spend all that time with us, and on a common basis, well not very common, but very uncommon basis—why, uh, it was just terrific and we all ate it up. And she was *there.* She was there for a long time. She wasn't just "quickie over and quickie back" like so many of the tours were—not to knock any of them because they were all a thrill, but nothing compared with this. She did so much for our confidence. I mean, after all, how many little guys can write home in their next letter and say, "Well, Marlene Dietrich was down to see us today and I talked to her," and all this stuff? And she spread herself all over the place, so thinly that everybody was exposed to her, and the kids loved it. It was like stuff they'd just read about before in screen books and things like that, that they'd never imagined it was gonna happen to them. And here it was happening right in their front lines. And as for me, finally relaxing around her and being able to talk to her without trembling was kind of a wonderful thing. It gave me a confidence to approach almost anything in life that I have faced since.

In the meantime, the general, James Gavin, uh, loved the fact that I'd done this. And of course I introduced them, and made it possible for them to become friends. There is no doubt that Marlene Dietrich became a huge factor in both of our lives, certainly, at the time. And I guess if we had to evaluate, later we'd have to say, uh, for all time. Shortly after the war, Marlene's mother died suddenly. Marlene was in Paris and asked General Gavin to work it out so Josephine could get buried. There was still no contact allowed between the Germans and our people so it was complicated. But Barney Oldfield, a PR man on the general's staff, saw to it. I remember when Maria [Marlene's daughter] arrived in Berlin for Josephine's, her grandmother's, funeral. Maria was in a USO show at the time. Her stage name was Maria Manton, I think, and she'd come up from Stuttgart and into Berlin for the funeral, and to be with her mother. And that was definitely an experience. After it was over, I was asked to take Maria back to Stuttgart 'cause she had to get back to her show. Well, this meant going out through the Russian corridor, the corridor that we had through the Russian zone, and then driving down into Stuttgart. We went in an open jeep. It was pretty damn cold, and it was a terribly long drive. It was about three hundred miles, I think. I had to ride in the catbird seat in the back 'cause the driver, of course, had to take the jeep and so he and Maria were up in the front. And, of course, I was envious because they were having a good conversation and everything. I was back there freezing to death. But, I guess they weren't too warm either.

But, anyway, we drove back and got down to Stuttgart and she returned to her USO show. And lo and behold, a Red Cross girl that was involved with the show suddenly appeared and turned out to be an old girlfriend of mine from Michigan. So that eased the pain some, and I guess that was the last I heard of your mom. But we had some good conversations on the way about her mother, Marlene, and her grandmother Josephine. Maria looked a great deal like Marlene, although perhaps a bit more substantial.

Then the director Billy Wilder arrived in Berlin to set locations for the film *A Foreign Affair.* He kind of adopted me I guess, and we ran around and I was sort of his assistant. We went to all the nightclubs in Berlin, which were kind of beat-up. I mean, it was a really bad time for them, but some of these places were still up, and we'd go in and I'd write down all the Airborne and local American expressions for him, and stuff like that. He was just one of the guys then, this was before any of those other films, he hadn't worked with Jack Lemmon or Walter Matthau or any of those people yet. Actually, he really didn't know what he was gonna do then, for sure, what kind of film. He just knew that he was gonna do something on the Eighty-Second Airborne, and probably on post-wartime Berlin. And so he gathered all this background stuff, and then later he decided that he really wanted Marlene for this show, *A Foreign Affair.* They said she played a Nazi woman, but I didn't think of her character as that simple; none of us did. All of us had at least fantasies about an affair with some German girl and all. Even though it was against the law for us to fraternize, we all had girlfriends in Germany, so she was just the epitome of the girls we already knew. I thought her role was great. I thought she stole the whole show. And, of course, Jean Arthur was also in it and she was a high-powered actress, and Marlene just made mincemeat out of her. It was kind fun to watch. I could see Billy Wilder enjoyed this, too, and I think that's probably why he did so many films later on the German situation, like Nuremberg and things like that, and had Marlene star in them, of course, or vice versa, whichever—whoever engineered the things.

But, no matter what, it was a rebirth of her whole career. She had literally just dropped out of Hollywood completely for, I guess, two years while she was overseas and stayed with the troops and just stayed over there.

She didn't just run over and come back like the other movie stars did—not criticizing them. But she just stayed with us and stayed so, eventually, she became an integral part of our fabric, part of the whole war. And we all felt very strongly about her being one of the group and things like this. Then again, I have no way of personally knowing her relationship with the general, General Gavin, but I could see that it was very special. I'll leave that to someone else to talk about. But it was special.

But in the meantime, she built me up as she did every GI she met, I think—built me up so that my confidence could stand anything and, as I found out since, especially as the executive director of the Swimming Hall of Fame. Being involved with competitive sports the way I have and things like that, it's your confidence that's the most important thing you can have.

Marlene had a way of not only being nice to a person and being involved, but also built you up so that you thought you were a better person than you ever thought you were before.

And, uh, so, she may have looked on us as war heroes, but we looked on her as, well, sort of our "war mother," I guess, not that they [*he laughs*]—not that they regarded her as a mother type! But, I guess I sort of did.

And I, among other things, remember driving around Berlin with her in the car, and she, of course, would tell me these stories. She told of her life before Berlin, or France, and even about before the war. But, anyway just knowing her, and the fact that she was spending time with me, I just stood in awe of her. And I've always thought that this was the kind thing that Barney Oldfield and I had in common. We weren't just publicity men looking for some sort of shallow surface thing, although I tried a lot of things with Marlene, which I didn't tell you about, which were not too deep. Like, I wanted to get her famous legs in the Berlin Stadium, which we controlled as the occupying troops in Berlin. So, I tried to get her down there. I asked her to pose with her famous legs in the box like Jesse Owens. I thought that was a great photo opportunity.

Well, that was the biggest bust I ever came up with. And nobody—no paper [*he laughs*]—ever used it or anything. But, anyhow, that's one thing we did.

After they left Berlin, this was at least a year later, Marlene and Wilder were in Hollywood doing inserts and finishing stuff on *A Foreign Affair.* I had already gone back to the States, to Michigan, to finish my degree. Around Christmastime I went to see the Rose Bowl game in California, which my team was in. We won forty-nine to nothing by the way. Anyway, while we were there Marlene invited us, the whole team, to visit the *Foreign Affair* set. So, I brought the football team and we went to the studio for a tour of the thing. Marlene was great with them, too, even the coach, Fritz Chrysler, who wasn't the violinist, but the other Fritz Chrysler, and all our great football players. And of course we got to watch a few scenes being shot. Suddenly, in the middle of a scene on the stage she caught sight of us, and right on the set in front of Jean Arthur, who was sort of a different kind of a movie star, John London and all these other people, she told Billy Wilder that I was the brightest young show-business maverick that she'd ever known! Now, she may have exaggerated but I ate it all up anyway, and then she added that he'd better get me a job in Hollywood because that's what I was born for, that they were missing the boat, and that I'd done all these fine things for her in Berlin that took talent, and on and on.

Well job or not it did get Billy Wilder to invite me to S. P. Eagle's New Year's Eve party in Hollywood—his was known as the greatest party. He had a tent in the yard and had decorated his house and all. When I got there, I found Billy Wilder, who was with Evelyn Keyes and Marlene.

At midnight I looked around and I kissed Bogey's girl, Lauren Bacall, and some other people—Evelyn Keyes, Marlene, and some other people. But I get this tap on my shoulder and Bogey says, "What do you think you are doing, kid?" And I said, "Well, this *is* New Year's Eve," and so he, well, let's just say he put a stop to that.

The last time I saw Marlene in person was when Judy Garland made her comeback at the Palace Theater. Judy had been sort of down and out, and she'd been ill and so forth. She made this marvelous comeback there at the Palace doing her one-girl show for about two-and-a-half hours. During intermission, I went down into the lobby with this girl I had been dating. And like a lot of people, I had told her a lot about Marlene and the rest of the stories, and one thing or another, but she had thought that it was all a little suspect, that I was just a blowhard, you know? So, we got down there in the lobby, and suddenly, from all the way in the back of the room, this voice called out, "Lieutenant Dawson! What are you doing here? Come over here! I'm over here. Marlene! It's Marlene, I'm over here!"

So, I go over and she introduces me to Joe DiMaggio, which was a great experience for me 'cause I'd always wanted to meet him. You know, it's kind of small potatoes, but I always thought later on, when they made all this fuss about Joe DiMaggio and Marilyn Monroe, that I met him before he'd ever met Marilyn. And I thought, well, Marlene probably built him up the same way she did me, so he had the confidence to go out and pursue a movie star like that.

So, this girl that I was with, the one I had told all the stories to, she just sat there in awe through the rest of the show. We were up in about the third balcony. And she just kept shaking her head saying, "I never believed any of your stories, and you really do know Marlene Dietrich," and stuff like that. It was just all part of a wonderful thing called Marlene Dietrich.

So, um, these things were all just great. Nobody better . . . well, if anybody ever knocks her to me, they, you know, I'll have to straighten them out. I'm getting a little old for any rough stuff, but I'd try to straighten them out.

FELIX MOELLER

Historian and biographer FELIX MOELLER studied politics, history, and communication science in Munich and Berlin. In 1994 he received his doctoral degree from the Free University, completing a dissertation about the diaries of Joseph Goebbels. He is the author of several studies of Nazi-era films, including *Der Filmminister: Goebbels und der Film im Dritten Reich* (The Minister of Film: Goebbels and Film in the Third Reich). Joseph Goebbels's infatuation with Marlene and his reaction to Marlene's avid anti-Nazi stance are discussed in our interview.

Propaganda in the Third Reich was like that of all totalitarian systems and states. The nation centralized all the planning and direction. A gigantic apparatus was set up to manipulate public opinion, which would prove to be historically unique. Goebbels, the man, was surely unique, too. He was in government leadership, but really got involved in propaganda at every level, mastered all the details, and got every branch into tip-top shape. Third Reich propaganda included film, newsreels, press, and radio. Goebbels liked to call his ministry the "largest culture concern in the world," because though it was not generally known, he had secretly bought up film studios and publishing houses in France, Denmark, and Sweden. This way he could manipulate public opinion beyond the borders of Germany. It was a system for opinion engineering, and not limited to Germany. Hitler and Goebbels were both such master showmen in soothing and manipulating the media that many say, had not both these people been at the helm of Nazi Germany together, it would have been far easier to defeat the Third Reich. The Propaganda Ministry controlled all the branches of media and culture of Germany, radio, press, film, and newsreels.

Naturally he thought that it could be similar in other countries, and he went to great efforts to buy newspaper publishers and film studios in other European countries. That was easier when the war started, and they had governments of occupation in those countries. Goebbels and Hitler were also thinking about the time after the war and were thinking, maybe someday we will let those countries go, but the media will belong to us. That was their long-range perspective. Without the talents of Goebbels and Hitler personally to relate to the international press and manipulate them, without this skill, it might not have been possible for the Third Reich to cause such death and destruction with impunity.

The heyday of German films was already over when the Nazis came to power. It was not the case that total upheaval was felt immediately in 1933. Hugenberg, the German nationalist, had already bought UFA. He had already had several very reactionary films produced. In that respect, after the Nazis' takeover in 1933, they had no program for what they wanted to do, how the new Nazi film should look. In those first years, Goebbels was very dissatisfied with the films in Germany. He didn't like a lot of the films, and Hitler was pressuring him all the time. Hitler said, it's about time we were making films, where you can see that it reflects *our* ideology, and not just patriotic films in general that a German national studio could have produced. We want to see *Nazi* films. For this reason, Goebbels had studios like UFA and others like Tobis bought up. He didn't feel powerful enough yet to believe that he could push his goals through at all levels of the film firms. That was one of the reasons that the media and the film studios were nationalized.

Of course they knew what they didn't want anymore, what should be forbidden. And it was clear that the daily social realities should be glossed over. But for the moment they had no firm concept. In the first years, from 1933 until the beginning of the war, Goebbels experimented with various forms of propaganda films, which had all the types of German ideology like racism, militarism, anti-communism. But many of these films were not great successes. It wasn't until after the war began and during the first war years that the Nazi film reached its perfection, its brutality, and this penetrating power that we think of when we talk about Nazi films. *Jud Süss, Ohm Krüger, Ich klage an* [I Accuse], and other well-known films. At this pinnacle of Nazi film perfection, Goebbels ended the strategy. He recognized that during the war there was no point in stirring up the people and inciting them. He thought that entertaining films with subtle indirect propaganda should be made, containing political messages that reached the public subliminally as a form of psychological warfare. That was the innovative film concept that made the German film propaganda such a success.

For example, there were these films with Zarah Leander. Elsewhere, they were great entertainment films, with songs that were sung by millions. But when you look carefully, there are a lot of skillfully done dramaturgic details that put the viewers into certain rules of behavior. One example is the famous scene where the great star Zarah Leander is sitting in the air-raid shelter with a lot of normal, everyday German people, and beforehand she was always saying, "Terrible, to be sitting in the air-raid shelter with all these awful people." Then you see her in this place, where millions of Germans didn't like to sit, with complete strangers, and she says, "Oh, it's really not so bad here, it's a kind of community of people here in the air-raid shelter." That was unbelievably skillful, because it took the problems reflected in the everyday life and tried to solve them along the lines of NS [National Socialist] propaganda.

In the '30s the position of the Nazis regarding Marlene was not always clear. Goebbels mainly wanted to convince her to return to Germany. But there were also party organizations under the SA [Sturmabteilung] who boycotted cinemas. There were protests against Marlene's films because they were made by Jewish directors like Sternberg. To that degree there was no clear guideline by the Nazis on how to conduct oneself with Marlene and with Marlene's films. The press covered her more likely with the tendency to say, "Yes, Marlene is the big star, a great German actress, but she had the wrong roles, she had the wrong directors, the influence of the Jews in Hollywood is too big." They didn't criticize her much personally; they tried to separate it out—she has been misled, she is on the wrong path—and naturally in Germany they would bring her back to the right one.

There was a "Home to the Reich" campaign, designed to get German minorities to come back to Germany. This also included actors who were living elsewhere and working with foreign directors. They were supposed to return to Germany to strengthen its film industry—they were needed. Lillian Harvey, Rudolf Foster, and G. W. Pabst came back for a bit, and Marlene would have been considered the biggest prize. Goebbels himself really marveled at Marlene. He saw all of her films that he could, and he tried many times to win her back. The last time was in 1937, when he sent Foreign Minister Ribbentrop and director of the German theater Hilbert to Paris to get her back. It wasn't clear what roles she should play in Germany, what image they wanted to give her there. But mainly it would have been a

Germany's biggest star defies the Nazis by joining the Allies on the front.

huge propaganda coup if Marlene returned to Germany even for one film. They would have seen it as a victory by Nazi Germany over Jewish Hollywood. Contrary to later reports, Hitler himself was not so obsessed or fascinated with Marlene. He was only slightly interested in her. When he met people who had worked with her, like Emil Jannings, he asked what she was really like. The well-known director and actress Leni Riefenstahl said that Hitler saw private screenings of Marlene's films at the Berchtesgaden chalet. Actually, neither Hitler nor Goebbels met Dietrich personally. Hitler was more a fan of Greta Garbo. Goebbels wrote in his journal that when Hitler saw Greta Garbo films, he sometimes was so moved that he broke into tears. That didn't happen after Marlene's film.

Marlene's image in the '20s as a vamp and self-assured woman didn't really fit in after 1933. If Marlene had returned to Germany they would have had to try and mold her in Hitler's image of women. Hitler said that the battlefield for women is the delivery room and her workplace is the kitchen. This concept would have been hard to reconcile in the new German film landscape with the Marlene of the '20s. The picture of women had changed. They were supposed to sacrifice, to support the man as a helpmate. Hitler also had this preference in films for the "noble sufferer" roles, for mother roles. This image would have been a hard one for Marlene if she had made films in Germany again. Goebbels didn't even like the film *The Blue Angel.* He wrote in his journal that it was a terrible film, but somehow it must have had its influence on him. In a speech in 1944, I think at the Sport Palast, he adapted a phrase from it to say, "We are set for war from head to toe." Who knows whether he still remembered it, but in this case he must have had this film in mind somehow. But no matter what their own likes and dislikes, Marlene Dietrich was *the only* great worldwide German star, even after the Nazis came to power, and they wanted her back in Germany.

When Marlene applied for American citizenship there was naturally a furor in the German press. The word traitor hit the Nazi Party's press and Hess's [later Streicher's] paper, *Der Stürmer.* But mostly the reaction was not as strong as you'd think. Even then Goebbels did not give up hope that he might get her back to Germany. So there was a somewhat mixed reaction. Ah, maybe she doesn't love her home anymore, but, well, that could change again. Finally, when Marlene put on the American uniform, when she worked for the USO, even when she spoke out against Hitler, the German press stayed surprisingly quiet. You'd think it would have been an opportunity for a heavy propaganda campaign against the traitor Marlene, but obviously Goebbels thought that at this point in time the Nazis were already so weakened within Germany that this could have backfired. Of course, the outside foreign propaganda aimed at Germany was very, very limited. It is not clear how much people knew about her. Many people listened to Radio London secretly, and of course she was heard then. And rumors from outside Germany were sometimes spread in Germany quite effectively later in the war. It was a danger that Goebbels recognized, but the penalties for even *listening* to foreign propaganda, for listening secretly to the radio, were so draconian—including the death penalty—that not very much from the outside got to the people. Perhaps in the cities, but for most of the people certainly not. So to begin a campaign against her may have revealed more than people even knew at the time. The Germans still knew and loved Marlene, and if it was said that she was on the other side, then they might have asked themselves *why.* On the other hand, if you consider how much Marlene was hated after the war, maybe a propaganda campaign by Goebbels would have been a big success, and people would have begun to hate her even before the end of the war.

Nazi propaganda ignored Marlene during the war. There was no campaign against her for working for the Americans. That is probably a reason why her mother and sister in Germany were left alone. Often the friends and family of the Nazis' opponents were sent off to the camps. That didn't happen here, because no one wanted to even bring up the subject of Marlene during the war. Marlene said sometimes, "If I had stayed in Germany, if I had come back to Germany, maybe I would have had some influence on what happened. I could maybe have talked Hitler out of his plans for expansion, his anti-Semitism, and so on." Of course this is pure theory, and I don't think she could have changed an iota of what happened in Germany. On the contrary, the danger would have been very real, that she would only have served the Nazis as an instrument of propaganda. She would probably not have been able to accomplish much in Germany. She surely accomplished more by being against Hitler and against Germany and by working on the Americans' side. Hitler never let anybody tell him anything. Leni Riefenstahl couldn't tell him anything either.

Marlene Dietrich and Leni Riefenstahl were always the counterpoints. The one was a symbol for the ones who left, who went into exile because of their opposition to Hitler, because they were against the regime, because they knew they could also be successful in another country.

And Leni Riefenstahl was the opposite; she not only stayed in Germany but actively made propaganda for Hitler. They embody the different possibilities which some stars, in literature, music, and film, had. The question is, which did the Germans hold more responsible? You had the impression after the war that the Germans hated Marlene more than Leni Riefenstahl. The one left and spoke out against Hitler, and the other basically never really regretted what she did, even after the war. The counterpoints between Leni Riefenstahl and Marlene Dietrich essentially continued after the war. The one was met with hostility because she was *against* Hitler; the other experienced the same because she made propaganda *for* Hitler. But one wonders if Germans didn't hate Marlene more than Leni Riefenstahl. There is a real question whether the Germans hated Marlene more because she stood on the other side.

But no matter what, Marlene Dietrich remains perhaps the only German world star. Throughout her life, from the whole period of Berlin in the '20s and through Hollywood in the '30s, and finally at the front in the '40s her legacy will remain unique. She was a very courageous woman who showed that there's a different way; that you can stand up against Hitler and speak out. I believe that this contributes a lot to her mythos. I hope that someday there will no longer be, as still happens here and there, the attitude that somebody who worked for the other side was a traitor. I can only hope that someday the Germans come around to seeing Marlene only in a positive light.

COL. BARNEY OLDFIELD

As the most celebrated war correspondent and press officer in the European Theater during World War II, **COL. BARNEY OLDFIELD** had the questionable honor of "handling" Marlene's needs and wishes when it came to Berlin in the last months of the war. Part of the team that found Josephine von Losch, Marlene's mother, and then reunited them on a bleak airfield in Berlin, Barney always maintained a sense of the dramatic. Because he worked with Billy Wilder to prepare for *A Foreign Affair,* he was intertwined with Marlene and their friendship lasted for over forty years. As a favor to Marlene and General Gavin, it fell to Barney to bury Marlene's mother when she died suddenly, almost immediately after the U.S. occupation of Berlin. Barney had to sneak Josephine's body out of her apartment under the cover of darkness and find a private place to bury her, as he was defying strict standing orders of "no fraternization." The story is both an amazing footnote to historical conditions at the time and an ironic twist, as had he not chosen the final resting place of her mother, Marlene would not be interred only twenty feet away. He determined both of their resting places, and I think of him and that lonely night back in 1945 each time I visit Marlene's graveside.

My name is Colonel Barney Oldfield. I was fifteen years in the army and fifteen years in the air force. My first meeting with Marlene Dietrich was at the old Paramount Studios in the middle '30s when she had just come to the United States as a protégé of Joseph von Sternberg. I first encountered Marlene Dietrich after going to Hollywood on one of my annual swings when I was a newspaperman to get interviews that would last me throughout the rest of the year. It was at the time when she was making a big sensation with trousers, covering up those glamorous legs with trousers of all things. And the press agent who was leading me around the lot had an incredible name of Murphy McHenry. And, uh, he was telling me how strange it was that she wanted to wear trousers when she had such great legs, and so he was building up the glamor factor greatly. And so he took me out on the Paramount lot and said, "I want you to meet this gal because under the trousers are some great treasures for the studio if we can just get her to use them a little bit more." And so [*he laughs*], I had no idea what to expect. When I first came upon her, she and Joseph von Sternberg were sitting on a bench outside the studio door. As I came around the corner she had an eighteen-inch-long handful of German sausage in one hand as she was gesturing with the other. As I came closer she put it in her mouth and went down with a crunch that must have taken off an inch and a half of it, and began chewing [*he laughs*]. And right then and there I knew I was dealing with a rather basic, earthy creature. [*He laughs.*] It was not the most glamorous pose that she ever made, I think, but it was kind of a delicious read on this all-ranging, widely ranging woman that she was. It wasn't a very glamorous introduction. But to see her in that kind of a setting and make-believe was surreal when you think about what the road ahead had in store for us, some of the most incredible and awful things that a war can produce. To be together in both of those time frames was a life-changing contrast. The experiences shared gave clarity to both conditions.

Darryl Zanuck was the only studio person in a power position when the war was coming on who knew anything about a war and could do something about it because he'd been on the staff of the original *Stars and Stripes* soldier newspaper in Paris, in World War I. So he had an idea that film should play a more important part in what was going on, and his idea was to make allotments of films to the other studios so they would come on and could function in the role of morale support at home. There would be pro-war-type movies, like *GI Joe* and things like this. But he couldn't get the army to listen to him. They only talked about training films, just training films. Finally in desperation he said, "Tell me the worst subject you have. I'll make you a short for free on that subject, and let you know what the difference is between professional production and letting somebody in the Signal Corps do a film for you." Well, they all looked at each other like, "We got him," and they said, "Venereal disease." So, he said, "Okay, I'll do it." He went back to the studio and here comes John Ford across the lot, between pictures. Zanuck said, "John, you're gonna make a picture about venereal disease." And so this was how the famous VD film came about, and it was done in such a great fashion because you had this hotshot guy from the city playing pool with the farm boy. And the guy says, "I'm not gonna stick around for this guy. I'm going downtown where there's some action." And they hit the pool cue, and here comes the eight-ball up on the screen. Well, this captured the audience, and then of course, it went into all the physical characteristics of syphilis and gonorrhea [*he laughs*], this kind of stuff. They used to have to have a nurse on duty every place they showed this, and every man had to see it within thirty-six hours of coming in to the induction center. And you wouldn't believe it but they fainted. They couldn't stand this kind of thing, and it became a bigger hit than *Gone With the Wind.* Everybody [*he laughs*] saw it—you had to see it.

So, *then* the army began to talk to Zanuck about his idea that Paramount would do one film, Metro Goldwyn Mayer would do one, Warner Bros. would do one, and so on, and then we'd have this home-support thing keep working on the public.

Of course, all the studios went into training films also. General Hap Arnold, the air force chief, came out to Warner Bros. and he said, "Jack, everybody wants to be a pilot. I can't get anybody interested in being a navigator. I can't get them interested in being a gunner or a crew chief, any of it. Can't you make me some short subjects that would make heroes out of these people so everybody will be important so we can establish the crew positions?" So, Jack Warner picked up the phone and called Owen Crump down in the short-subjects department and says, "Owen, you just joined the air force." Owen said [*he laughs*], "I what?" "You just joined the air force." And he said, "Ronald Reagan is gonna be your star." So, that was the beginning of the first film unit for the air force. And subsequently those training films that were made by professional writers and professional actors hastened the readiness of the soldier more than had ever been done before. The mobilization and the quickness with which they were oriented on what they had to do in order to perform their particular mission was hastened by the motion picture.

In the wake of all this, the movie star's role came into focus. Things like the "Hollywood Canteen" or "Command Performances" on the American Armed Forces Radio and Television Service all became star outlets. And here was Marlene, one of the first volunteers for this stuff, who had gone through her recent political-poison business with the box office. Suddenly this gave her a reference point where she could still have visibility. Her career might not be in the best shape, but at least she was kept alive in things like this. So, for her, the natural thing was to lead to service in the USO, and then to go to England. And that's where I picked up on her because she was a part of the propaganda apparatus on what they called the ABSIE Propaganda Station, the American Broadcasting Station in England, and she had a weekly hour called "Marlene Sings to Her Homeland."

Marlene Dietrich was not a stranger to London. She had lived there before the war in an apartment with Douglas Fairbanks Jr. During her stay there, and at one of the moments when she wanted something and he wanted to please her, she got the bath changed to fuchsia pink, a fairly loud color. And the moment that you walked into this place, the bathroom dominated everything. And of course, only a short time later, the apartment turned out to be where General Eisenhower had his office. When we would go up with photographers to do some shots with the general with some dignitary or whatever, one of us would always have to go close the door to keep the fuchsia bathtub from showing because it didn't look too much like a foxhole.

Well [*he laughs*], when they moved me into the same building to write the tables of organization and equipment for the press camps, who were now following the field armies, they had so little office space left they put me up on the sixth floor, two little dinky windows, and that was where Marlene's trunks were stored. [*He laughs.*] So, my introduction to her in wartime was more in the porterage area than it was in the palpitating-heart department. And yet I met her at functions, and I would say, "Ain't as nice as it was at Paramount, is it?" And she'd say, "Oh, *depends.*" [*He laughs.*] And so, she was lighthearted about it.

Anyway Marlene had this weekly hour called "Marlene Sings to Her Homeland." This was how Marlene's mother, who was still living in Berlin, kept track of her because they couldn't correspond with each other with any great degree of assuredness that the postal service would, on both sides, let their mail get through. And this led to her performing for the troops when the war started when Marlene found a role that really picked her up in spirits, made her feel important again. She saw in the eyes of the people that she entertained that they appreciated what she was doing. And they did. I mean for someone like her to come halfway around the world and perform under battle conditions when you could have stayed at the Beverly Hills Brown Derby and just talked about the war was admirable. Just sitting around didn't appeal to her. She was an action-oriented person, and of course deep down, I think, she had the wish to somehow find out whether her mother was alive.

Marlene had many advantages that were not easily recognized by other people. She knew about power. She knew where it was. She knew how to find the way to open doors with her own agenda being served while she did something almost to obscure it because she did this other thing, which is perform for the troops. And, of course, the generals were fascinated with her, and she was in their age bracket, so this was sort of a grand fit. She was such a high-voltage person that she could change her personality to suit whomever she was talking to.

If there was anyone who could come up with an instant rapport it was she. She had an instant connection with both young and older people. She had the "mother" thing, and the glamor figure that was a little bit beyond that. So each person had his own picture in his mind of *her,* which suited him exactly. She was extremely clever about all this. She may have known many men, but she learned a great deal about what their interests were, and how to make them feel good about themselves if they did something for her. And so, she was really never "off." She was always "on."

When it came to the USO and performing for the men, she knew how to push the limits better than most. If she wanted to go a little bit farther toward the front lines than the others were allowed to do, the driver looked the other way and they went a little bit farther than they were supposed to go. And that had its rewards, too. As you go forward to where the troops are most exposed, the surprise that greets you in their eyes is palpable. I mean, here they are in some wild, forlorn place with bullet holes in the trees all around them, and here is this glamorous figure from Hollywood coming to visit you. You know, you kind of have to pinch yourself to realize that you're not having hallucinations. And then she had this charming kind of an act, with a musical saw and those long legs, and of course, to make the saw really work, she had to spread her legs and use them as a kind of a foot pedal. Well, all these guys were sitting out there with their eyes boggled at the scenery before them.

And so, the men in her audiences were constantly entangled with a creature who could make them feel warm about her having come to visit them, and then feel another reason to be warm in the heart by what they were seeing.

But I remember that Marlene had tremendous ordeals in terms of cold. For her to perform wrapped up in an overcoat wouldn't have been effective at all. She wore a thin sequined gown for all of her appearances, even when she was driving around. So, you could almost see the gooseflesh come out on her skin as she would perform because she had no protection at all. When you're in an environment where you have humidity and the atmosphere is constantly filled with moisture, it's a most penetrating kind of cold on this earth, and you feel it clear down in your bones. But she put that whole thing out of her head and performed as if she were sitting under a sunlamp in Beverly Hills. So, I think you could say that she was not only a great actor but a great endurer.

Marlene was a deeply committed person. She didn't do things by halves. She didn't move into her dressing room if she didn't bring her—her cleaning, uh, fluids and to clean it all up before she would declare it fit to be lived and to work—be worked out of.

So, she wanted to be useful. She had this hausfrau instinct that came up at certain times, and if somebody needed caring for, she wanted to be in the caring business. So, she was remarkably adjustable to whatever seemed to be the right thing to do.

Part of Marlene's magic was that she was improbable. [*He laughs.*] She would find herself fitting into special niches that were so unexpected.

For a soldier, if you're sitting in a place like the Ardennes Forest—all those trees, that entire miserable atmosphere—and you're in a uniform, you're the most anonymous thing on earth. It's almost like being an earthworm because you have no face; you have nothing except a serial number. And that gets hung on the cross that they put over the head of your grave, and that's what you are, the serial number.

Well, here was a woman who came and looked them right straight in the eye and, in effect, was saying, "You mean a lot to me. You mean something to me. I hope somehow I get through to you that I want to be here with you." And, uh, it didn't take long for that to soak in.

So, she was able to take [*he laughs*] people like "monkey see, monkey do." Whatever the mood was that she was setting up, they found themselves wrapped up in it. She was quite a magical person.

But Marlene was also seen as a threat to a lot of women, wives of the GIs back home mostly, in the beginning. There were some newspaper pieces about how women objected to the type of show she was doing, that it was too risqué. But she won them over too, eventually. Marlene had an advantage over mothers at home because she knew the soldier as he was *after* having encountered streetwalkers in London and in other places along the

Marlene and General James Gavin share a moment together in Italy, 1944.

way where there was a tendency to be grateful and show it in some charming ways. These were not the "boys" that had left home. Marlene knew what their current interests were much better than their mothers were willing to admit. So, we had to make allowances for the fact that there might be some innocent out there who would write home and say, "Marlene Dietrich was here today and she told some really kind of raunchy stories," or something like this. And so the mother would immediately go to the village preacher or priest, or whoever, and say, "What are they trying to do, like giving free beer to my boys to get them to be drinkers?" and all this. And [*he laughs*] by that time, the boys had gotten enough free beers that they were willing to go after it themselves. But the mothers hadn't been with them during that period, and Marlene carried over into where their interests were now. And these were people who didn't know whether there was gonna be a tomorrow, you know? So your "now" interests were the next fifteen minutes or the next day. And whatever there was that could make you feel better about yourself, warm you up inside, was the equivalent of a St. Bernard dog with a wine bucket under his neck who comes to [*he laughs*] rescue you at the last moment and save your life. So there was a lot of that kind of thing, but if any mother had seen what many of the sons were writing on the walls in the hovels that they lived in, indicating what their fantasies were, they would probably have been surprised, and maybe even washed their mouths out with soap. As I said, they were not exactly the same kids who left town barely able to shave. Oh, they liked her very much because if they wanted to talk sentimentally about home, she could be sentimental as any mother might have been. If they wanted to tell her their own brand of jokes, she could listen and laugh at them, and make them feel important. She took them out of the uniform, which reduced them to a statistical anonymity, and they suddenly became individuals again, had a personality, each his very own. And to be able to draw this out of an audience that had normally been so bashful individually, that they wouldn't have known how to talk to somebody, she had a way of making anybody whose eyes caught hers feel that she was only talking to that person. Marlene once said that after having performed for soldiers at the front, no other audience could ever measure up to this experience. How could a handful of soldiers measure up to a world audience? Well, when you're impressed by what you see out there—you see all these little package deals who, together, won a war, it has to be an impressive audience. It's like a Kennedy Center experience, where you're honoring people who did it better than anybody else.

Of course, the older guys liked Marlene, too. I'm not exactly sure when she first met General Gavin, but I believe it was during a lull, when his division was out of line and he'd gone to Paris for one of those interminable conferences that they had at the Eisenhower headquarters. And he would be billeted at the Ritz Hotel, where she was in residence. So, it was not hard for them to meet each other. And Marlene was fully aware of the magnetism of not only power, but also young reliance on power. Gavin was one of the youngest generals of them all. If you were going to cast him in, let's say, terms that people could see generally, Jimmy Stewart would have been sort of a bashful type of character that would have fit in the role very well.

When they did the film *A Bridge Too Far* they cast Ryan O'Neal as Gavin, and they had him carrying a pistol. The Eighty-Second Airborne Division almost all wanted to go jump in a river because he looked nothing like Gavin. Gavin never carried a pistol in his whole military life. He always carried a rifle. He wanted something that would shoot accurately and shoot far, and it became his brand. You could see him lugging that Gerand rifle around just like any other GI because he was not so far from the front that he sometimes didn't have to use it to win the day on a moment.

It was sort of natural that they would have dinner together. I don't know what else went on, but it would not be unusual for something to have happened. She liked the idea of men who were courageous enough to be so eager to get at the enemy they would jump out of a plane suspended by thirty-two nylon threads at about 750 feet above the ground—so anxious to get out they came at them from the air. People like this attracted her, she thought these were real men, not Hollywood men. These were not actors playing parts. These were guys that if they went for your throat, they went for your throat and came away with a handful of what used to be there. So, these kinds of things were pretty heavy after the many make-believe situations in which she had lived the bulk of her life, and probably were refreshing in a way. And she had to be just as real as her service went on, just like the rest of us.

Marlene once told me a story about when she approached the boundaries of Germany. As you well know from looking at the maps, Holland and Belgium frequently had a village that was split right down the middle. And on one side of the street was Germany, and the other side was either Holland or Belgium. And often she would be on her side of the street, and the German kids on the other side would point to her and say, "Marlene—Marlene." [*He laughs.*] It really got to her because it meant that their parents were still talking about her, or the kids wouldn't have known about her, or perhaps they'd shown them her picture. And now the kids could run home and tell their parents that they had actually seen Marlene Dietrich. So, it sort of established her roots again, no matter whether Hitler and Goebbels had taken her citizenship and thought she was a traitor and all the kinds of things they came up with. In the hearts of many people she was still one of them. And maybe because she was, if they could talk to her, the people she was now with would be kinder to them when they became vulnerable. Who knows what goes on in the minds of people who see the darkest time in the world closing in on them after all the great promises had failed them one by one? The country was coming apart, and who would it be who would be most sympathetic, to help you get on your feet again? Marlene sensed all these things.

Maybe it's related to this, but I was in the first column that entered Berlin on July 1, 1945. And almost immediately Germans who spoke English came up, curious as to why I had to come there. I had a goose egg on the map of Zehlendorf, the parched suburb, which was not far from Babelsberg, where the film studios were—a lot of professional people lived there. I had to find six hundred beds to accommodate the war correspondents who were coming in two days behind me, who would cover both the occupation of Berlin and the upcoming Big Three Potsdam Conference fifteen days later. The moment I started down into Zehlendorf, I had a problem because [*he laughs*] I was thinking, if I take those people who live in those houses out of those houses and then they bring in some people who don't know anything about the houses to run them, there probably wouldn't be much left. Because the nonfraternization rule was on, we weren't permitted to be in any contact with the citizenry, but I wanted to help our guys and not destroy anything, so I sort of winked at it and said to the Germans who were all standing in front of their houses, "I have to take your house, unless—"

"Yah?"

"—[*he laughs*] you will move in the attic or move in the basement and take care of us so you will have your own property properly supervised, and let the people who we billet here use the main floors and the main bedrooms."

So, everybody said, "Yah," and suddenly they're coming at us way down the street saying, "Come on down here and take our house," because they all wanted to keep the place they lived in.

I had gone in thinking it was gonna be like Rommel said about D-Day: the longest day. But I suddenly had more housing than I knew what to do with because of this "adjustment."

One of the townspeople was a very skilled interpreter, and he told me that he'd worked on many government missions as an interpreter for high-ranking Nazi people, and that he would like to be my interpreter and explain to the people so they would understand clearly what was involved. We had, perhaps, gone about halfway down the block when suddenly in front of me stands a famous German comedian named Heinz Ruehmann, and apparently the word had been sent to him that I was there, and what I was up to, and who the people were who were coming in with me. He wanted to prove to the American press that he made not only propaganda pictures but regular films. He wanted me to let him do a screening of a couple of these films in the theater, in the Zehlendorf area there. And I said, "Why not? Let them make their own judgments. They probably won't treat you kindly, but you can give them an idea of what they've been writing about in terms of speculation." So, I began to meet a great many of the local people, even though it had to be all business.

As luck would have it, I was in the first column to enter Berlin. I had all the communications equipment that was going to be used for the occupation of Berlin and the Big Three Conference. With me was a major paratrooper-photographer, named Al McCleery. He was a great friend of Marlene Dietrich and had been in one of the many sessions with her where she would talk about finding her mother. And so when I turned into Zehlendorf to find my housing, he said, "Bye-bye, see you later," and off he went. And he went straight to the address that he had. And he was the first to find Marlene's mother, which was a surprise for both of them. As he got to the address, he was suddenly confronting this terrified little old lady who didn't speak English very well. He had a driver who spoke German, and he said, "Are you Marlene Dietrich's mother?" And she said, "Yah." And he said "Marlene sent me here to find out if you were still alive so I can get word to her. She wants to come up from Paris." She said, "No. Marlene dead." And he said, "No, she's not dead. She's in Paris." She said, "I used to hear her sing on the radio from England, no? Goebbels said London is in flames, so she must have been killed in the fire, no?" She didn't know about the logistics of moving to Paris. And so he said, "We'll get word to her." Armed Forces Radio set up a call between them and then two days later, I get the message from Marlene that she was on the shuttle coming up from Berlin. And I grabbed two of our GI photographers, went to the home of Marlene's mother, Josephine, and took her down, put her in the jeep in the front seat, the photographers in the back, and we went bangety-bang to Tempelhof Airport. When we got there, I drove around in that huge cement expanse, where the aircraft approach the gates. And I put her alone in the middle of the place, and I told the control tower, I said, "Bring that plane in up to meet the little lady who's standing out in the middle of the ramp area." And the plane came up rather slowly, and stopped. The props had to stop turning before they would let you open the door. The moment that prop stopped, Marlene came out through that door in her USO uniform, and it was the greatest family reunion picture I ever saw in [*he laughs*] my life. And you would have had to have a heart of stone not to be moved by it.

One of the other visitors to Berlin shortly after we began the occupation was the famous film director and writer, Billy Wilder. And, of course, he'd been a ballroom dancer in the old Hotel Eden in Berlin before the war, and it was a big sentimental return for him. He had an idea for a movie that he was going to call *A Foreign Affair,* to star Jean Arthur and Marlene Dietrich. And he came to me and he said, "I can't bring a whole crew over here to Berlin. I need to have pictures of the rubble so we can construct the sets at Paramount and do it there." So, I gave him two GI photographers and he did nothing but roam Berlin for almost six weeks getting those rubbled buildings, some of which became sets at Paramount. And it was a fascinating time for all of us who knew that we were participating now in some aspect of the life we'd known when we were all at home doing whatever peacetime thing we were doing. And to be a part of that transition back to the good old times was a very nice moment for all of us.

We placed our so-called fabulous Press Club of Berlin in the residence of what had been the home of Hitler's Reich minister for economics, a fellow named Walther Funk. And, of course, you *had* to have a bar if you have a press club, and it turned out that a friend of mine was liquidating the stocks of the Potsdam Conference. He had $3,200 worth of leftover stuff, and we drew it. When my sergeant came back with a truckload of gurgly fluids, he said, "They gave me a hard time." "What do you mean?" I asked him. He said, "It can only be signed for by people who attended the Potsdam Conference or their representatives." So, since he had all the stuff with him, I said, "Whose name did you sign?" He said, "I took half of it in the name of George C. Marshall, the Chief of Staff of the U.S. Army, and the other half in the name of Harry Truman." So I knew we had to clear the accounts rather quickly because if the word got out that those two people had spent that much money on booze, heaven only knows what they would have said about the Potsdam Conference!

But this was August 10, 1945. At the same time, the Japanese were making overtures about surrender, and it seemed like half of Hollywood was there. USO shows all came to town so they could say they had been in Berlin. Marlene Dietrich hung around there a great many times, both for lunch and for dinner, and so it was one of her stalking places for one of her enterprises she was pursuing at that time.

But almost from the moment Marlene and her mother had been reunited, she changed into an entirely different person. She was on a mission. And her mother took her to see her home—well, she lived on the second floor in a little bitty flat and she was taking care of her ninety-five-year-old aunt, and they were almost starving because they didn't have any power. They were just two old women. Younger people were getting the rations.

And so, Marlene went on a literal crusade for the family. She had found that the parents of her husband, Rudy Sieber, were in a refugee camp in Austria. She said to me, "I want you to take me out to Zukov's headquarters." Marshall Zukov was the tsar of the Russian zone, and really a mean, tough cookie. And I said, "I can drive you up to the front, the zone, but I can't go in. My papers don't authorize me to go in." She said, "That would do all right. Just do the best you can." So, I drove her out there to Potsdam, and she went in. She went in with the determination of somebody who'd just found termites and she was gonna kill them all with her bare hands. And she was in there for two hours. I don't know whether it was all spent in bickering or they were wrestling, she never said. But when she came out, she had a pass, signed by Zukov himself, which permitted her to take a jeep and a driver across the Russian zone to Austria, and if she found Rudy Sieber's parents, it authorized her to pick them up, bring them back to Berlin, install them as a complete family in Berlin, then get the green ration cards—the best ration cards you could get—so they would be a family again. And she went at this almost like she knew nothing else was important in the world at that moment for her. But when you think of all the looting, and the number of people in the Russian forces who were scattered throughout that territory, drunk and up to anything. . . . And in those days if you had cigar coupons sometimes you could fool a sentry and he'd let you by—what did he know about Zukov, except there was a rumor or somebody way up yonder. And so, she risked all that, but she did go, she did find them, she brought them back, and she got them installed.

Marlene with General George S. Patton Jr.

After she had done all this magnificent [he laughs] nuclearizing of the family, on November 5 General Gavin and I were in London to say goodbye to the people who treated the Eighty-Second kindly when they were in residence, and we were in the middle of a press briefing when the phone rang, and it was Marlene from Paris. She told General Jim that she just had word that her mother had died. And she said, "I wish you could help me." And he said, "We'll take care of it."

And so, as we got on the airplane to fly home, he kept saying, "I'm too visible for this." "The antifraternization rule is still on. It does not excuse association with Germans, whether they're dead or alive. So, you take care of it." So, I had to recruit four paratroopers, each armed with a shovel, and I went to the Schöneberg Berlin Cemetery, which was as near as I could figure to the neighborhood where Josephine von Losch had grown up. So, when it got dark enough, we went in there. It was a setting much like you'd think to start a Dracula movie with because in all the artillery that the Russians had rained down on Berlin, and the bombings of the RAF and the American Air Force, many of the graves had been blown open and the coffins were standing up on their ends, and the partial remains were hanging out of these coffins. And the smell of death was all over the place. It wasn't a place where you're likely to be interrupting anything, so it worked quite well for us. And we dug the grave, and I went all around like as if I didn't know where the heck I was, uh, just being sure that we didn't have any visitors or anybody being curious about why Americans were in there. And we went off after the grave was dug under the trees at the side of the cemetery, and waited until two o'clock in the morning. Then, under cover of darkness, we took a truck over to Josephine's tiny apartment and we brought her body down the stairs, down that narrow stairway, in the coffin and put her in the truck, and took her over and put her in the grave. And then we went back under the trees. A German cemetery is not really a cheerful place in the best of times. It has all the atmosphere of brooding, an unpleasant feeling of things being ripped apart. The conformity of the gravestones makes absolutely nothing out of the residents who are below. And it's just, in the end, a procession of erasures. And to have this complemented by the smell of dead people, and to be working furtively like you were stealing something when all we were trying to do was do things quickly and get out of sight so nobody would be curious and come in to find out what was going on, well, it's hard to describe. So all of these things: going up those stairs to her apartment, and the casket was so light because she was so small, and to horse it down those stairs, and get it in the truck and think of her bouncing along, in not what you would call regal hearse-like splendor because we needed to conceal the identity of our cargo, and then to slip her into the grave, and then move away so if anybody came we could warn them off. If they didn't come all was well, and that's the way it finally turned out.

The next morning, here came Marlene with William Walton, the *Times* bureau chief, who, because he was a member of the press, could mix with the Germans and there would be no problem for him. They had three professional mourners, and they did the usual writhing and groaning, and things that went along with a traditional funeral. And Marlene just sat there looking at the coffin. When the time came, she dropped the earth on the lid, and Walton did, too. And then he took her by the arm and she turned her back. She never looked back; she just walked away. So, we sat there until darkness, and then went over and covered the grave. But I will say that Josephine was the only one in the Schöneberg Berlin Cemetery that was truly buried six feet down that day. Everybody else was partway up out of *their* graves. But at the very end of it, two weeks after this had happened, a military policeman came into my office and said, "I've got an old German out here. He's very nervous, but he has a bill." And I said, "What's the bill for?" And he said, "It has to do with Marlene Dietrich's mother." And I thought, boy, this is never gonna go away. I brought him in and he gave me the slip. It was for fourteen deutsche marks, and the interpreter explained to me, "It says here, 'For washing the body.'" So I paid the fourteen deutsche marks, and that ended the story—until Marlene herself died.

Because Marlene had said often that she always wanted to be buried near her mother, it always kind of spooked me that without knowing what I was doing, I picked the last resting place for both of them. Marlene's grave is actually about thirty-five steps from her mother's in that little dark place we found in the middle of the night.

Ironically, two months after you were able to take Marlene back for burial in 1992, I was in Berlin for a reunion of the Luftwaffe [*he laughs*], of all the incredible changes of things, and I went out to visit her. And that's when I was looking at both her mother's headstone and hers, and this German lady came up to me and she said, "You knew Marlene?" And I said, yes, and I told her about it. She said, "They did not want her here. They said she was a traitor. But she got the movie star's revenge." She said, "When she came back, there were more cameras in this cemetery than there are tombstones, and the flashbulbs were going off in every direction." So, I guess Marlene won the day, big time. For those who thought well of her, they were glad she'd had her say, even though it was a silent, "I'll show ya." [*He laughs.*]

GUY STERN

GUY STERN, distinguished professor of German and Slavic Studies at Wayne State University, has become widely known as one of the originators of the field of exile studies and as founder of the International Lessing Society and the Lessing Yearbook. As author of numerous books and articles on eighteenth- and nineteenth-century German literature, he has received many awards, both from the United States and Germany, the country that he fled in 1937 during the Hitler period. Among his American honors is the designation as Germanist of the Year and an honorary doctorate from Hofstra University. The Federal Republic of Germany bestowed on him the Grand Order of Merit and the Goethe Medal. His chance encounter with Marlene Dietrich in the last years of the war became one of his most memorable events during his exploits in Europe as a member of the U.S. Army. Driving around together in an open Jeep speaking German in the middle of the U.S. Army advance has always been a picture that again profiles the incredible irony of war and that in Marlene's life in general.

My wartime encounter with Marlene Dietrich came right after the Battle of the Bulge in 1944–45. As you will recall, the Germans had staged a counterattack. We had to withdraw. We withdrew, luckily, on the road to Eupen, not to Malmedy, where Sepp Dietrich had amassed SS troops. They became known as the executioners of the famous—or infamous rather—Malmedy Massacre, where many American troops were killed after being captured.

But we got out of that region and withdrew to a city in Belgium called Huy. Now, this city featured a large fortress on a mountaintop. And that's where we established our prisoner-of-war enclosure, after having been as far forward as a city on the border of Belgium in Germany called Welkenrad. That's where our prisoner-of-war enclosure had been, and it went from there to the city of Huy, which was further in the interior of Belgium.

While we were there, the Germans were beaten back, and so we were really in much better spirits and our morale had lifted. And then one day, it was lifted even further because we got news that a USO show was coming by starring the one and only Marlene Dietrich. It was scheduled to take place at a restaurant, which had a large catering hall. And it was only about twenty miles away. So, we went to our superior, and I said, "Could we drive to see Marlene Dietrich perform? He said, "Sure. Take one of the jeeps." So, two of us jumped into a jeep—my friend Fred Howard and I. He also came originally from Germany as I did, but he came from Berlin. And there we were. We arrived in the town near Huy, found the spot where she had chosen to give her performance, and it was magic. There were no chairs—we were sitting on top of our helmets, and the hall was *packed*. You could have dropped a needle and it would never have hit the ground. There was an upright piano on stage. And we all sat there expectantly. We waited about fifteen, twenty minutes. And waiting wasn't easy, not just because of our anticipation but also because we were, despite our raised morale, physically quite miserable. During the German retreat, the water supply had been tainted and we all had contracted a disease, which was known by a slang name as "The GIs." I needn't further explain, I am sure. So, we were sitting there on the helmets and occasionally someone had to climb over everybody else to hurriedly leave for destinations known.

But before long all of a sudden, the hall went

quiet—the noise completely stopped because Marlene Dietrich appeared, and she appeared in her GI clothes, dressed just as we were. Before she began her performance, she stepped up to the mike and said, "Fellows, I may have to break in the middle of a song and excuse myself, and, heck, you know the reason why." And so we all laughed, and she had won us over as a performer with one sentence that showed that we all shared the same "misadventure." Fortunately for her, that break didn't actually happen. She stuck out the whole program. She had one intermission. But it went very smoothly. She had a piano player who accompanied her who looked far more uncomfortable.

I cannot remember the repertoire, except for one song, which just stuck in your mind, as memory will help you sometimes, and sometimes it won't give you the whole story. I do remember she had that famous saw between her legs, and was performing with that. But this one song, "Go See What the Boys in the Back Room Will Have," really hit home for us. We all could have used a drink at that time so it really struck a nerve in me and all the other fellows. We, because of the retreat, had run out of alcohol. What we had brought from Normandy was an impossible drink, which did more to you than one would really, normally intend [*he laughs*], and that was a drink called Calvados. In fact, we brought in bottles upon bottles of this lethal stuff, hidden in our jeeps and in our duffel bags, but we had run out. And so now, when Marlene Dietrich burst into that song, "Go See What the Boys [*he laughs*] in the Back Room Will Have," well, we all applauded because that's exactly what we were thirsting for! The applause was thunderous.

My adventure story really started after the show. My friend, Fred, had far more guts, and initiative, and a little bit of chutzpah beyond mine and he said, "Let's go backstage." And so we did. "Backstage" is an exaggeration. It's merely a theater term. We went into that little dressing room she had, which was converted out of some improvised, tiny room in this inn. Fred was a talker, I wasn't, and he said, "You know, Miss Dietrich, you must have known my mother in Paris. She talked about you, she moved in the same circle." And by some chance, he knew the circle in which Marlene Dietrich moved when she lived in Paris. So, he mentioned that name, and she, lady that she was, polite as she was, she said, "Oh, yes. Yes, of course. I remember your mother." And he gave the name and she couldn't have known her because later on, Fred told me that was a cock-and-bull story. But it was enough for her to take an interest in us. And then Fred said, "You know, we are twenty miles away from here, and we are prisoner-of-war interrogators. Our enclosure is twenty miles away from here at the fortress in Huy. How would you like to come along?" And she said that might be very interesting. She had some people with her who were her escorts or guards, but she didn't even notify them,

Marlene and "her boys" walk through Stolberg, Germany, in January 1945.

she just shouted to somebody—I think to the piano player—and said, "I'll be back in couple of hours." And so, we filed into the jeep, just the three of us, and we drove through Huy and up that winding road that led up to the fortress.

I have to describe the enclosure for a moment. On the left-hand side of this huge fortress, there were barbed-wire enclosures on both sides, with a walkway in-between. On the left side were the captured enlisted men, and on the right side, the captured German officers. Scarcely had she taken a few steps into this walkway in between the two enclosures when the word spread like wildfire: "Marlene Dietrich is here." And the officers as well as the enlisted men to the left side and the right side rushed to the barbed-wire fence to get a look at her. She waved, but she was also taken aback by that mass of Germans [*he laughs*], the storming of troops toward the center of the walkway. And the excitement began to spread, and they were all anticipating her walking farther, so they all rushed to the barbed wire. And, taken aback, Marlene stepped back a few steps. They couldn't get into the walkway but ran to the borderline marked by the barbed wire.

After a few moments, when the outcries of the German prisoners reached the command post, the captain of our military police detachment, which was there to guard the prisoners while we interrogated them, came storming out. His name was Captain Amacher. He was the captain of our military police unit guarding the prisoners, which had accompanied us all through the war, from Normandy on. He came storming out and he said, "What the heck is going on?!" He used stronger language than that, which I don't dare repeat here, but basically he said, "What the blank is going on here?!" And then he saw what was going on, and he shouted at us, "Get her out of here! We can't have a riot here in the prisoner-of-war enclosure." And then when we tried to explain, he became apoplectic. He kept shouting, "Get her out of here! I'll have a riot on my hands." And, of course, Marlene Dietrich completely understood, and so we were properly chastened and that was the command, "to get the blank out of there," so we asked her to "please come back to the jeep with us," and she did. We piled back into the jeep and we calmed down a bit because Captain Amacher seemed to be calming down now that we were leaving. We had seen him before at great rage, but not like this! So we drove her back to the inn, to the catering hall where the performance had been, and where her accompanist was on the stray piano. Waiting for her at the inn was her military police escort, probably none too pleased.

But on the way back, she told us a wonderful story. She said, "I am not surprised really that the German prisoners sort of took a delighted interest in me because I had a similar experience just a few days ago."

I ought to tell here that we had just taken—the First Army had just taken—the first German city. It was the city of Stolberg, not far from the Belgian border. And here she decided to visit the first German city that had been taken by the Americans. Stolberg had been heavily shelled and previously been bombed, and many of the buildings were down, she told us. These people of the town had lost much of their goods. They also didn't have all that much to eat. This was now a town occupied by the Americans. And she went in there and she was very curious, perhaps even anxious, as to what the reaction would be by the German population.

So, she was a bit apprehensive, she told us, and she said, "While I had left Germany, I had come over to the American side, and I thought there might be some very strong resentments."

So, Marlene Dietrich ventured forth, as she told us, and she was prepared for a very hostile reception, because after all, she had left her native Germany, a voluntary exile, and she was prepared for at least indifference, but the exact opposite happened. And she told it in a sort of sense of triumph.

She had encountered first one housewife, who immediately recognized her, and she sort of clapped her hands together and said, "Why, you are here, Frau Dietrich!" And she then rushed from one house to the next—food and everything else in Stolberg was in very short supply. She went from one house to the next, gathering ingredients for a cake, and the citizens of—or the women of—Stolberg baked her a cake. And I think, the way she talked, it was the nicest present or the nicest delicacy she could have gotten. And, of course, she was used to Parisian gourmet food, but she was really excited that the people had done that because it augured for her that people accepted—even applauded—her for what she had done, in leaving a tyranny for the free country of America.

So, we drove while we were talking. She told us some of her experiences with the USO; that she had appeared in many shows, although we had ascertained this even before that. And she told us that she gloried in this activity, that really this gave great meaning to her, taking part in the war effort.

Then we arrived back to that very same inn, and as she left the jeep we said good-bye. And I, of course, didn't expect to see her again. I was just a student who had finished his sophomore year at St. Louis University and I was not in the league to ever meet Marlene Dietrich again.

Afterward at the castle, in the course of interrogations, when you had, obviously, a very cooperative prisoner, I asked whether he had seen Marlene Dietrich. Most of them hadn't—only those in that first rush had. Those who were farther in the back of the enclosure missed seeing her, as it all happened too fast. But there were a couple of cooperative prisoners who brought up the subject. One of them said, "Did I see right? Did all my friends see right, was that Marlene Dietrich, the famous Dietrich? All my friends said, yes, she was the genuine article." Many, of course, were too seasoned not to see that she was the genuine article. One prisoner was so astounded that a world-famous performer and actress would be at a prisoner-of-war enclosure. He was a young fellow who was very doubtful. He couldn't quite believe it. So I assured him. I said, "That was Marlene Dietrich." And he asked me, what was she doing here? And I told him that she was doing these USO shows and had spent a good part of her time going through France, having, as best that I knew, also appeared in England. And so, that satisfied him, and he told me that it was a wonderful experience. Three or four others echoed this sentiment.

And I think that was a significant sample or cross-section of prisoners, as it occurred from the enlisted men as well as from some of the most sophisticated and high-ranking officers that I had to interrogate. Their shared feeling was that they were astonished. It was a great surprise to see her in a prisoner-of-war enclosure, see the famous Marlene

Checking out the soldiers' legs.

Dietrich. And it also was for some, I would guess, admiration. Of course here I may be interpolating or extrapolating what their feelings were, that she would come so close to the front and entertain the troops, but I don't think so.

In many ways it's difficult for us to understand sometimes how the enemy, especially captured soldiers, could be as positively affected by someone who, in a way, helped the other side. And even though we don't know the answer to that, I think the troops were far more favorable than some of the later reactions you heard—you know, from Berlin, where there were was criticism of her that she had voluntarily left Germany because she could not associate with the Nazis. And I think the prisoners took it for granted that somebody had the right to choose sides. And, of course, they were also used to camp and camp entertainment because Germany had an equivalent, or the Germans had an equivalent to our USO. And we have criticized, and I think rightly so, some of the Swedish stars who came to Germany—Zarah Leander was one of them—who entertained the German troops. But I think also the German troops at that time had seen the futility and the tragedy of the war by that time. And I think out of that first, let us call it, "shell-shocked experience," they were far more amenable to understanding someone who did not want to share in the dreams of conquest and terror that Hitler had imposed. You have to remember, these were soldiers coming out of the front lines, captured, had the shock of capture. And many of them, in a way, came to their senses. Of course, some of the stories we heard were opportunistic, concocted to please us. But I think in many cases it was genuine. I have to say we were seasoned interrogators by that time, as we had done it from Normandy all through France, till Belgium, and sizing up a prisoner, whether he was sincere or was giving us a story or was trying to curry favor with us, well, we were able to spot that. These people were genuinely converted in a way. Many of them, too, at that time, when the Battle of Bulge failed, were deserters.

One of the most fascinating prisoners I had was a young Austrian sergeant who had deserted to us and had brought a diary along with him. And it was such a fascinating diary, showing the decline of morale almost day to day, which he had written down—the failures of the battle, and the mud, and dirt, and slime that he was enduring. It was a brilliantly written diary, written in shorthand, which I had been trained to read. We attached an episode of this diary to our intelligence reports, sort of in installments, which went to forty different agencies. This diary gave the morale story of the Germans, and it was written from that perspective, of a defeated group having come to disillusionment. And I think that word ought to be underlined—*disillusioned,* prisoners who were not looking at it with the grand hindsight of later generations, but these disillusioned prisoners who were happy to see Marlene Dietrich. Because it certainly gave them something. It gave them a lift. Not the same type of lift, of course, that we had experienced during the USO show, but one that showed that civilization, even German civilization, was not gone completely. And this was powerful for them in their dreary circumstances. These camps were not comfortable. They were primitive. They were improvised. The food they got was C rations, which they rather liked, I must say. But they were delighted to see a sense of civilization and the appearance of civilization coming into their war enclosure.

My impression of Marlene Dietrich during our encounter was that she had given very serious thought to her identity. And that came through because Fred, the more aggressive of the two of us, did a role reversal in our interrogations—"good cop, bad cop." I was always the tough guy, but in personality he was far more aggressive. And when he started talking to her and he addressed her backstage, he talked to her in German, not in English. And when we continued the whole trip in the jeep, we spoke almost entirely in German. And that set a certain ambience in our conversation, which, indeed, hearkened back to the days of prewar and pre-Hitler Germany. She was not condemnatory of Germany as a whole in side remarks, but rather also saw the culture out of which she came and out of which I came, and out of which Fred came. Ultimately she found the positive aspects of her very fine culture that once was and was now destroyed by Hitler. And her responses to that when we talked about, like Berlin in the '20s, for which both Fred and I were far too young, but when she talked about it, it was in no way trying to superimpose the catastrophe of the '30s upon the significance and importance of the '20s.

The complex question is: Why was there a spontaneous favorable reaction to Marlene Dietrich, and then later on a far more ambivalent one? I think the answer lies in the fact that the prisoners whom I interrogated, and even sometimes talked to just by chance or in passing, referred to Marlene Dietrich with, I would say, unreserved approval. Why was that?

There were essentially three reasons why the people of Stolberg and the prisoners that encountered her for those brief moments had an absolutely favorable impression of her, and approved of what she had done in leaving Germany.

The first was because these soldiers were dispirited and disillusioned, and had gone through a demoralizing war, and the last stand of Hitler at the Bulge had been repulsed. They were shell-shocked, many of them still. And so now they had a different perspective. Even those who might have started out as fervent Nazis now understood that that was the wrong road for Germany to take. And they approved right after that war experience what Marlene Dietrich had done, and in that context.

Secondly, many of them remembered her from a time, which they saw now in retrospect, as a very positive one for German culture, cabaret, film, and the like. And remembered her from her days before the war. It was a sensation for them to see Marlene Dietrich in the flesh, right at their prisoner-of-war enclosure, a true reminder of better times.

And thirdly, her presence was, in itself, an unheard of thing—that a world star of the stature of Marlene Dietrich would come close to the front lines or close enough. They were surprised that someone of that great magnitude had come to the front lines to entertain American troops. They were astonished by it. Their remarks were, "My God! What else! These Americans have it all."

I think the reason why the encounter with Marlene Dietrich meant a great deal to me is that though we came from entirely different backgrounds, there was a certain congruence of our fates. I had left Germany at age fifteen in order to get away from Hitler, from being persecuted. Marlene Dietrich had vol-

With the guys on the front in Europe.

untarily taken the same step of getting away from an intolerable, tyrannical government. And so we met out there in the field as two new neo-Americans, very close to the battlefield where the nationalities of our past and present were fighting. And so the impression it made, this encounter, is one that will really stick with me. It's indelible. Here we were, we were talking in German. We were sharing the same fate—I'm saying that without wanting to be presumptuous because she is of such great stature, and yet, there was this immediate empathy between the two of us. I was a refugee from Germany. She was a voluntary exile. And those two fates really coincided and overlapped. And I venture to say that she felt something like it when I introduced myself and when my friend Fred told of his background, which was identical to mine. He came from Berlin, I from a provincial town in northern Germany called Hildesheim. We both had to leave, Fred and I, and Marlene Dietrich also out of moral and ethical convictions. So, we understood each other. I think that was a moment that really, beyond all the warfare, was a sense of emotional touching one another that happened at that moment in the vicinity of the Belgian city of Huy at that inn where she had performed.

It's well known, of course, that since that little-known time of this spontaneous acceptance of Marlene Dietrich things have changed. And there was a really serious division and some hostility in Berlin and elsewhere when it became known that Marlene Dietrich wanted to be buried in Berlin. There were protests. And I'm trying to analyze why things have shifted so much. I think one of the things that changed was simply a matter of time or generations, where younger people no longer understood the moral necessity of fleeing Hitler, of fleeing the Third Reich.

Secondly, I think it is also that some people have shifted again toward a more rightist position. And out of this neo-fascist position of a small minority of Germans, trying to rewin World War II—of course, a futile undertaking—there comes a poisoning of general opinion. I would say it is a very minority opinion that is protesting against Marlene Dietrich or against other exiles that voluntarily left Germany. Democracy has triumphed in Germany. The idea of traitor—no. The German chancellor recently said, "We won the war by losing it." And that is exactly the attitude of the majority of Germans. There was recently a demonstration against the hatred, the xenophobia, of some Germans, a large demonstration that illustrated once more that this group of people who cannot accept what happened forty or fifty years ago is on the wane. And I am convinced that it is a small group that is still harboring these feelings of resentment.

But in the wider picture, Marlene Dietrich is again a big star. Her movies made in prewar Germany are being revived and are being shown. Her American movies are being shown, some for the first time, in film museums. Sooner rather than later, I think we are going to see the treasure that the exiles possessed in toto, and people like those Marlene Dietrich represented will be more valued as time progresses.

Prior to World War II, Marlene tried in vain to convince her mother, Josephine von Losch, to leave Germany. For the duration of the war, Marlene helped raise millions of dollars to buy bombs that were then dropped on Berlin where her mother lived. She also did many radio shows designed to demoralize the German citizenry. How this affected her family was unknown as there was no communication possible between them. Marlene was unable to contact her mother until the Allies entered the city in 1945. This is their first conversation, recorded and in English for security reasons. It was found in the bottom of a box in Marlene's living room marked "Cleared by the War Department."

"Lena!"
"Mami!"
"Lena!"
"Mami, my sweet, we have to talk in English."
"*Ja,* my lovely Lena, I am so glad to hear your voice."
"Mami, Liesel is alright . . ."
"What? Liesel?"
"Yes, and the child too. Her son is alright."
"Did you see her?"
"Yes, I have seen her, and I'm coming as soon as I can."
"Ah, *ja,* and I am so glad and so thankful for all . . . what you have done."
"Mami, you suffered for my sake. Forgive me."
"Yes, my love."
"Mami, take care of yourself."
"Yes. Goodbye."
"Goodbye, Mami."
"Goodbye, my heart. Goodbye."
"Goodbye."
"Goodbye."

ELIZABETH MCINTOSH

ELIZABETH MCINTOSH was a women's page editor stationed in Hawaii on that fateful day in December 1941 when the Japanese bombed Pearl Harbor. From there, her career led her to the newly formed Office of Strategic Services (OSS), which was the first organized intelligence service, later to become the CIA. During her tenure with the OSS, Elizabeth participated in many operations behind enemy lines in the Pacific Theater of war, in stark contrast to her almost motherly manner. During her career as an OSS agent she also worked closely with "Wild" Bill Donovan, the founder and head of the service, and formulated and conducted a system of disinformation programs called Morale Operations (MO). Many of these new ideas included Marlene and utilized radio and rumor to great effect. Elizabeth's book, *Women of the OSS,* offers insight into this early period of clandestine work and also explains how, in the middle of a war, a German national like Marlene was given such latitude and secret duty. Much of Marlene's work remained secret until after the war, when the State Department permitted Marlene to release an album of her wartime musical contributions called *Songs of the OSS.*

I was living in Hawaii before the war started, and I happened to be in Honolulu the day that the Japanese bombed Pearl Harbor. It turned the islands from a tranquil little sort of a resort community to an armed fort right in the middle of the Pacific. It was about seven o'clock in the morning, I guess. I was just listening to the church choir, and all of a sudden a voice cracked over the wire: "The islands are under attack. This is the real McCoy." And I thought, "Oh, here's some more army maneuvers or something," and I didn't believe it. But if I'd looked out my window, I would have seen the second wave of Japanese planes flying over Cocoa Head on their way to bomb Hickham Field.

But at that point, my photographer—I was working for a newspaper then—called and said, "We've got to go down. Something's happened. We're on assignment now. Pearl Harbor's been attacked."

It was such a beautiful day, I just couldn't believe it. As we went into town, you began to feel the tension there. There were sirens. Buses were stopping on their way to church. We passed an open market where the shells had just sort of leveled it, but there was all this Christmas stuff scattered all around. And there was one little kid in the middle, playing with all these beautiful Christmas ribbons and things. My photographer said that it would make a great picture. But he said, "The kid's smiling, can you do something about it?" So I said, "Well, okay." I went up and I pinched him, and then he started to cry. We got the picture and I think *Life* magazine ran it.

I was not allowed to go to Pearl until the next day. They sent me to a hospital to report on the wounded coming in. This is when you first get the feeling that the war is beginning, seeing all those wounded and bloody people from Hickham Field. I was one of the few women reporters, I guess, that were allowed to go to Pearl Harbor to see the terrible casualties and the dreadful effects of the bombing.

I went out and saw the ships that were still burning, the smoke and the smell was everywhere, and oil was all over the water. You could look out and see bubbles coming up from the ships that were sunk, most with their men still in them. When I was walking along the streets of Pearl Harbor, there was something else that hit me, too. It was even more poignant; I looked down on the streets and there were the bodies of hundreds of dead birds that had been killed by the concussion of the bombing. There were sparrows, mynahs, and doves that were just lying there, all ruffled and dead. It had a terrible and rather bittersweet effect on me. It was a very sad day, but also in a sort of strange way, there was a wonderful feeling, too, to know that we were perhaps going to get into the war because they had just attacked an American outpost.

And so, to me it meant that a whole new life was beginning for all of us, which it did. And it did mean that we were getting into the war, which we'd all been feeling that we had been preparing for. We were very, very much aware of what the military had already been doing.

I remember once I went down to Manila on the ship the *Republic.* We took the New Mexico National Guard down, that was May '41, and we were bringing back women and children. Now, that was long before the war, and you had the feeling that something was going on, really happening, and especially around Hawaii. The Red Cross was being organized, and there was just a feeling that something was building up but we didn't quite know what.

Prior to Pearl Harbor, a lot more troops were being sent in to us and a lot more troops were going into the Philippines, but now that we really knew, we also knew we had to get in and fight to the finish. And so it was, in a way, an inspiration to have seen this happen and to know what was going to come from it. And for me it meant working for the intelligence service.

The Office of Strategic Services, or OSS, was the first organized intelligence system during the war. And it was headed by a general named Wild Bill Donovan, who had been a great hero in World War I. He had the imagination and the ability to create something that was very unusual and different from the usual for our wartime period. And he ran up against the military establishment, of course, because he was sort of a nonconformist, but his ideas went over with President Roosevelt. The two of them worked together with Winston Churchill to produce a worldwide organization, except in the Far East, where MacArthur held us back. [*She laughs.*] But we were all over Europe and the Middle East.

I knew General Donovan quite well. During the war he was something of a hero to all of us. He was a New York lawyer who had been in World War I. He had more decorations than General MacArthur—and I think this was part of our problem with later not being able to work in the Pacific! But anyway [*she laughs*], he was a wonderful man, Irish with bright blue eyes. He was sort of, well, I called him "penguin shaped" once and he almost hit me over the head because he was quite proud of his looks!

But he was the sort of man who could imagine things and get them to work. He was a good lawyer, but had an organizational ability, too. It was a little bit different from what the military was used to. And when he came up with ideas like having Morale Operations in the front lines, the military were rather, well, not quite sure they approved of it.

But General Donovan was eventually able to organize the Office of Strategic Services, which later became the CIA. It was initially a multiunit force with not only the Morale Operations people but also included the units who went behind the lines and sabotaged, the ones that blew up ships, and the ones that did the counterintelligence work, usually with the British and the Chinese. The general was always behind everything that was happening. He knew what was going on all the time and he was always there when we needed him.

And we had quite a few jobs. The first one was research and analysis. When we got the information, our analyst would sit down and decide what we could use it for, and where we should be going with it. This was very, very important. These were the people who stayed at home and did all that. And we fed them the information.

Then, overseas, we had special forces and operatives, people who would jump behind the lines and then work with the French or the Chinese, fighting the enemy in their own field. There were also the maritime units, which would work attacking shipping, sometimes by placing limpet mines on the hulls of enemy vessels to blow them up.

Then there was X-2, another type of intelligence unit that would try and infiltrate the enemy's intelligence system and find out what was going on and then hopefully be able to anticipate what's happening or was going to happen. The British were very lucky in that they had cracked the German code and toward the end they were using that to great advantage.

Finally, there was also something that I was in, which was called the Morale Operations, or MO. And this was a sort of a "disinformation" unit. Its primary purpose was to throw off the enemy, keep them off guard, disturb them, or endeavor to make them confused.

The effect of what we called Morale Operations against the enemy is hard to determine because you don't get a body count when people change their minds or go over to the other side. But we had a feeling always that we were doing something significant, especially the radio work that we did with the British. That started in 1944, and continued right through to the end of the war.

Top secret, our radio station broadcast to the Germans all night long, from eight to eight, supposedly from German territory. They never did know where this radio program was coming from, but they assumed it was a German station, that the whole thing was German.

And of course, the material that we broadcast was always slanted. The messages were subtle so that they wouldn't fully realize what they were hearing. But here and there, there would be snide remarks about how Hitler was, well, perhaps not doing the right thing by going into Russia, for instance. Or just the hint of the idea that the people he was working with were not competent, or that the German people elsewhere were suffering with no food, things of that sort, things that would bother the Wehrmacht soldiers in the field—get to them, make them worry. We tried to make the German soldiers get homesick, war weary, want to give up. But the station was also heard in the cities, and when it was, it also had a very demoralizing effect.

One OSS part of the radio operation was to create the music and entertainment that was broadcast in addition to the news that the British put on. Some of the music made fun of the regime, sort of the way you can with naughty songs. And then others tried to make the people become generally melancholy, or make the soldiers not to want to fight the war. We would just sort of try and demoralize them by playing songs that would be just a little bit changed from the original tunes.

Donovan was a great admirer of people who worked at the front, on the front lines. He, of course, had been there himself during World War I. The fact that Marlene Dietrich was out there with the troops in uniform, in her own fatigues, and got as close as she could to the border, just to be there and help raise morale, well, it impressed him terribly.

When the groups of singers and musicians were organized in New York in 1944, he personally said that he felt that Marlene Dietrich would be one

Marlene begins to look the part of a resistance fighter on a USO tour, 1944.

that we could talk to, that we could bring her into the *secret* part of it. We could not do that with any of the musicians or any of the other actors or singers that we were using for security reasons. But he felt that he could trust her and that she would appreciate what we were doing. So she was the *only one* that he really told the whole problem to, and she worked out beautifully in the program. And I think Marlene made it better *because* she knew, and because of how she contributed. The recording studio was in downtown New York and it was very secretive. You could only get in with a pass and special orders and all. They had this big orchestra that would be playing for the recordings.

They had a lot of great singers from the opera and others, including Marlene's daughter, Maria Riva, and they were all very well-known names. And they would come in and out, thinking that they were doing something for the Americans' cause by singing these songs, most of which were very kind of patriotic. But they never heard the songs recorded in German and never knew their English recordings were for anything but American GIs. But Marlene and Maria knew that some of these songs were being changed, especially the German versions, to influence the thinking of the Germans. And so Marlene helped to rewrite and change some of the things. You can hear that in the recording that we still have, the OSS Columbia record. You can read some of the words they used and you can see how they'd be rather wicked and mean to the people listening to them and how the other side would be kind of disheartened.

The secret songs were American tunes by our great writers, but all in German, and some German songs that fit with them. And one of the special ones, of course, was "Lili Marlene," which didn't need any transcription at all. It was so, so very beautiful. It was so poignant. Even the Americans and the Allies loved to hear it.

Somebody described the song as a spy that worked on all sides because it was so poignant and so beautifully sung, and it was just soul-wrenching to everyone. [*She laughs.*] It made everyone kind of homesick and war weary!

I understand from people I've worked with that to the German officials, this radio program was very offensive and that they were furious. Marlene Dietrich was, I guess, an anathema to a lot of the Germans, as an American would be to us who was working for the Germans or the Japanese. We would resent it terribly.

German officials felt that Marlene Dietrich was a traitor, betraying her country by singing these songs that so upset so many of the people listening. And yet, we heard, too, that these songs seemed to be very popular, as we found out later from the German soldiers who were captured. Many said that they were very, very much overcome by this music and they used to always listen for it. They said they still used to love to hear her voice, that she was such an important person in their lives. And the actual fact that she was singing these songs broadcast from the enemy didn't seem to matter when they found out because of the beautiful quality of her voice and what she was singing to them. As we talked to the German prisoners more about it later, they admitted that these songs really got to them. Officially they hated her very much but they secretly listened to her music.

And this, I think, is quite wonderful when you think of how much the German High Command hated her and our broadcasts, things they really wanted to do away with but were never able to. We kept playing her all the time, and she was just a terrific woman. And we had a very good cover, too, that we were able to maintain.

It seems sort of strange to say that I heard Mar-

Marlene releases her wartime songs originally made for the clandestine services.

lene Dietrich singing in China, and this was when I was in northern China with OSS. I was stationed behind the lines, but it was rather lonely because we were virtually protected by our air force, the Fighting Tigers. But we were working with a group of Chinese mainly and were really isolated. And so, occasionally a plane would come in with a couple of singers or a band, something that would sort of be entertaining. We could hardly believe it; it was so wonderful to be able to relax. It was a little like going home again. And that's probably, too, why they'd send us so many records, just to get our spirits up.

We used to get her recordings on these great big records, and we'd play them on a very squeaky record player. And sometimes we would be able to dance to some of the music. But whenever she came on, we'd always kind of—the men and women, if we were sort of having an after-dinner dance or something—we'd all sort of stop dancing and listen. And it was just a magical feeling that we'd get about this voice coming over, especially when she was singing songs like "Lili Marlene." I do remember "Lili Marlene" because it just got to me. It—it grabbed me. It was something that kind of lifted you up. And so to me it was something quite wonderful to think that she was able to affect us as well as I know the people fighting in Europe were affected, on both sides. That was just one memory that I have of her, far away in China.

I think that these women in the war proved themselves. The ones that were in the WAVEs, the WACs, and the other female units not behind the lines were the ones who were in the spy trade, as it were, both British and French as well as American. Women seemed to have a feeling for how to really fool people, how to dissemble. Some of the French women were just terrific when they were captured by the Germans. I remember one time this lady had a radio in her suitcase and the German said, "What have you got in the suitcase?" And she said, "I've got a radio." Just boomed it out at him. He said, "Oh, sure, of course," and let her go. There were quite a few women all over the world who were working with Morale Operations. One lady in Italy was working with German prisoners of war. She got about ten of them together finally, and she was able to train them to go back behind the German lines with our material to convince the other German soldiers that the war was coming to an end and that they were going to lose it. She did a very good job of it.

I mean, it's this sort of thinking that I think gives women sort of an edge over men occasionally. And we were also able to think of a lot of gossipy things to do for MO that men never would have thought of. Like organizing a group of women in Germany who would pose as women welcoming their men back. All our agents had to do was to wear what would look like a proper identification, and then they would be met and welcomed in Germany and have nothing to worry about. They were accepted by onlookers as husbands or brothers or whoever. This is the sort of a thing a woman can think of. A friend of mine actually did it and it worked out beautifully. It was reported, actually, back in America, this kind of thing. [*She laughs.*] I don't want to brag about women, but we *can* sort of feel how we could hurt people better, maybe, than men could think of, in terms of what we might be able to do. And a lot of our MO rumors and little leaflets and things that we passed out were that sort of business.

One rumor we came up with was that Hitler had decided to further increase the German population by issuing special little lapel pins to certain Wehrmacht troops going home on leave. The story went that if these "selected" soldiers simply just showed this pin to *any* woman "back home"—now this could be *your* wife, your sweetheart, or even your *mother*—that they could go to bed with her, and the woman couldn't refuse. This would be the open arms and free love that the Führer had instituted to increase the population! This is [*she laughs*] the kind of rumor that sort of went over really well!

General Donovan believed in us, that we could do things that perhaps the men couldn't do at MO. And I don't mean the Mata Hari types [*she laughs*], but we just had ideas about rumors, feelings—how we could get people thinking about or worried about what was going on "back home." And music and songs and how they were sung were a big part of that.

So, I think the women who participated in Morale Operations like Marlene Dietrich made a great deal of difference. It may not have been noticed as a great victory militarily, but she was doing something that was getting to the hearts and the minds of people. And I think that she believed in what she was doing, as we all did. We believed in the cause, and it was a different type of life and a different reason for living in those days. It meant that we were fighting for something we believed in, and I believe that's what she did, too. And I think it made a great deal of difference, the *way* she approached the situation. I think many other women did affect people but perhaps not as dramatically as Marlene Dietrich did.

MARKUS WOLF

MARKUS WOLF is the son of physician and author Friedrich Wolf, who was known for his socialist-oriented dramas and prose. In 1933, the Wolf family emigrated from Germany via Switzerland to France, and, in 1934, from France to the Soviet Union. He attended school in Moscow, and in 1940 he began studies at the College for Airplane Construction, followed by attendance at the Komintern school in the Soviet capital. He later became an announcer and commentator for the German Freedom Radio Station (Deutscher Freiheitssender) until the end of the war. The station was housed in Moscow and broadcast Russian propaganda in German. In May 1945, Markus returned to East Berlin where he was employed at an East German radio station for several years before he began work in the Ministry for National Security of the German Democratic Republic. For a long period he functioned as deputy minister in the East German cabinet. Markus ultimately became the infamous chief of foreign espionage of the German Democratic Republic, but has since retired. His work during the war was largely propaganda much like what Marlene was doing for the OSS. Markus wanted the world to know that there was a good side to Germany during the Nazi years, a "Germany in exile" and Marlene's efforts were a big part of his message.

By the time I began to be active in the fight against Hitler, the German resistance was practically decimated. In Berlin, for example, there was a resistance organization that later became known as Red Chapel [Rote Kapelle]. A small core of this group worked before the war with the Soviet News Agency. There were various splinter groups all over Germany, partly Social Democratic, partly Communist. We found out very late about the popular revolt by officers on July 20, 1944. These people attempted to kill Hitler, but this attempt also failed. All in all, there was no strong opposition in Germany, as opposed to France, Yugoslavia, Italy, and other German-occupied countries. But there was also an attempt to do something from exile, outside of Germany, to support the resistance.

That was the beginning of my activity with the radio, in the summer of 1943. In Moscow, besides Moscow Radio, there was a station called German Peoples Radio [Deutscher Volkssender], Voice of the International Freedom Movement. That was the station identification that I announced until May 1945. And that was an attempt to politically influence and support the anti-fascist resistance groups in Germany. It was one of the many radio stations that attempted to support the resistance in Germany in any way possible, which at that time in mid-1943 was scarcely noticeable any more. There were other stations in the west. Our model in some ways was the British station Soldiers' Radio Calais, who like us gave the appearance of broadcasting within Germany and supported anti-fascist resistance there. And we did that, too. We know that this station, like other radio propaganda stations outside Germany, was being heard. Nowadays you'd call it an underground station. We gave the appearance of being *in* Germany, transmitting illegally from the resistance. We did programs for that. We'd break off transmission because of the danger, which was fictional. There were all kinds of different programs, which we tried to keep entertaining and colorful. We had a speaker who came from Berlin, and she portrayed a Berlin woman. There was a man who portrayed an SA man in a very earthy way as an attempt to reach SA people, similar to the way the Calais station did. Almost every day, every hour, I announced, "You are listening to the German People's Station, the Voice of the International Peace Movement." Of course it was interesting and sometimes exciting for us to learn from our western counterparts what was happening, from the Voice of America, the Soldiers' Radio Calais, the BBC, and what they did to find programming that was entertaining, sometimes with music, which we couldn't do. Moscow Radio had it too, but our station didn't. And sometimes we read in letters that were found on prisoners, or from field mail that came into the hands of the Red Army, that these programs were indeed being heard.

That was the beginning of my activity in radio, which I continued after 1945. We followed other programs with interest, naturally the Nazi programs. We argued directly against them. I learned to write commentary from that. And I wrote and broadcast the so-called front commentaries; my counterpart on the Nazi side was a Mr. [Kurt] Dittmar, who did Nazi propaganda. Naturally we followed all the Nazi broadcasts carefully, as well as the programs of the western Allies, especially, the Soldiers' Radio Calais, which was broadcast out of England, as I later learned. It was established and led by a very capable journalist, Sefton Delmar. I later met him at the war criminal trials at Nuremberg. The programs were done in a very interesting way.

They also did it as if it was the resistance within the Nazi Party, the SA, who were against Hitler's leadership, against corrupt Nazi leaders. They were good programs, and they also had a demoralizing influence, as we saw in some of the letters that we got hold of from Germany and also from soldiers against the Hitler Army [Wehrmacht]. We listened to the Voice of America and also to the BBC broadcasts. We were also happy about German contributions. We listened to them with great interest. There were the broadcasts by Thomas Mann, I think, on the Voice of America. And there was great excitement when we heard a recording in German of a message by Marlene Dietrich. I remember one day a woman who worked in the station's recording section where all the programs were put together came, all excited, and said, "Marlene was speaking." Whether or not she sang, I don't remember, I don't think so. But she was using her authority as Marlene Dietrich to do the same thing we were doing—to urge the women, men, and soldiers of Germany to stop this meaningless, criminal war. That was our main purpose. Our older editors, especially the women, knew her films and songs. I know we had a record at home with the famous song from *The Blue Angel.* My mother had brought it with her from Stuttgart.

That was the work that I did until May 1945 at the front, when I did radio propaganda. And of course we tried like the others to pep up the programs. We had an editor from Berlin, who gave Berliner messages to reach the women; I think her name was Miss Werneke. There were similar programs at the Soldiers' Radio Calais. We had no musical programs, but got the tapes of the BBC, the Soldiers' Radio Calais, the Voice of America, and so on that were taped in Moscow. We heard them with great interest; we tried to reach Germany using casual programs, with songs including the famous ones from Marlene.

My brother Konrad did radio propaganda *right* at the front. He was drafted into the Red Army at seventeen and went that entire difficult way from the Caucasus to Berlin and beyond, right at the leading edge of the front. There were special loudspeaker wagons, radio wagons with special equipment, and he took the microphone right in front of the wagon. Or else, it was connected to the wagon with longer cables, because it was quite danger-

Marlene singing on Armed Forces Radio, broadcast to the front and into Germany, 1944.

ous. As soon as the propaganda began, they were usually shot at from the German side. He said his short texts in German, urged the soldiers to give up the senseless war, and to turn themselves over. They were also promised that nothing would happen to them while in captivity. The messages had to be short, because the Germans fired at them right away. It was a dangerous thing. And in order to get their attention, they played records of well-loved hits. I remember that my brother, I think he wrote it down once, that among the names of the singers on the records was Marlene Dietrich, probably the famous song from *The Blue Angel.* I suppose that was when the Red Army was coming into Germany. They looked for records, and they took whatever they could get to take with them. There were only five records or so. They couldn't take more with them. But one of the records had Marlene's voice on it. That was also an attempt to shorten the war. For a long time he had scarcely any success. But then toward the end of the war during the big battles, where German troops were in a hopeless situation, these radio messages did help to win over troops. At the end, entire fighting units gave up the war.

After the war, my brother became one of the most well-known film directors in East Germany, and one of his films, in my opinion his best film, titled *I Was Nineteen,* was about his final war experiences in 1945. He was sent to the Soviet-German front in the Caucasus, and he made the entire trek from the Caucasus to Berlin, and beyond Berlin. He was a radio propaganda man, but directly at the front. With German speakers like my brother, he portrays this activity during the last weeks of the war. The film shows how this radio propaganda worked, how dangerous it was. At the end of the film, his commander dies, a likable officer, shot by the SS, who were already retreating at the end of the war. That was also a kind of radio propaganda, different from how we did it in the "West," and using Marlene. But all had the same goal: to shorten the war. We had some feedback with letters and so on that the programs were being heard in Germany and also by some soldiers at the front. They wrote that it was very dangerous and secretive. But in retrospect, I have to say the effect was probably minimal.

The Americans were very involved in the so-called front services or front propaganda, if you want to call it that. I didn't know that at the time, but I found out about it later. There are also very impressive recordings [or photos] and documents. It was also very widespread on the German side, among Hitler's Wehrmacht. We knew more about that. We learned it from prisoners of war. The German propaganda was thought to be very important for entertaining troops, encouraging them after their terrible war experiences, and using entertainment to influence them. It was well known that there were entire companies of singers, musicians, and bands who were entertaining troops at the front or just behind it. There were well-known hit singers like Lala Andersen and Zarah Leander and so on. We knew about them from German prisoners. I imagine that when you had such a well-known actress and singer, who was famous before Hitler, and she was participating on the American side, if you will, in the war against Hitler, it must have made a difference. How much of one I wouldn't know, I was too far away. But the indirect effect was seen after the war.

From 1951 until 1986, that is, for thirty-five years, I was head of the espionage service of the GDR, or the East German Espionage Service, if you want to call it that. My duties were directed chiefly toward the "West," and so you had to figure that any prominent person visiting from the "West" was seen by many people as representing

The song "Lili Marlene" became synonymous with Marlene, and it was broadcast to the front lines and into Germany almost daily.

"Western freedom." For this reason you had to show them special support. You would see demonstrations that could be characterized as hostile, or they could be created. I always saw that from a certain distance, but I know that that was the case. Naturally I knew something about how prominent personalities from the "West" were handled during their stay, above all their entourage, and the effect that their presence had. It was not my job exactly, which was more directed toward the west. But I assume that when Marlene Dietrich appeared in a socialist country, that it caused a certain effect. I also know how visits of such prominent people as Marlene were followed by the internal services of the socialist countries. Such visits always caused great excitement, because nothing should happen to them. Some people probably saw her as a representative of Western freedom, and that was a drawing force for such people in these countries. Of course that was reflected in various files and descriptions and reports; I do not know of anything that was directed at Marlene personally. In Germany and in the eastern part, that is, the GDR, Marlene was not simply a star but also a personality in the anti-fascist struggle who was met with great respect and admiration. She was a representative of the anti-fascist resistance. Of course the appearance of Marlene Dietrich was greeted by her admirers and the people who knew her from before, the older generation, but also younger ones, who had already heard about her and seen her, and I as well. I don't know when I saw *The Blue Angel* and where—whether it played in the GDR, but I think so. There was her participation in the film by Stanley Kramer about the Nuremberg trial. I took part in the case myself; I think it is a good film, which also captured the atmosphere of the trial. And of course there was Spencer Tracy, but also Marlene Dietrich. They were actors back then that we were enthusiastic about. I was in Nuremberg at practically all of the main trial, and in my opinion the film captured the atmosphere in Nuremberg very authentically. Its message also represented what we in the eastern part of Germany wanted, namely, that this trial, and all that it expressed, would contribute to having this never be repeated. With the songs that she interpreted so wonderfully after the war, Marlene is still alive for me.

When Marlene came and appeared in Germany again, it didn't just cause enthusiasm. Many were enthusiastic, and many of the older people still knew Marlene Dietrich. My parents' generation knew her very well. *The Blue Angel* was shown in Germany fairly quickly after the war. But there was also a counterreaction, which was a reaction to her participation on the American side of the war. Some saw that as betraying Germany. We others experienced much the same. After the war, my brother was just twenty and still in his Red Army uniform. He was in Halle to give a speech to students about the future of German youth. Behind him on the blackboard someone had written in chalk, "Fatherland Traitor." I experienced similar things, like many other émigrés who returned to Germany who had actively spoken out and fought against fascism. So there were some similarities between the fate of Marlene and other anti-fascist German émigrés.

It is hard to estimate the effect Marlene's appearance had on Germans in *Germany.* The fact that she turned her back on Hitler's Germany was surely an important fact. Many representatives of German culture, like authors and filmmakers, had left Germany. A good portion of them wound up in America; others like us went to the Soviet Union. There weren't any other countries where one could find exile, except perhaps England. But it certainly had an effect, especially with the generation who knew her. The fact that it had an effect was shown by the negative reaction that Marlene found when she appeared in Germany again after the war. Certainly there was great support and enthusiasm for the wonderful actress that she was known to be, and as a wonderful representative for the art of singing with her marvelous songs. Maybe the most important thing was that in the rest of the world and in Germany, people could look and say, "There is another Germany." There was not only the Germany of Hitler and Goebbels. There is also a Germany in exile, a Germany of the anti-fascist resistance.

But as I said, after the war there was also rejection, and many viewed her, like they viewed many of us emigrants, as a traitor. We felt it the same way. And similar things happened to many who like Marlene were in America—Thomas Mann, Heinrich Mann, Bertolt Brecht, Lion Feuchtwanger. I remember when Thomas Mann appeared in Germany in Frankfurt on Main and in Weimar. He encountered almost the same thing as Marlene had. But I think the Germans' approval of her grew as they understood that Hitler was a great disaster, that this was a path in Germany that must never be traveled again.

When I think about Marlene, the thing that fascinates me the most—she was a great personality, one of the greatest of the last century—but it was she herself, the person. Of course she was a wonderful actress, who also interpreted the most diverse roles. For us older ones, it is still *The Blue Angel.* But besides this there is her conviction of what is necessary in order to be true to herself. She demonstrated that by not staying in Germany, while many had to adapt and did so. She showed that during the war, and I experienced it firsthand after the war, through her performances. "Where Have All the Flowers Gone" is interpreted over and over, but has never been communicated like Marlene—"Tell me where the men are, where are they now," the way Marlene did it. She could convince you with her personality, and I believe that brought her closer to me as with many in the east.

ALFRED HENS

ALFRED HENS was a rear-echelon soldier for the German army during the last days of World War II. During this time, he heard Marlene on the radio, the result of both the U.S. Armed Forces broadcasts as well as broadcasts from the "Soldatensender," a fictitious radio station reputed to be aired from inside Germany and organized by the then secret service known as the OSS in collaboration with British Intelligence. Alfred recalls much of the controversy surrounding Marlene, the tall, blond, blue-eyed woman who epitomized Aryan looks but was a traitor to the Third Reich.

Marlene Dietrich became known to us for the first time, especially us young people, through her film *The Blue Angel.* The "vamp role," as I think I'd have to call it, was unknown to us in Germany before that. She had a spirit that was new, too, especially for a woman. Shortly after that film, Marlene Dietrich went to America and started what we know now was a world career, which to us Germans was conflicting. Some believed she went to America for all the money that she was earning. But others believed that in Germany, Marlene would have had all doors open to her. It was also very well-known that she was the daughter of a Prussian officer. To the National Socialists she was an example of *the* German woman, blond and blue-eyed. Somehow it was always believed that Marlene Dietrich would give only a guest appearance in America and then would return to Germany. When it didn't turn out that way, before the war but then especially during the war, Marlene disappeared into the background, on purpose, because of the propaganda.

If you heard something about her, it was, "Because the American film industry is in the hands of Jews and has unlimited capital, she allowed herself to be bought," and so on. Others went so far as to say that she was a traitor. And then, like many Germans, we listened to the BBC in the evenings and in this context we heard Marlene Dietrich's songs and thought, "But why, for what reason, is she making propaganda against us?" Later we were propagandized to believe that Marlene was not acting against the leadership of National Socialism only, but against the entire German populace, the German people. That's how a divided opinion arose. Even among young men of my age, some said, she's clever, she did it right, but the others went so far as to say, "She's a traitor." Then in the final wasted months of war we all had our thoughts on other things, other than Marlene Dietrich or any other woman for that matter.

Back then at the end of the war I was nineteen when the Americans marched in. On the one hand we were relieved and happy that the bombardment was at an end. On the other hand we were dealing with emotions that were against the Americans, because we had gone through the Allied bombardment for years, but in all we were relieved that this situation was finally over. Of course for years and years we were painted pictures of the big plans of what Germany would become, the "Great Germany" encompassing all of Europe, but now, at the end of the war, the disappointment was total, everything destroyed. We were afraid of what would happen now. What would the future look like? On the one hand it was linked to the hope that maybe now there would be a chance for a new beginning. But we were, I have to say, afraid based on what we were told to expect from the enemy. I remem-

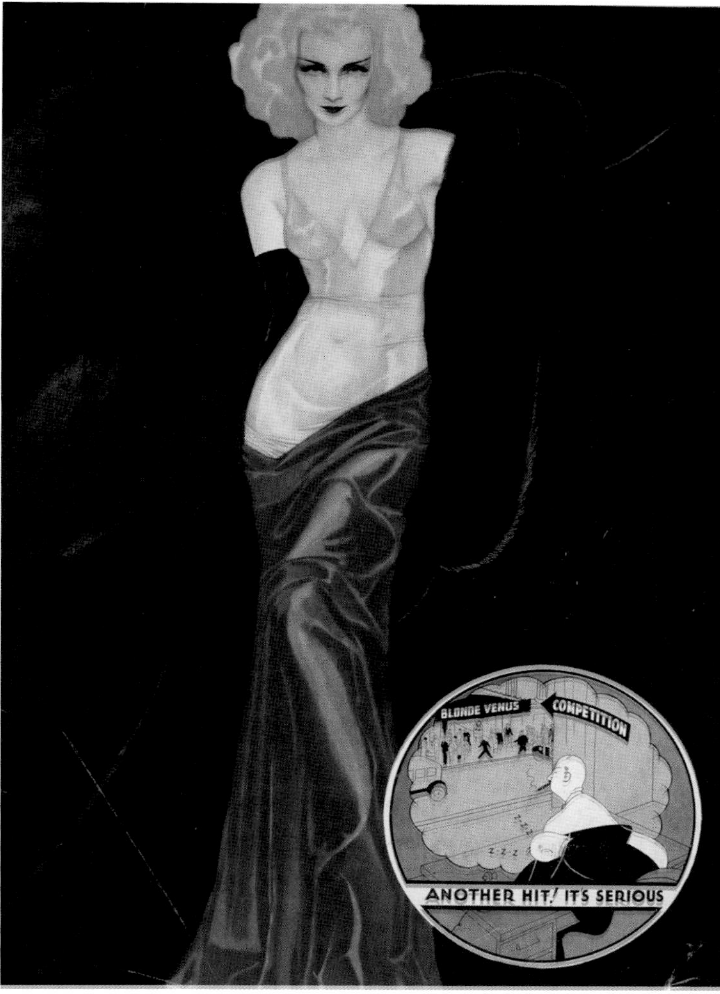

A poster for *The Blonde Venus* juxtaposed with an altered and derogatory version of the poster from a Nazi propaganda paper.

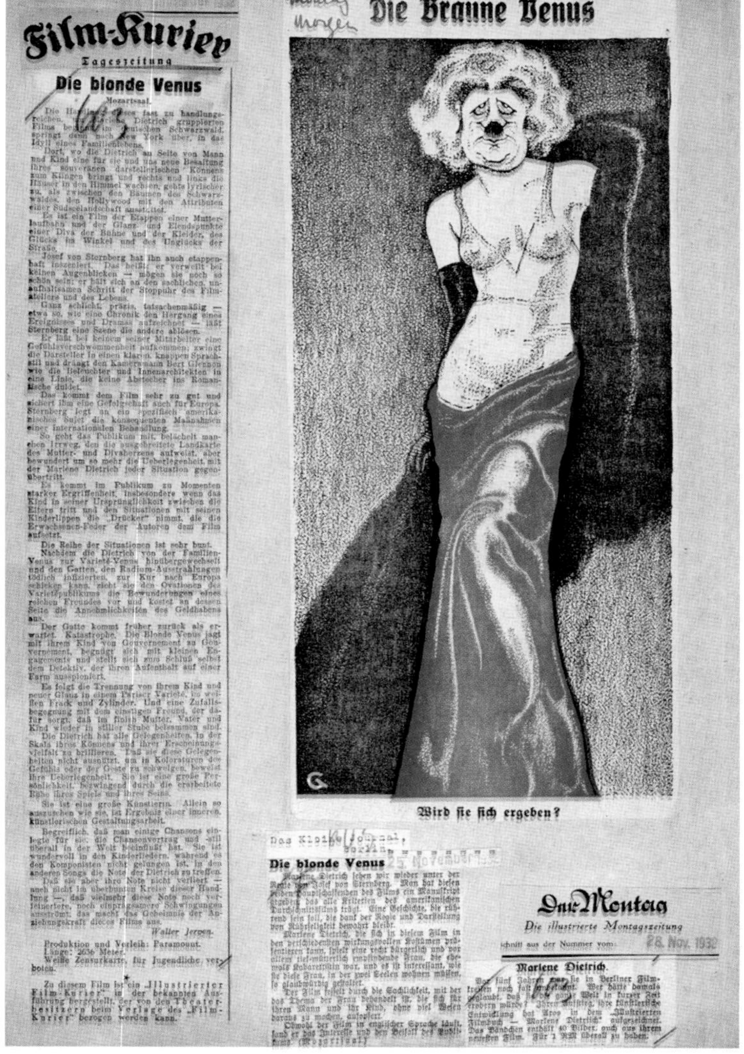
Film-Kurier
Tageszeitung
Die blonde Venus

Die Braune Venus

Wird sie sich ergeben?

Die blonde Venus

Der Montag
Die illustrierte Montagszeitung

Marlene Dietrich.

ber the first Americans that I experienced, after the fighting—they gave us food, something to drink, and I had the impression, I and my fellows, it can't be as bad with these Americans as the propaganda had been telling us for years. I'll never forget the beginning of that day. We had already thrown our weapons away beforehand. We were then taken prisoner by the first Americans, and I was very surprised when the first thing an American did was offer me a cigarette. I was having these thoughts, "I am a young man, what is going to become of me?" Then after all the things they had told us, like things about colored Americans, I was surprised all over again, that another American came up to me and offered me a piece of chocolate. Already you had this thought as a young person, "It can't be all that bad." In the final analysis we were happy to be captured, that the bombardment and shooting would be over. And then as to Marlene Dietrich, after the war we could see her films and were clear about the entire thing and what this woman had become.

Then in 1960, I think, she came to Germany for a first guest appearance, and we again had these divided opinions here in Germany. The one side cheered for her, the other booed her away. I suppose we will always be divided over her. But she was definitely a German through and through, like her or not.

JOHN DOLIBOIS

JOHN DOLIBOIS was an interrogator during World War II who worked extensively before and during the Nuremberg Trials, the subject of one of Marlene's most successful films, *Judgment at Nuremberg.* What took him to Germany and his insight into Marlene's legacy from that film bears looking into. We met in Washington, DC, on Veterans Day 2001, and his take on those dark days of World War II were a real lesson in "reality versus art." He remains an authority on attitudes during that time, some of which Marlene was destined to immortalize on film. Unlike Marlene, he is still not sure whether the German populace knew about the wartime atrocities. Despite her character in the film, who says "We did not know," Marlene always said that "everyone knew damn well."

As a boy growing up in Luxembourg, when I was only just beginning to see movies, the stars in those days were Tom Mix and Hoot Gibson, the cowboys, and Willy Fritsch and Lillian Harvey, the romantic couples, and, of course, Marlene Dietrich. Those were the actors with which I became familiar. I had no idea, even during our stint in Nuremberg right after the war, of the role that Marlene Dietrich played outside of an entertainer. It turns out she had been working with the OSS, the Office of Strategic Services. The man who coached us, to a certain extent, was Wild Bill Donovan, the head of the OSS. As a matter of fact, at one point he had recruited me for the OSS, and then found out that I was married and had a child and so he—they—were no longer interested. I was too much of a risk.

So, I knew who Wild Bill Donovan was, but I didn't know of any official relationship that Marlene Dietrich had at that time. All we knew was that she was an entertainer and she sang for the American troops. We thought that was the full extent of it.

My military career actually started when I was drafted in November 1942. That particular day the army happened to need tank drivers, so when I arrived at the induction center at Fort Thomas, Kentucky, the young man who was behind the table in the personnel section asked me what I could do.

I said, "Well, I'm a college graduate, and I can speak German fluently because I was born in Luxembourg. And I would like to get into military intelligence."

And he said, "Did you ever drive a truck?" And I said, "No, but I can speak German fluently"—I wasn't gonna give up so easily. But neither was he, so he said, "But did you ever drive a bus, or a tractor, or a plow, or something heavy with air brakes?"

The outcome of it was that in spite of my desire to get into military intelligence because I spoke German, I ended up in the armored force at Fort Knox, Kentucky, where the army promptly proceeded to make a tank driver out of me. So, I became a tank driver that day. If I had been inducted the day before, I would probably have been a cook and sent to bakers' school in Texas somewhere. If the day after, to an artillery school in Kansas.

Anyhow, I started my career in the armored forces and, after basic training, attended the Officers Candidate School, and graduated in 1943 with a commission as a second lieutenant in the armored forces, or mechanized cavalry, to be exact.

Then I was assigned to the Sixteenth Armored Division, Camp Chaffey, Arkansas, which is where Elvis Presley did his basic training, so it's one of our national shrines. I was resigned to spending the next two or three years, or the rest of the war, in the Ozark Mountains when somebody finally stuck a pin in the right hole and my card dropped out and they suddenly found out I could speak German fluently.

At that time we were just getting ready to invade North Africa. It occurred to somebody in Washington that we would now begin to have personal contact with the enemy, and they hadn't made any preparations for interrogating the POWs.

So, this is why the sudden cry went out and, regardless of where you were in the service, if you could speak a foreign language, they yanked you out and transferred you to military intelligence. So, this is how I ended up in military intelligence on three hours' notice, from Arkansas to Washington, DC, and then up to Maryland. The Maryland National Guard camp had been selected to train military-intelligence personnel. I was put into a category called IPW—Interrogator of Prisoners of War. And so, for the next two months, I went through a crash course of the techniques of interrogation, the psychology of dealing with the human "personality." I had majored in psychology in college, so that opened a door for me from that standpoint. I was trained to be an interrogator, taught the German Order of Battle, the organization of the German army, their characteristics, personalities of the high-ranking Nazis, and the history of the rise of National Socialism—at least as much as we knew. We really didn't know too much about what was going on in Germany at that time with the result that at the end of the two months, I was to go overseas as a member of an IPW team to interrogate prisoners taken on the battlefield and find information about their unit, and whatever.

But I didn't go yet. Because I'd had this background in the armored force, the army decided I would be more useful as a teacher. So, I became a teacher, training others to be interrogators. And as a teacher, you learn more than you do as a student. So, I became a specialist in one area of what they called detailed interrogation. We had two kinds of detailed interrogation: the tactical, which was unit to unit—you want to find out what's across the river, how strong are they, or what kind of weapons do they have. But I went into the other type, what is known as strategic interrogation. When I did go overseas, my assignment was to interrogate at a higher level and on a wider basis. We were interested in interrogating German scientists to find out what the Germans had done in developing an atom bomb. We were interested in interrogating those who were working on the rockets—the V1 and V2—and then chemical and bacterialogical warfare. We wanted to talk to people who had personal contact with Hitler, Himmler, Goering, or any of the other high-ranking Nazis.

We had a special detention center in the northernmost tip of France, almost into Belgium. It was actually a hunting lodge, and prisoners taken on the battlefield who were screened and had the potential for having that particular background information would be sent to this hunting lodge in the Ardennes where we would do our work.

For the rest of the war, my job was to go around to the various battlefronts where there were prisoners taken and weed out which POWs had some potential for information that we were interested in exploiting. For example, if I found somebody who knew something significant, like where Werner Heisenberg or a Nobel Prize–winning physicist was, if we found people like that, we shipped them off to the hunting lodge. We also included any high-ranking prisoners we found. Then we went back and did detailed interrogation. In this way, slowly but surely, we began to get more and better information about the enemy. We also began to understand more about a new thing for us, the Nazi program of organized, state-sponsored propaganda.

From the propaganda standpoint, of course, we knew even less about this part of the German organization than we did about the military aspects. Donovan of the OSS was only just beginning our version of the program, but in Nazi Germany it was already in full swing. Slowly we learned more about Goebbels, Hitler's chief of propaganda, and how he had organized his propaganda campaign. His first function, as we learned later, was to sell the high-ranking Nazis to the world, particularly people like Joachim von Ribbentrop.

Von Ribbentrop was a former champagne salesman who had impressed Hitler because, first of all, he was an expert in champagne, so he had to know something about diplomacy. Furthermore, he impressed Hitler because he was a linguist. He could speak English fluently and French quite well, and even a little bit of Italian. That impressed Hitler. In addition to these qualities, he had also inherited a title; he became a "von" at the age of thirty-two after being adopted by an aunt. Titles impressed Hitler even more. In any case it was for these kinds of people that propaganda played a crucial role. Goebbels's Propaganda Ministry went into play to convince the world that von Rippentrop was an expert in foreign diplomacy and foreign affairs and, incidentally, a perfect example of the Aryan, the master race, the superman, not a drop of Jewish blood in his veins, that kind of propaganda. Within Goebbels's circle each had his individual area of expertise. A man named Rosenberg, for example, played a very important role as editor and publisher of a Nazi Party journal. The anti-Semitic aspect of the propaganda play was primarily the purview of Julius Streicher. His propaganda was everything anti-Semitic, his job to expose the Jew, whether German or not.

So, the anti-Semitic propaganda came through Streicher. The philosophy of Nazism and the purity of the race argument and so forth came through Rosenberg. And then Goebbels, of course, had the political propaganda. It was his job to sell National Socialism and everything else that was necessary in the rise of socialism.

A lot of what we heard after the war was new to us. When we started, we actually knew very little. Keep in mind that there were very few immigrants coming from Germany during the Nazi regime. Nobody was leaving Germany, except Jewish refugees. When they came to the United States they started telling stories of what went on, about Kristallnacht, for instance, and about the Nuremberg Laws—they

One of the international posters for *Judgment at Nuremberg* signed by Marlene.

were a set of laws that required Jews to wear the Star of David, prevented them from marrying Germans or even associating with them, denied them citizenship if they came to Germany after 1914, and denied them the opportunity to hold office in the government. That kind of story came to us from Jewish refugees. I would guess that 50 percent of what they told us was dismissed as propaganda, and we decided, well, those are just the usual stories, the kind of stuff we had during World War I: atrocities that the Germans were committing, and that kind of thing. So, it was written off as propaganda. There was a very definite "America First" sentiment in the United States at that time. So that information coming from refugees never became, really, the foundation for what we knew about what was going on in Germany. Toward the latter part of the '30s, America didn't even accept Jewish refugees anymore. You know, we actually turned them away, which is sort of a dark spot in our history, too. I'm pointing this out because, as a result, we had no source of information on what was really going on. Our intelligence gathering as such was very poor, and so we knew nothing about what was really going on in Germany until the fighting and the invasion of Germany itself began. We didn't learn too much until we started to interrogate prisoners and found out more about what was going on behind the lines. Later, of course, we started to run into the concentration camps and liberate people who had been forced into slave labor or who had been inmates of concentration camps. Then we became fully aware of reality.

While I was at the hunting lodge interrogating prisoners in the Ardennes, I got a letter indirectly from the leader of the German Labor Front. He indicated that he had some very special information that he wanted to release. He trusted me, and he would give that information only to me. The letter was addressed to John Gillam—that was the false name I used. I had two brothers in the German army, so I went by the name John Gillam at the advice of General Donovan, who said, "Don't use your name, 'Dolibois,' use a different name—any other name." So, I picked a good Luxembourg name, Gillam.

So, that letter was addressed to Gillam. As a result of the letter's contents, I was transferred on temporary duty to Nuremberg; I probably would never have gotten to Nuremberg otherwise. It was thanks to the leader of the German Labor Front that I went there to get that information from him.

While I was at Nuremberg, the prison warden, Colonel Andrews, pulled all the strings to keep me there 'cause I'd worked for him in Luxembourg, so now he had me back in his clutches. I resisted it because I was tired of interrogating prisoners. I didn't want to do it anymore. I didn't like the prison smell. I didn't like Nuremberg, the ruins.

I wanted to get away, so I was pulling strings to leave there, but nevertheless, Colonel Andrews was a colonel, and I was only a first lieutenant so I ended up staying in Nuremberg.

So when the war ended, I found myself assigned as an interrogator in preparation for the Nuremberg trials. During the summer of 1945, our group actually had all of the high-ranking Nazis, those who were to be tried at the first session of the tribunal, and also those who would serve as the witnesses for the defense and the prosecution. All of them were gathered in a special detention center, in the Grand Duchy of Luxembourg, the little resort town of Mondorf. At this detention center, which went by the code word Ashcan, we had all of these, a total of eighty-six high-ranking Nazis—members of the German General Staff, members of the Nazi Party, the Alte Kaempfer, the Old Fighters—who helped Hitler come to power, and then were rewarded with a position that had the power of life and death—and also those who had served in the German government, some during the Weimar Republic, and some had even worked for the kaiser in World War I. They had become Nazis and kept their plush jobs in the German government during the Hitler regime.

The first thing we found out was that we knew very little about the Nazi organization. We knew very little about what the SS, the SA, and all of the other paramilitary organizations were doing, even so far as to what the different ranks in the military even stood for: you know, what was an Obergruppenführer, or what was a Reichsführer?

The prosecuting staffs of the four nations said, you know, "We're gonna have problems trying these people, we really don't have a handle on them. We know very little about their background—what makes them tick, what do they really want, and what did they try to do, and why?" Consequently, it was decided that they would all be brought for further interrogation to Ashcan, our special detention center before the trials.

And so, during the summer of 1945, all of the high-ranking Nazis, anybody who was anybody in the German General Staff or in the National Socialist Party organization in the German government and had been taken prisoner or had voluntarily surrendered, were all gathered together and brought to Luxembourg.

Actually, Ashcan was a four-story resort spa hotel that we had taken over and turned into a prison. There was a barbed-wire fence around it, machine-gun towers in each of the four corners, all the best security, including klieg lights overhead, military police, and so forth.

When I arrived from France I really didn't know too much about what was going on; in fact, nobody knew. Everybody was sort of writing his own ticket. I learned that I was to be one of five interrogators, American interrogators, who would work with these prisoners during the summer of '45 on behalf of the Nazi War Crimes Commission. The commission members were the people who prepared the case for the prosecution on behalf of the United States, headed by Supreme Court Justice Robert Jackson. They would prepare briefs and questionnaires about particular prisoners or organizations and send those questionnaires to us in Luxembourg. Then we would interrogate the prisoners to get the answers to those questions and write up our intelligence reports, all of which together became the basis for the conduct of the trials in Nuremberg later on. So, we were what you might call the pretrial investigators. You know, when a crime is committed, the prosecuting staff has investigators whose job it is to find out more about how the crime was committed, by whom, why, and what the motives were. And we actually played that role, although not in a legal sense; we did it on a military-intelligence basis. And even if we didn't do strictly military interrogations anymore, we were still gathering intelligence, partly through visiting and interviewing the prisoners' families. I would actually go out and visit Hermann Goering's wife and his daughter, Edda, and Kesselring's wife, Jodl's family—we just continued to gather information.

I worked for Colonel Andrews as sort of a welfare officer and assistant. Then a prison psychiatrist came on the scene, American, who conducted a Rorschach analysis, the inkblot test, but he couldn't speak German. He found out that I'd majored in psychology in college, so I ended up being an interpreter for this Major Douglas administering the Rorschach test. This gave me a chance to really get to know a lot of the prisoners quite well, very personally.

But every waking moment I was in Nuremberg,

I did my best to leave because I wanted to get away from it. I wanted to get home and be with my wife and my child. Finally, we made a deal that if I could get a replacement, I could leave. The replacement was Gustave Gilbert, who wrote *The Nuremberg Diary*. He is considered the authority on the Nuremberg trials because immediately after the trials, his book came on the market. And it is footnoted by just about everyone.

So, during the summer of '45, that was my job: to get the answers to those questions. I remember that the first prisoner I met was Hermann Goering, the vice marshal of the Third Reich.

When the movie *Judgment at Nuremberg* came out, we, of course, those of us who had been there, found that it was a little bit farcical because it wasn't really the way the trials were conducted in Nuremberg.

First of all, we were critical of the fact that there was a civilian judge in a military court, and the defendants were judges who were being tried for crimes they had committed against the German people. Now, why an international tribunal would sit in judgment of German judges for crimes committed against German people just didn't make any sense because that would be, well, illegal—from an international standpoint.

But the film's take on the German psyche was of particular interest to me. When I first came back to the States, I got a lot of invitations to talk about my experiences at the war crimes trial. And an amazing number of Americans thought *Judgment at Nuremberg* was an actual documentary portrayal of the way the Nuremberg trials were conducted, which, of course, is ridiculous. What the movie showed was Spencer Tracy as a civilian judge in a military court—now that was typical Hollywood! Why would an international court try Germans for committing crimes against fellow Germans? It really didn't make any sense if you looked at it. But many Americans thought that it *was* the international war crimes trial. So, those of us who considered ourselves experts on the trial, having been there, laughed at them. We really didn't take it very seriously of course. It was a good movie, good entertainment, but it really was not a true portrayal of what the Nuremberg trials were all about, yet I would guess if you had conducted a poll at that time, 99 percent of the American people would have said, "Oh, yeah, we saw the trials in the movies. We knew what was going on." And so everything in the movie was believed, too. Marlene Dietrich had the line, "We did not know," saying that the German people didn't know about the camps. Tracy fires back, "I can't seem to find anyone in this country who did know." So the film says that they all knew and just said nothing. It was a powerful thing to hear, but probably not as cut and dried as that—factually.

The attitude of the German people as it was portrayed in the movie *Judgment at Nuremberg* actually aroused my interest because one of the functions we had, during the last days of the war, was to get the German viewpoint. We wanted to know what the German people were thinking after the war: what was their attitude toward Hitler, and so forth.

So, two of us—actually, there were two teams, two men in a team—traveled around Germany for a period of about six weeks. We were pretending to be Germans who'd been prisoners of war and were on our way home having just been released. I pretended to have come from a camp in Felsberg, because I could still speak the dialect, Saarlaendisch, which my family spoke at home when I was a boy. Wearing tattered German uniforms, we talked to people we met along our way. We would sit in railroad stations and talk to displaced persons, and we

Marlene listens to the verdicts in *Judgment at Nuremberg.*

talked to German housewives, and other German people on the street.

So, I got firsthand information from all walks of life. The answers were a normal curve of reaction. There were those who were still very sympathetic to Nazism, who thought that Germany was a superpower and Hitler had brought it to that particular point. And now they deplored the fact that the war had been lost and believed it was mostly because they ran out of supplies and manpower. These individuals clearly wished it could have continued and that if it had Germany would have been victorious.

Then there were those who professed total ignorance. They didn't know anything about what was going on. I think some of them were sincere. They were either ignorant of what was happening, or they were afraid to talk about it. Hitler had managed, during the regime, to establish a fear psychosis, making people afraid to talk about what they did know. So, everybody pretended not to know anything, and after they did that long enough they convinced themselves that they really didn't know about the concentration camps in their own communities.

Others would say, "Yes, I knew there was a camp and I figured there were some things going on there, but I didn't want to hear about it. Everything was just going fine; we all had jobs and we were very happy with the way things were going. We didn't ask any questions."

There were women who deplored the fact that they would no longer hear the marching and the goose-stepping of the handsome German soldiers, and they missed that. They lamented the days of glory, when the men in uniform were marching down the street and Germany was rising toward being a superpower.

Then there were the noblemen, the barons, and the counts—those connected with royal families, who, of course, were the archenemies of Hitler and of Nazism itself. They deplored the fact that they never got revenge. They had lost their positions of power under socialism, and now they remained totally unimportant.

So I got the opportunity to ask many different types of Germans about a lot of things. Yes, I would have to say that the German people knew there were concentration camps. But if you asked them about details of what was going on in those camps, in their community, they often honestly didn't know any more than you might know about what was going on in the state prison in your state, or even in your county jail. They really didn't, they honestly didn't know much of the time. If they did know, they were afraid to talk about it, even after the war. Through the Nazi regime and their organization, there was an effective and rigid system of people spying on people, people listening to what other people said, children winning brownie points in school by reporting what their parents were saying at home. The very real result of such reporting was that people were sent to concentration camps. If they went there and were released—sometimes people would stay in a camp just six months or so—when they came back out, that fear psychosis had been so firmly established that they were, to put it mildly, afraid of talking.

So, yes, people knew but they were either afraid to talk about it, or . . . they—they didn't really have the true inside information. They only knew a little bit about, yes, there is such a camp, and I honestly don't know anything about the inside of it. Or I can't ask questions.

What we as Americans have difficulty understanding is that there was no free press. You know, we have CNN, and we have our investigative reporting, and our newspapers. Today these sources will report everything under the sun, every little detail, even more than you want to know. There was no freedom of the press in Germany. There was no freedom of exchange, only the government line, and the propaganda from the Ministry of Propaganda, from Goebbels. So, the German people were really not as well informed, or if they were, they were too afraid to talk about it. Whatever "judgment" we came to at Nuremberg, the fact remained that there was more to it than any film could grasp.

I tried to remember what it was like at Nuremberg and although they were there at the same time I never saw Marlene Dietrich or any of the other actors. I would have enjoyed them, meeting Spencer Tracy, too, in those circumstances.

HANS GEORG WILL

The son of Marlene's only sister Elisabeth, **HANS GEORG WILL** spent his formative years in Bergen-Belsen, where his parents operated a movie theater during the Nazi regime. Marlene publicly distanced herself from Hans Georg, a member of the Hitler Youth, and his family because of their complacency during the war. Marlene's staunch anti-Nazism made their relationship impossible, but despite their divergent political views, she helped the family financially when she could, and vouched for them to the American and Russian forces after liberation so they could maintain their movie-house business. Prior to setting up this interview, I was unaware I even had a cousin. Marlene had completely disowned them, publicly at least, and Maria, out of respect, maintained silence on the subject also. When we met we found much in common with each other, and formed a lasting friendship. War tears families apart, and Marlene's was no exception. Hans Georg continues to work in the film business in Germany.

Well, I'd say that my mother was always in the shadow of her extraordinary sister. My grandmother, Josephine von Losch, did favor Marlene. And I believe to her this was not unusual. In certain families, as one is always saying nowadays, everything is discussed, but the von Losch-Dietrichs were a typical middle-class family, or maybe even an upper-middle-class West Berlin family, and some things were not talked about, or at least not in front of me, the child. Keep in mind, this wasn't a three-room apartment, where everybody sits around the kitchen table. So I can only reflect upon it, drawing on impressions that I had then, although I wasn't a child, as many may think. In earliest childhood, I had already become independent. I never carry my life experience around with me. Instead I lived in the time in which I lived. I know that the closeness of my grandmother to Marlene "rained down" onto the phone bills [*smiles*]. And Marlene was always calling up, and my grandmother called her, too, and my mother was tied in with that. But how does a child live? When I tell you I was born in '28, then I was seven or eight, the war began in '39, there was the way to school, play, and I can't talk about specifics, but Marlene simply meant everything to this family, was its alpha and omega. The fact that my father was maybe a little more distant to Marlene, that was also because Marlene was distant to my father. It was reciprocal. And my mother was a very loving, highly educated woman, but my sense is that she was sometimes a helpless woman caught between two fronts—strong fronts. And the one in this family who lost the most was Elisabeth Will, my mother. My father got his way; I swam my way, free, prevailed. And the connection with my grandmother, that is, her mother, Frau von Losch, who lived here in the Friegelstrasse [sp], was of course lost upon her death in November of '45. My mother was basically her whole life long a lonely woman, whom I see differently and more painfully now that I've reached that age myself. But back then for me it was *my* life, *my* leaving from Bergen near Celle. You've got to imagine, we were in Berlin, and had to move. My father was moved against his will with his wife and me, his son. We had to settle ourselves in Bergen-Belsen. Then I went to school in nearby Celle to the Hermann-Billung Gymnasium [upper school]. That I had to leave this place, Berlin, well, that was something that I regret, especially as it pertains to my mother.

How did I get there, or how did *we* get there to Bergen-Belsen? I'd have to say, for me, it was my mother. Before the war, the German Wehrmacht was building a troops training ground in Bergen.

My father had an opportunity there. He had come out of the theater, near where we are now, over there in the Tingel-Tangel. He was there from '33, until that was closed, when the Theater des Westen [of the West] took it over in '36. When the war began, I was in Waldsieversdorf in my boarding school. In '38, no, it was already later, '39 it was, General Schumann, who was the training ground commander, said, "Will, this can't continue with your family not here. That's not right, and we don't want that." So that was our departure from Berlin to Bergen near Celle—it was called Bergen back then.

The war was on now. And we were in Belsen. I rode to school, was bused, rode every morning on the omnibus to Celle, got my education, home in the afternoon. That's how the days passed. Materially we were doing well, we were also in a place away from the bombing. There was food and drink, the boring schoolwork, but twice a week there was the Hitler Youth, where one preferred to go. Swallowed it later in the bad Latin grades. [*Laughs.*] That's how the years passed.

And I myself grew up during this time, and at sixteen one could volunteer for the military. And given a choice of military excitement over boring schoolwork, well, it was a very easy choice. Any time one would choose the military; better than to ride to school. In retrospect I've regretted it, but then I didn't know. Still remembered by all. And the impression of my choice was naturally even more relevant when I became a soldier in the spring of '45. Became a Youth soldier. RAD [Reichsarbeitsdienst] Division Schlageter and up there, of course, Berlin and Pomerania, too. We were supposed to fight the Russians, with our laughable numbers, naturally! Looking back at the children's army, more often they made in their pants.

I don't remember much of your mother, Maria, or the rest of the extended family. Memories just based on pictures. Still, I believe, in '36 or '37 before the war, we all met again at Lake Geneva. Marlene came with Maria. And after that, of course, nothing more, because when Marlene came to Germany after the war was lost, in order to see her mother or to help *my* mother, I was still a youth soldier in Mecklenburg. That's why I can't really say much about the time *before* the war, but that doesn't change the memories. When I was five, five to six, it started in Germany, with Hitler, so I grew up during that time, and I admit it, with all its ideology as well. When the war was over, then, in '45, my father had had a large cinema for years in Bergen-Belsen near the concentration camps, and my aunt came there and testified for my mother and my father, so that they were allowed to stay, and then I joined them in May. Then we heard a lot from each other of course, but not in person.

Marlene's sister, Liesel, with her son, Hans Georg, in the late 1920s. They would not meet again until the war was over.

And when I came back home, I came out of the chute from being a prisoner of war. [*Becomes emotional.*] And came home, to Bergen-Belsen. By now of course the concentration camp was opened. We already knew by '42 that in a clearing three kilometers away from the military grounds there was a mill, actually a work camp, where the workers were housed in '36. At first they brought Russians down there, even *that* was wretched, the way they were brought in trains to the unloading ramp and were herded down it. I had noticed it myself as a Youth Nazi, and my father absolutely very much disassociated from National Socialism, but since he knew that Hans Georg was a staunch Hitler Youth, not much about it was discussed. You want to protect yourself. The shock, I already mentioned it before, the shock where the bottom fell out for me was to come the end of May and to experience this troop ground now filled with sick and wretched people, I have to say. And then there was, well, I was supposed to go to school, no, I didn't want to so much, and didn't even go. So this English bombardier officer said, "So do a little something." And so I was a youth electrician in these buildings and had to help to renovate [or tear down] things. I'd like to say, too, the misery I saw there and the dying people [*drops his head*]—I will never forget that in my lifetime. As I have said before, nobody can tell me about the "magnificent" things in the Third Reich. Whatever was done, that we did, nobody can make it good, but one thing, well I'll say that too, you can cut it out if you want as far as I'm concerned, one shouldn't keep talking about it now. It's beginning to get a little difficult.

But, well [*straightens up*], afterward, the way it was for me afterward, nah, I didn't want to go to school again, my mother of course up in arms. Tante Lena, Marlene, was supposed to get me into television in Hamburg—if I'd only done it. I didn't want that either, so at first I worked for my father at the cinema and was therefore in Bergen-Belsen and found the position and managed both the cinemas for my father that we were allowed to operate, one for the English military with the AKC, and one for the displaced persons, as they were called then. Yeah, but over time that didn't go so well and I couldn't gain all that much. So, I swung over and looked for a position in the German cinema business. I eventually came then, not in the end, but then, to UFA Theater AG and was there for several years. Now I do cinema advertising—and had the possibility to come into German Railway advertising as a purchasing manager in Düsseldorf. And, well, I was there then for twenty-seven years, well, even longer, and now I am retired.

Just after the war, I became aware of Marlene, because now the world had become completely different. And when she came back, as I've already said, it was gratitude from my mother, my parents, that Marlene was there, vouched for them. It was the good fortune that my father was not a Nazi, and my mother was absolutely clear. But from then on Marlene was naturally in my thoughts. I did more pondering about Marlene because after the war, I was sixteen or seventeen—far older than before, when I was still a child in Germany. But I've said, I am relatively egotistical myself and fight for myself, and so it was that in '45 my own life was in the foreground.

How the news came to Bergen-Belsen, I don't know, but we found out Josephine died, my grandmother. Don't forget, it was six months after the end of the war, in November 1945. We still had an aunt in Potsdam, where she still lived and I suppose my mother found out by letter or maybe by phone. But to get through from Bergen in Lower Saxony to Berlin was nearly impossible, and I have to tell you, my mother was not a dynamic self-actualizing woman like we read about in magazines all the time nowadays. She was bound up in this "situation" in Bergen-Belsen, and there at first we had plenty to handle ourselves. Afterward there was enough aggravation about the inheritance terms because, you know, Frau von Losch was a co-owner of the timepiece store Konrad Felsing in Unter den Linden. But there again was Marlene, my aunt, and she took care of things some, so that everything was cleared up. And today the grave is here in Friedenau. And just this spring I had the headstone renovated, for the memory of Frau von Losch to Oma in memoriam for Maria and to Marlene. Frau von Losch was the root, this entire thing; she kept all the women together.

My mother's reaction to the death was terrible. Great loss. It was, of course, the next to the last thread connecting her to her family. Then of course Marlene was still there, thank God, but throughout her life, in any difficulty, her mother was more like her sister. She was, or supplied the strength needed. Frau von Losch was a force who, incidentally, like Marlene, knew her way around the world too. [*Smiles.*]

My relationship to Marlene was really *no* relationship. Naturally, I had a certain connection after the war. I was enthusiastic about her. Maybe I already sensed it, this difficulty, Marlene and Germany. Don't forget, when I came back from Mecklenburg, from my time as a soldier, to which I sent myself voluntarily—I did grow up in this Third Reich—I came into a camp with 20,000 Jews, freed from the concentration camps. The Hitler Youth—*that* was the breaking point with Nazism and the Third Reich. That was gone real fast. I had met Hans Sachs, a young Berliner who was as old as me, from Berlin here in the Kaiserallee, where I come from, Friedenau. My mother told me, of course, that Marlene was there immediately and vouched for us to the English occupation force, the troops, so that my father and we could stay with the cinema. That was our livelihood, and we could stay there, otherwise we'd have been gone. That's how I got closer to Marlene and the problems, when she came to Germany around 1960 to appear here. And maybe we learned more later, but even back then, I know, I was in the advertising business, in cinema business, I was with the UFA Theater executive offices, there was some media business involved, and I was aware of the shock when the Springer Press began to pit itself against Marlene. Because I believe—even back then I had this foreboding that something would go wrong. Springer with his *Bild-Zeitung* newspaper was already powerful in Germany, and although he was always pro . . . yes, the Springer Company is pro-Jewish. I was surprised that it didn't happen then. Maybe Marlene made a mistake that she was not accepting enough of the *Bild-Zeitung* paper, or didn't *grovel* enough to them. That was 1960. I attended two performances of hers, in Cologne and in Düsseldorf. Since I was working for the UFA Theater AG, I had the opportunity, and both times I was totally enthusiastic, but both times, not just in retrospect because I'm smarter now, I had doubts whether the German masses would understand her chansons [cabaret songs], the whole thing. This typical black-and-white thinking—you are my enemy or you are my friend—it was already starting then. And only a certain elevated segment of the press could make distinctions about that. At the moment where the *Bild-Zeitung* paper, or later *Die Welt,* had the songs described in their pages [or labeled them amoral] it was already done, because the human being, still today, looks for black-and-white contours, not gray—it seems just too difficult, and Marlene was a victim of her time back then. Indeed there were still enough, are enough cultivated people. To me after the war, Marlene was a chanteuse for *cultivated* people. That hurt me a lot to see it develop like that. And then when Marlene appeared here over in the GDR, in East Berlin, that was it. Well, you can imagine that the West Berliners, the German, the stirred-up German citizen, the East-West problem, that was it. Lindbergh, he could still carry it off; it was a whole different world, even twenty years later. So it really hurt me. And of course then around midnight in the hotel, the Park Hotel, when I saw my Aunt Marlene, well, we didn't talk about it, it would have been too much. But to meet again and a part of the family, maybe family, maybe I should have kept it up with her a little bit in the final fifteen years. Maybe I could have still given my aunt a little help. But then again I can tell you, our relationship, well, I can only say, Marlene was also [*smiles*]—uncompromising. Surprise! I suppose that if I had had anything to do with Marlene *before,* maybe she would have turned me into someone different. Just after the war, my mother was over in Paris many times to meet with her. I remember my mother almost had to be forced by Marlene. She would say, "Here's your air ticket, you're coming to visit me." It was, I think, because my mother was always stuck fast to Bergen and didn't want to leave. And when she was in Paris, after our child Axel was born, Marlene gave presents to my mother to take along. "Here, you don't have anything for your grandson, here take that for Axel." When Marlene appeared in Düsseldorf and in Cologne, I was there with my wife. After the appearance, we met Marlene in front of the Park Hotel, and there, too, I can only describe what great warmth we felt, but a *disciplined* warmth, one shown to a stranger, my *wife.* Here again she was uncompromising, "Where is the child? Did you leave your child Axel alone in bed to come here?" She did this kind of thing, she could do that. And that was it, really. After the death of my mother the connection thinned out, and I never, well, I admit it, I didn't give it much effort. Well, after my mother's death there was nothing anyway. Maybe it could have been different. But also, I don't think that Marlene would have been especially enthused about her nephew either, if he had stepped closer. I believe that by maintaining a strong reserve, that I maybe did her a favor. And I was not so loveable either, was not the charming young man who got close to people. I was very much preoccupied with myself, but it must be said that she didn't do anything either.

I would have, maybe should have, taken up contact with Maria. I thought sometimes, though, how it would look; "Here is Hans Georg, now he's presenting himself, he wants to be in the shadow of a famous family." Ugh! But I tried once more to telephone Maria about a year before Marlene's death. I have a little book of my mother's with all the personal telephone numbers and all the rest, I have it with me, but she didn't pick up, or that wasn't the right number. Well, but enough now. But let's be happy that Marlene has come home, here to Berlin and has found peace near her mother, her final rest. I was at her grave yesterday morning.

We have always thought of Marlene in good terms. She was not the enemy to us. But during the war you had to speak more carefully. After the war one could talk more openly. But above everything that I am saying and thinking about Marlene, there is the gratitude of my mother and also my gratitude for the help that she gave her sister, materially and otherwise. Marlene's work for the other side was absolutely no issue in our family. My father thought, at most, *less* of the Third Reich—just did his cinema businesses—and my mother was a product of this middle-class family from Berlin. I was the outsider there, being enthusiastic about this Nazi business. Not that there was total distancing, but the ideology was not the same. But no, my aunt was not thought of as a traitor in our house. Marlene Dietrich was an artist, and why should this woman, who was naturally not associated with

Nazi Germany, not continue to be an artist in the United States of America? Think of Thomas Mann. The ones who were over there, they were not traitors, that was cheap propaganda from the Third Reich, but propaganda that is still in the heads of many Germans today, namely, this black-and-white thinking, and no ability to think in shades of gray. In between black and white there is more, and between black and white is where artists live.

Recently there was a German-produced film about Marlene. Well, after Ms. [Katja] Flint made this film, I heard from friends, and it began the discussion all over again. I have said that this particular film did not serve the memory of Marlene Dietrich—on the contrary. But in any case, there is no doubt that the persona of Marlene Dietrich has always polarized people. Otherwise she couldn't be anything. Her songs are more conciliatory, more sentimental, more geared toward peace and "we want to be fellow humans." But it polarized us. And I experience in my circle of friends, well, this way, or that. This extraordinary woman, like other extraordinary people, did not always have it so easy. They're put into boxes. But they are too complicated for that.

But later my aunt Marlene, rightfully so, asked us that in the initial inquiries to interview us—my mother or me—we not talk about us, the aunt, or the sister of Dietrich. And we've held to that to this day. I have not given any kind of interview about Marlene. I've been—a closed door up until now.

It was my Aunt Marlene's wish for us not to go public. After Marlene's death this whole thing that happened was a case for the Riva family. I did not want to be a bother to them. Or be involved. The third point, I've saved it, was an emotional thing, from the point of view of Marlene, and I think Maria Riva made the remark that I was of course a Nazi. Whether I was, nobody can judge, but nowadays others judge others very quickly. So I said, then—no.

When the German government took my aunt's belongings for a museum in Berlin, I didn't visit the Marlene Dietrich exhibitions. Even though the director of the museum, Mr. Werner Sudendorf, sent several invitations. Thank goodness Mr. Sudendorf had a persistent secretary who stayed after me, and one day the Marlene Dietrich exhibition was in Hagen—that's no distance at all from Düsseldorf. I drove there and saw it, at first without identifying myself, and then I was introduced to Mr. Sudendorf, who made a pleasant impression. It made him happy that his secretary wrote over and over again with success. And I've found in Mr. Sudendorf a partner, a middleman to Marlene Dietrich, for this legacy, who is to my liking. And now the letter from Mr. Sudendorf came, about meeting you, and whether I wouldn't speak of my aunt after all. Well, now I'm over seventy, and I can see the horizon of my life appearing. And when the horizon comes, you turn around more. You look back at what was. So I said, good, tell me a little more, if I do it, we'll see. My wife had a few photos of the family, which we looked at and that's how it happened. I didn't know that I would have the pleasure of meeting my extended family again.

In the end, it was important for me to come. It was an homage to Marlene, a thank you to Marlene, and it was also an homage to their grandmother in common, Frau von Losch. That's why I was happy to come, and I have to say, staying here in West Berlin on the Kurfürstendamm is a help for me, to pick up the thread to my youth in the Bundesallee, the Kaiserallee back then in 1935, because everything stems from there, be it Marlene or be it Elisabeth, and me, too.

MARIA RIVA

Born in Berlin in 1924, MARIA RIVA was beyond question Marlene's most constant companion, as well as her daughter. Every moment of Marlene's life unfolded in full view, and even when distant, Marlene always kept Maria duly informed if not involved. Maria was Marlene's confidant, her agent, her manager, and her only constant family. Maria has never wavered from her belief that Marlene was a brilliant performer despite Marlene's other shortcomings. Maria herself also did her part for the Allied war effort as a member of the USO, performing plays and routines in Europe during the last days of the war. She returned to the United States in 1946 to continue her radio and stage career, eventually entering the new medium of television, for which she was nominated for several Emmy Awards. There were always two things that my mother, Maria, held above all else. The first was being an American. Having become a citizen along with Marlene upon their arrival in the United States, she was a model patriot—right down to putting American flags in our school lunchboxes on presidents' birthdays. The second was being a mother, for which she gave up her successful career. Much of her dedication to motherhood undoubtedly came from her not having what most would deem a "mother" in Marlene. Marlene was a lot of things, but a nurturing maternal force she was not. To Maria's credit, and without the benefit of example, she overcame this obstacle. She raised four boys reasonably well, and stayed happily married to the same man for over fifty years. She remains a creative force, now writing her third book, and is still the kind of mother only Norman Rockwell would have conceived of. She is universally loved by all who know her, including me.

You know, even before Hollywood movies brought America to the world, it was America's music that changed things. There was jazz in the Roaring '20s, in Berlin. American music always had this bouncy youth to it and embodied a type of freedom to allow you to do what you wanted. It extended out from there to everything in art and society.

My mother was always amazed by the puritanical attitude of the Americans about women in trousers as she was the first woman, so-called, to wear trousers. She said, "But we *all* wore trousers in Berlin." It was Sodom and Gomorrah in Berlin. Everything went. There were no holds barred. Some of the greatest performers in Berlin of the 1920s were women who appeared in tuxedos. And I think that it was this freedom, this wildness, and this androgynous attitude of Dietrich's, born in those days when anything was possible, that later became so much a part of Dietrich and her legacy. It was nothing really new as far as Germany was concerned—it was simply startling when it came to America.

During this period, the new form of "film" began to take hold. My mother was not particularly interested in the mainstream opinion at that time—that work in the "theater" was the only respectable path to follow. She wanted to earn money and try new things and so she auditioned for anything. On one of these many casting calls she met my father, which I think was the real turning point for her, personally.

My mother had heard that there was a casting call for petit moderne and a demimonde. And in those days, a demimonde was only sort of slightly removed from a streetwalker, and so she put on very long green gloves and a feather boa, and did the whole tramp bit.

And my father, Rudolf Sieber, who was the assistant director on the film, walked down the line of all these hopefuls and saw the green gloves. He always maintained that it was the green gloves that attracted him to my mother, and nothing else.

This whole relationship between Rudolf Sieber and Mrs. Sieber, also known as Marlene Dietrich, well, to begin with, nobody ever understands unless they're European, you know? You have to be European to sort of understand that the husband knows that the woman is having an affair, and as long as she comes home and makes dinner, it's all right with him, you know. There was never any fight between them, husband-and-wife kind of fights that, you know, people would think would be normal, or that he would accuse her of being in love with another man or sleeping with another man. There was never that.

It was really a tremendous friendship. There is a photograph of my mother and father, which is in my book, but also is quite famous, where I say they look like brother and sister; they're so beautiful together.

But it went much further than that. He was her mentor, and he was the one who guided her. And what was wonderful about Dietrich, and that is something that goes through everything, is that she always recognized perfection when she saw it, and followed it, whether it was von Sternberg doing her key light, and what he wanted her to do, or a designer, like Travis Benton, or great writers, like Remarque. She always recognized quality, and embraced it, and respected it, and went along with it. And my father's quality for her was that he only wanted what was good for her. He never steered her wrong. She followed him wherever he led her in her attire, in her attitudes toward people.

The important thing to realize about my father is that he was the greatest friend that she ever had, although von Sternberg was her creator and the greatest friend she had as far as her image is concerned. Her husband was the greatest friend she ever had for herself as a woman and as a human being. He protected her at all times, even when she was very lax about protecting herself. She would leave love letters from people on desks and in dressing rooms, and my father was the one who always went and collected them. Or she would show them to him, but he would never return them to her because he would always say, "There's a *maid*—there are people in these hotels. You know, they can make a living out of these things if they sell them to the scandal sheets." Even then we had scandal sheets.

He also had incredible taste, and everyone thinks that Dietrich had great taste. Well, she didn't when she started. Her taste was a bit uninteresting, and at times, a bit, as one would say in German, "zusammengewürfelt" which is a wonderful German expression that means sort of accumulated together, you know, but it doesn't really go together, but you have a piece here, and you have a piece there.

And he was the one who would always say, "Let me see what you're wearing" in Germany. Even as a child I remember that very distinctly. And whenever he found anything that was beautiful, that he thought that she should own, he would be the one who would always say to her, "This is something for Dietrich. This is a Dietrich item. This is what you should have." And she would look at it and say, "But for $5,000?!" And he would say, "It doesn't matter how much it costs. It's your image that is important. Dietrich would never use anything that is less expensive." And he taught her. In the first few years when he came to visit us in Hollywood, he would always go through her cupboards and he would say, "Why did you buy this? How can you possibly wear this?" And whenever he said anything to her, she listened.

And of course, when I arrived, I helped manage the "family business" of Dietrich also.

I'm often asked how it was possible that I grew up the way I did. And I have to explain about "duty," which was the guiding force in my mother's life. Always duty, whether it was duty to von Sternberg, or duty to the camera, or duty to her fame, or duty to me as her child, or her duty as far as the war was concerned against Hitler, whatever—it was what she defined as her duty that motivated her. And therefore, this entire spectrum of duty was such a *gigantic* force in my childhood that I never questioned it. I never questioned the fact that we weren't a normal family. I never questioned the fact that my father was rarely there. Duty was everything, and I followed that duty.

Marlene and Maria, Berlin 1925.

And as far as the family was concerned, in my family, my mother was the queen of our household, and I was there to serve her in the best way possible. Whether as a dresser, or as a child, or as a confidante, or as a secretary, it was always a duty to her.

And when she took up this fight against Hitler, and I was then twelve, I took it up as well. This was not because I followed her blindly, but because I respected her intelligence. She was a very, very intelligent woman. And one of the reasons she hated being a movie star, I think, was because being a movie star didn't need intelligence, as far as she was concerned. You know, she rather looked down her nose at all movie stars, anyway.

And so, the fact that her mother was in Berlin, and that my aunt, her sister, was in Berlin and might suffer really never quite came into the spectrum of what she saw as her duty. It was her duty to fight Hitler; therefore it was my father's duty, my duty, and anyone else who wanted to be a friend of Dietrich. I mean, if anybody said *any*thing that was even slightly pro-Nazi or pro-war, uh, you know, against America and England, or anybody made any remarks whatsoever, it blew, and they were never seen again. They were ostracized from her intimate circle immediately.

You know, very often people have asked me, "How is it possible to turn your back on a mother, a sister?" It can be understood that you can turn your back on something that is evil within your country, and therefore you can turn your back on your country, as my mother did, "but how can you justify turning your back on a mother?" This is another nagging question I am asked. And you know, my mother's attitude toward that was always that this was what her mother would have wanted her to do. She was convinced that her mother would want her to turn her back. And if you think of it in that frame of mind, it's understandable because my grandmother was very proud of what my mother did in the war.

But regardless of others' opinions, when my mother returned home from Hollywood after having made *Morocco* and *Dishonored,* she moved us to America. That was 1931.

I think the first thing that one has to remember is that Berlin is always gray, and always cold, and always stark. And suddenly, you were transported on a very large ship, and your mother is being photographed wherever she moves, which was new to me because she had kept me away, you know, from the photographers and the fame. And suddenly, you come into New York, which was also dank and wet. But it was the train trip that I remember, that was so amazing. As we came into California, you could smell the orange blossoms. You must remember that it was before air conditioning, and so the windows were open and you could smell the oranges. That is the first impression that I had. They had a little balcony, which was the observation balcony on the back of the train, and you would sit there at night and you would smell the desert as you were coming into it, and the purple mountains. It was—well, it was magic. It was my . . . Disneyland. Hollywood was my Disneyland before there was a Disneyland. And it was wonderful. I think I fell in love with America because it was such an incredible fable. It was like reading a child's book of fairy tales, and I was living it. I was inside of it and it was beautiful. And everybody was beautiful: the house was beautiful, the trees were beautiful, my mother was beautiful, the men she was in love with were beautiful. Everything was beautiful—the clothes were beautiful, the studio was beautiful.

And maybe that's where I got my—you know, all my neuroses, you know, that I thought I was ugly because when you live in a world where the entire industry is for beauty, for the face, for the hair, for the makeup, for the whole allure, it's daunting, but very exciting. It's a wonderful profession, but it requires sacrifice.

Anyway, after every film we used to go back to Europe—this was the big thing. And when we went back, we always stayed in Paris, but my mother wanted to go back to Germany to see her mother, my grandmother, and her sister, my aunt. And it was sort of assumed that she would come back from America, go to Paris, and then from Paris on to Germany. You must understand that Europeans have an attitude toward imminent war because they've had war in their lives, and in their centuries, and in their generations so that war is always prevalent in the mind of a European.

When I was a child, I remember people coming to the Ritz, to the hotels where we were living, and they had diamonds and diamond bracelets, and loose rubies sewn into the hems of their dresses because these were the White Russians who were escaping out of the revolution in Russia. Every doorman of every great restaurant, in every great hotel in the 1930s in Paris, was a prince or a count [*she laughs*], all deposed Russians.

And this was prevalent, this idea that one always had to be ready to move, one always had to be packed, one always had to be prepared. My mother, for instance, had a vanity case that she hated because it was too heavy to carry just to the set. But it was always packed for immediate departure for somewhere one had to run to, you know? I was taught to always have everything ready at a moment's notice, even before there was any fear of an actual Second World War. This was just a mindset adopted through the centuries.

When we were in America, my father was in Germany working, and of course we always sent photographs to him of everything that was happening.

And she told him everything. But he was very aware of what was happening in Germany. When we arrived in Paris after *Morocco* and *Dishonored* he told us to stay put. My father, who was still in Germany [*she sighs*], was getting very nervous. There were firings going on in his department. He was working for Paramount at the time, in Germany, for dubbing. He was an excellent sound mixer and created a lot of new systems for dubbing. And suddenly Jews were disappearing strangely from the roster of his employees. And my mother became aware of this also because everyone who arrived in Paris, whom she saw, was already aware of what was happening. Now this was the early '30s. Things were going on long before the world and the press knew what was going on.

Soon, my mother's hotel room, her suite, at the Ritz, for instance, was a place where every refugee from Germany—particularly from Berlin—arrived.

A young Maria on Rodeo Drive, Beverly Hills, 1931.

They knew that they could get a meal. They knew that they could get money. And they knew that they would get employment if there were something like that, or they might even get transportation to America or a job in America or her vouching for them.

It was really like a refugee camp. I remember many of the suites with this rococo decor and all this glamor and this beauty, filled with these frightened people. And then I remember room service—you know, my mother would call down to room service in her *immaculate* French, which was always so beautiful. She would order these platters of ham, and platters of chicken breasts decorated as only the French know how.

As I say in my book, I was not a child. I was a hundred and five in a child's body, but I was always there. I was her constant companion so that I saw all of this. And in my child's mind, I saw all these people who were very worried. Some of them looked very poor . . . always in wrinkled clothes, I remember. And that was because they had escaped from Berlin in trains and wagons and cars even then. And my mother would take them under her wing.

And my father kept saying to my mother, "You're not coming into Germany." And that was the only time I saw her angry at him, because she said, "Of course, I'm going to see Mama!" And he said, "No. I don't think that is a good idea. Why don't you have your mother come and meet you in Austria?" You see, Austria was still considered safe at that time. Little did anybody know that it wasn't safe at all, but safe enough as it turned out. And she said, "Why do I have to go all the way to Vienna in order to see my mother? I want to go into Berlin. I want to see Liesel and the family."

Finally my father prevailed because she understood, not because she was always following his advice blindly. It wasn't that. She understood that he had a reason for it, and when she saw her friends and people she had known in the theater coming to her for help in Paris, she knew that this was not just an idle "Stay out of Berlin" or an "I don't want you here" kind of thing from my father.

So from then on we used to make this trip out of France, through Switzerland, into Vienna or Salzburg, and there I would see my grandmother and she would see her mother.

Often my children asked me at the playground, "How was it when you were a child and you were playing with other children?" And it always stuns me because I realize that I never played with other children, because I never knew other children. I knew my mother's lovers. I knew my mother's co-workers. But I rarely knew children, unless they were children of movie stars at the studio or on the set. The only time I remember playing with a child was when I visited Austria and my grandmother, my aunt, and her son came to meet us. And I was told to go out and play, which was very foreign to me, and said in German it's even more peculiar.

And here was this boy, who was supposedly my cousin—which meant nothing to me—and I think we had an instant dislike of each other for some reason. You know, that's easy in children of that age. And I think I knocked him down. [*She laughs.*] And I'm very sorry I knocked him down.

But, I never saw him again. And, for me, he was always just Tante Liesel's son. Later I was told what had probably happened to him during the war. It was something that happened to a lot of children who were innocent; they were warped by the Nazi system.

You know, it's always an interesting question, when somebody asks me about my family. For me, "family" means the family that I made through my wonderful husband. That is the only family that I ever acknowledge as a family. And I'm very blessed because of it. But I suppose there was other family too, that people thought was family. But my grandmother—the last time I saw her was in Austria. And at the time I thought it would be nice to hug my grandmother, you know. And she sort of backed away, and she looked at me and said, "You do what your mother tells you to do. And you do your duty to your mother." She didn't say, "Do your duty to your parents" and so I think my grandmother [*she laughs*] was quite aware who was the boss in our family. My grandmother sort of frightened me because she was rather tall, and very Victorian, and very straight-laced with those high collars, you know. But I always felt very close to my mother's sister, my aunt Liesel, because I've always felt close to the ugly ducklings of this world, being one myself. I always had a soft spot in my heart for her. But my aunt, she was sort of a soft little wren of a woman. And my sweet, poor aunt was the type of woman who followed wherever her husband led her, and so she ended up in Belsen—in the town of Belsen. And, well, that's another story.

And when I saw them in Austria, I didn't know it would be the last time that I would see them. My grandmother simply said to me, "You do your duty by your mother," and she wouldn't even let me hug her or anything. My aunt you could always hug. She loved to be hugged. I think that this poor woman never got enough love. And then there was my cousin, Hans Georg—I had a cousin, an actual cousin. You know, in my family today, to say that you have a cousin is a *big* thing, you know, because nobody thought about these things before. My mother didn't have this thing about "family." It wasn't part of her duty, so, therefore, it wasn't part of our lives growing up. And besides, you know, Dietrich needed to be in control, and if you loved or paid attention to somebody else or to somebody that was not sanctioned by her, well, you were in trouble, you know, even dogs. She never would have a dog around for that reason. So there were a lot of little innuendos and waves that were made because of affection for people, or for animals. So one learned quickly not to "do" family a great deal.

When I got married, one of the first things that my mother said to me was, "I suppose you're now going to have children?" And I said, "Yes, as many as I possibly can." And she said, "Oh, no!" [*She laughs.*] So it was, really, a very tenuous point.

But the wonderful thing about my grandmother was that everybody knew that her daughter refused to remain a German, that her daughter became an American citizen at the moment when Goebbels attacked her as a real slap in the face, that, uh, she, uh, entertained the American forces, the—the—the enemy, that, uh, she became an enemy to the German people. Everybody knew that Dietrich refused to come back and become the great star of the Hitler Reich, that her mother would remain in her house, in Berlin, and not be sent anywhere because who would dare to touch a Dietrich, or a von Losch? I think it was clear to everyone that my mother really got her courage from her mother, in a way! As a matter of fact, my grandmother was very proud of the fact that she lived through the entire war in the same house where her daughters had been born.

After our visits to see the "extended" family, we always returned to our home, a hotel suite in Paris. One morning my father shooed me out of my mother's suite and said, "There's a very important meeting here—children, out of the way." And I knew my cues, and so I went down the stairs 'cause my mother's apartment was—in this hotel—was up the stairs. But I was curious, as all children are. I don't really know what age I was, but I was a child.

Suddenly, these black-leathered apparitions marched up the stairs. They were actually very frightening. I remember them as being ominous, you know, a little bit like Darth Vader from *Star Wars,* you know? And they were all in leather, and it was shiny, and they marched in front of this gentleman—there were two of them—and they marched in front of this gentleman, who was dressed in what we would have called in Hollywood "straight from the costume department," you know. My mother used to always say, "They always look as though they're coming from another set," they're already dressed for a different part. And, this man, he had medals, and he had a uniform, and it was, as I remember, uh, very resplendent.

He walked into my mother's suite with the two guards. I assume they were guards, dressed in black leather coats, which we realized many years later were Gestapo coats. These two stood guard at this door, at this portal of my mother's suite. And, uh, it took quite a while, and I waited and waited and waited, and I thought to myself, what is going on in there? Because it was only very rarely that I was told to not be there. I was always that shadow, you know, the sponge that was absorbing everything.

And so, finally, this gentleman from the other set came out of my mother's suite and marched downstairs. And the guards marched downstairs with him. And I *scooted* into my mother's suite and my mother was pacing. My mother paced when she was angry. Erich Maria Remarque later would call her "the puma" because that's how she moved, you know. She was also smoking, and she was saying, "Now we know where they took all the Jews—to make their uniforms! That's where all the good tailors have gone to!"

And it happened to be von Ribbentrop who had come; he came quite often after that—to ask Marlene Dietrich to come back to Germany and be the reigning motion picture star, the jewel in the Nazi crown of moviedom. And so even though this happened quite often, my mother was absolutely furious that they even thought that she would be interested, that she might even consider it. But she used to always say, "Well, Hitler never got over that garter belt in *The Blue Angel,* and I'm stuck with it," you know. But she was absolutely furious, and that's how I remember von Ribbentrop.

You know, the European contingent in California was always geared to the war, even before America came into it.

And so then when Pearl Harbor happened, of course, all the expatriates who had not taken American citizenship like my mother had all felt guilty because here was America now involved in the war to save their country. Young men were going to die for their country, and they were sitting in Hollywood making pictures, you know. It was very difficult for them, I'm sure.

And for Jean Gabin, my mother's lover during that time, I think it was more difficult for him than for any of the others that I knew personally. It was only a matter of time before France would fall and he was a patriotic man. He felt guilty. He knew he was making lousy movies to begin with. He felt uncomfortable. The Little France that my mother had created for him sufficed at home for a few hours, but his guilt was tremendous.

My mother also felt that now that she was an American she should be doing something too, not just feeding refugees and not just always preaching against Hitler and being aware of the war, which we had been since 1933.

So now we were in the war, all of us, and sometimes, you know, it's been said that my mother finally pushed Jean into saying, "I've had it! I'm going back to fight for the free French." And sometimes we thought it was he who said to her, "I can't stand it anymore—I'm going." But whatever it was, I think it was that both of them felt the same way.

And he went back to fight for France. And she was very jealous of the fact that she couldn't also put a uniform on and fight for the free French, as De Gaulle was one of her great heroes. She loved him. She thought him a god. And anyone who was willing to stand up and fight against Hitler and what Hitler stood for was okay by her.

You know, in a country that is not being attacked by an enemy, to get young people to go and fight across the sea, even for an ideal, is not the easiest thing to do, although I think Americans are always ready to help anybody in trouble. My mother decided to help where she could, and at first this meant war bond tours and the Hollywood Canteen.

The first canteen opened in New York, the Stage Door Canteen, for all the military boys to have a place to come, who were lonely, who'd come from the heartland of America. Suddenly they were in New York, and they were going to be shipped out. And this caught on. It was a wonderful place for young boys to come there, to have one more moment of American life, to dance with an American girl, to have their doughnut and their coffee.

And so, one was opened in Hollywood. It was called the Hollywood Canteen. And Bette Davis and John Garfield were the ones who were the instigators behind it because by this time, of course, the Pacific war was going full tilt also, and everyone came. And the *idea* that you could dance with Hedy *Lamarr,* and you could dance with Betty *Grable*—I mean, the army boys and the sailors, well, I mean, it was a morale builder for the them. They had someplace to go, and they kept out of trouble. The MPs loved it because they knew that once the boys were in a place that was controlled like the canteen was, there wouldn't be trouble. The canteen didn't have any liquor, didn't allow any liquor, and was safe. Even the girls were not allowed to leave the premises, the starlets under contract to studios. And, of course, the big stars would certainly come there.

The Hollywood Canteen was really a place that was jumping. All the wonderful orchestras came there: Glenn Miller was there, Kay Kaiser was there, and Harry James. And the boys were dancing to this music with *movie stars,* and they would always say, "May I have a picture with you?" And, of course, my mother did the same thing, and so did Hedy Lamarr, except that they also had to help serve ham sandwiches, and cheese sandwiches, and coffee, and all this. And finally, one day, uh, my mother, who always had an apron on because she liked aprons anyway, said, "But who's doing all the dishes?" And she goes back into the kitchen, and from that moment on, you couldn't get her out, you know, because she was in a kitchen and she was washing dishes. And then, of course, Hedy Lamarr wanted to get in on the act also, which prompted that wonderful quote of Bette Davis, who said, "Get those two Krauts out of the kitchen!"

But it was a wonderful place. It was in full swing and everyone was ready, because at that time, and even before Pearl Harbor, all of Hollywood was geared toward entering the war and being helpful with the war effort. They were already making films like *Mrs. Miniver.*

So everybody was for the British because they were being bombed and we were sending packages over, "bundles for Britain." And children were coming over to America, who were being evacuated. I mean, all of Hollywood was geared to the propaganda. All the films, at the end on the screen, had the message, "Buy War Bonds." Everything was geared toward this *tremendous* war effort, even before Pearl Harbor. And, of course, when Pearl Harbor hit, you can imagine California, which felt it was going to be invaded that same day.

So my mother started selling bonds on the radio and at rallies all over America. Long before she went overseas, like every star and every starlet, she went and sold bonds. For my mother, it was very important to make the point to the people listening that she was a German citizen at one time who had become an American citizen because she was against what Hitler stood for, and what was happening in the world around her. But you should have seen the speeches that they wrote for Dietrich for the bond rallies that she went on. They had prepared these texts that they would hand my mother. In one she was an Austrian because they thought she wouldn't want to say that she was German-born, and then she was a Czechoslovakian—basically from any country. Anything to do with whatever Hitler had taken over it was okay to be, you know. So, first of all, she said, "What do you think, these people are idiots who are going to give money to win a war?" But it was very important to her.

Please remember that Dietrich was the *only* world-famous figure who turned her back on Nazism who was not Jewish, not married to a Jew, nor had any connections with the Jewish people. It was very important that here was this Prussian, this German Prussian, who had become an American citizen because of her hatred for what Nazis stood for, what Hitler stood for, what Goebbels stood for, and was aware of how evil they were and that she wanted to do something about it. This was long before she went overseas with the USO.

You know, when you joined the USO, you were not told where you were going, what country even, but you had your uniform made at Saks Fifth Avenue because you had officer status. And they were known as "pinks"—you had a pink skirt, and gentlemen had the pink trousers.

And before she had ever been overseas, I was always fascinated by the fact that my mother had her uniform made—this was before she had the Eisenhower uniform, that was the real one—as a summer uniform. Now how did she know that? When I went overseas we were issued winter clothes. Once we were on the ship, and even then only when we had reached the middle of the ocean, we were given tropical uniforms because by then they could tell us we were on our way to Caserta in Italy, and not to the North Pole, or wherever we were supposed to be shipped. So there was always a funny story that she really must have known where she was going beforehand. And I think that she did it only because she was so vehement about going over. She badgered the USO Camp Shows chief Abe Lastfogel, who organized the USO in the very first stages of it, that she should be allowed to go over because she was a German by birth, who had chosen to become an American citizen because of the attacks on her family, because of her stance against Hitler's regime, and because she felt she would be important as a figurehead. I think it was for these reasons that they finally did let her go. And when they did clear her with the FBI, and all the other things, they told her where she was going so she'd look properly dressed.

You know, when you're entertaining troops, everything is very structured. It has to be. You cannot send civilians into the battlefield, right? And the very first USO troop that she had, which was with Danny Thomas, was very structured. The Special Services would set it up. You were billeted. You were told when to perform. There would be stages. And the boys would be told, "Dietrich will be here tonight, et cetera, et cetera." And everything was very structured. Well, as soon as she got the lay of the land, right, she decided that this was too far back from the actual fighting lines. And so she started to finagle her way to the front lines and artillery batteries, with just a jeep and just one accordion player, or whatever she could dig up. She got very good at it.

And I know that one of the reasons that she became great friends with so many generals was not only because she liked generals and they liked her, but also because as soon as she had that relationship with a general, she could say, "Can't I just take the jeep and go and do this show over there?" And of course they would always say, "No, it's too dangerous," but she went anyway and they really respected her for that. It was known that if Dietrich were captured the Nazis would do terrible things to her for propaganda reasons. And although her rank was technically captain, if she was taken prisoner, it would be a nightmare for the American troops. But she always wanted to go to the front.

What for her was so important for the boys was that it was not an organized, plastic statement like, "Here come the Hollywood entertainers. You're the poor little doughboys, all full of mud, and with your purple hearts, and you're fighting and you're getting killed. And here come these little cutesy-pootsies," which, of course, came with other people, like Bob Hope, who always traveled with a cameraman and a pool of reporters. But she didn't like that for them. She wanted to be a soldier *with* them, to say, "I am here, and if you want to hear a song, and if you want to hear a routine, and you can flirt with me on the stage, and I can flirt with you from the stage, and you can have a little bit of sense that time has stopped still for just a moment. That's what I'm here for, not to parade, you know, cutesy-pootsy across the stage with a lot of jokes." And well, for her, that's what was the most important thing.

And I think the loyalty of the GIs was earned. Her greatest audiences in Vegas were ex-GIs who remembered her in the mud here, and under fire here, and when they had given up hope of ever breaking through a line—and suddenly Dietrich in a glittering dress appeared before them, you know, out of context, out of time, not because some Special Service officer had engineered it. That was the reason for her great following. They knew that she was not phony, that she was really there for them, and that she was ready to be with them in the mud.

And I think that was the basis of this tremendous devotion because I saw it through all the tours that we did. To her it was always, "the boys," and they were *her* boys. She always called them "boys," and by that time they were grown men, you know, with families and grandchildren. And she would always say, "My boys are out there! My boys are out there!" It was a love affair between thousands and thousands of young American boys and one woman who wanted to do it.

During the two times that my mother was overseas, when she already felt that she really should be in the trenches with a rifle shooting the enemy, the OSS, the Office of Strategic Services, came to her, which was very strange because it was sort of a secret organization.

What they had done was to take American songs that were very well known and had put German lyrics to these American songs. And what they planned to do was to pipe them through the underground and to the German public—not the Nazi, per se, but the German public. At that time, we still believed that the German public and the Nazis were separated by a large chasm, which we later found out they were not when we discovered Auschwitz and Treblinka. But in those days, the OSS was still trying to help the resistance, to give them fodder, to give them power by beaming these secret songs into Germany. And it was very interesting because the lyrics were written with a slant like, "Tomorrow it will be a better day," "Tomorrow there will be sunshine."

Because I spoke German and knew sort of the American rhythm, my mother said, "Why doesn't my daughter also do it?" because my mother said she never knew how to do anything that was jazzy, you see. So, she enlisted me at the time, and we recorded these songs in New York. I think I did four recordings, four songs, and she did four, or maybe even more. And it was all *very,* very secret, and I wasn't supposed to tell anybody about it. And I thought it was very weird because I knew I couldn't sing.

And so we sang "Wenn der Sommer wieder seinzieht dann bauen wir uns ein neues Haus," which means, "When the summer comes back, we will have a new home." This was for the Germans who were being bombed, you know. It said, "You're—you're going to find a better life once the Americans have saved you from the Nazis." This was the whole premise of this propaganda, and it was very secret—*very, very* secret. My mother recorded whenever she could between her USO tours in Europe.

I had my time with the USO also. I have to preface that a little bit by telling you that my mother was there during the war, the actual war, and when she came back on one of the trips, I was ready to go over with the USO, which was to perform in a play, not because I wasn't a star; I was just part of a company that did a play. And with the great intelligence of the USO, they took a play, which had all male parts, and put a lot of women into the parts so that the boys could see women. And I was given the part of the whore, and so everybody was sort of hooked onto the fact that I would be playing Molly Malloy in *The Front Page.*

And my mother came back and we were both in uniform and had been taken out to dinner at the Zebra Room in New York. Of course her uniform was the Eisenhower uniform, trim and beautiful and wonderful, and she was the real soldier, and I was sort of in a dowdy USO uniform, always be-

Maria and Marlene meet in New York at the El Morocco club just after both returned from overseas USO duty, July 1945.

ing too fat and too big, you know. And she said to me, "Now, sweetheart, when you get there, they will be so wonderful. They will be suffering, and they will be so brave. And you will be crying all the time—you'll be crying. But you mustn't show it—you mustn't show it." And she gave me this magnificent, really inspiring advice about what I would see—preparing me for this experience.

Well, I went over in '45—it was the end of the war and these wonderful, brave men were furious because they were waiting to be shipped to the Pacific, where war was still raging. And there was no heraldry. There was none of this wonderful euphoric thing that happens to people when they are under the threat of death. And I was looking for this experience that my mother had had, and of course it was not really there. And I felt for the boys because there were some that had five or six stripes already on their sleeve, which means that they had been over there for a long time and had seen the worst of the battle.

But I did have one great moment when we were in Italy. We moved through Italy, up through to the north of Italy and into Germany with this troop. And in Italy, I was the one who was told by the Special Service officer that the war in Japan was over, and that I would be the one to announce it to the boys in the audience.

Marlene coming home after being overseas.

And in the middle of the play, we stopped, and I walked to the front of the curtain of the little theater that they had built there in this compound, and I told the boys that the Second World War was over. And that was a . . . that was a fabulous moment, a *fabulous* moment. There was absolute silence . . . just ominous silence, like you get before an earthquake in this part of the world. And then suddenly, this explosion of life, this celebration that they had made it, that they were still alive to hear it, that they had fought, and that they were no longer in danger, and that they could go home, to the home that they had been fighting for. It was—it's something I'll never forget, and it was amazing, absolutely amazing. Of course, there was bedlam after that, and no play was put on for days [*she laughs*] after that. So, I had my moment of glory there, and it was a wonderful moment, a wonderful moment.

The following winter, I was with the Eighty-Second Airborne Division football team in Stuttgart when I heard that my grandmother had died. My mother was in Berlin. And I tried to get back—but I had no travel orders. And by the time I got to Berlin, my grandmother had already been buried, and I couldn't stand next to my mother and hold her hand, to see her mother buried.

It was a strange time for my mother because even though she had gotten back to Germany and she'd seen her mother right after the war ended, it hadn't been long since then. I knew my mother would be very lost and so I wanted to be there, but I couldn't. I thumbed my way through the Black Forest up into Berlin. But I wasn't there in time. But we always knew that the moment Hitler was defeated, my grandmother would say, "I've lived this long, I've outlived him, now I can die." And so it was not as tragic a death as it might have appeared to other people because there was this indomitable spirit of my grandmother, who had outlasted this "Devil." And so the war was over for her, and for my mother and me, too.

Coming home from the war was an interesting experience for my mother because, suddenly, everything was mundane—if you can imagine it that way. It started at the port when she arrived by ship. They took away the guns that the boys had given her: the Lugers, and the pistols, and the this and that. You know, they were always wanting to give her something. And for her, suddenly she didn't have a uniform to wear; she had to think about hats and stockings and, I mean, she hated this. And, of course, she suddenly had to earn a living because during the war she was not paid, as everybody knows. And so she, like everybody, needed money and she had none. She tried to write a check at the Plaza Hotel in New York the night she came back, and it, you know, bounced. They wouldn't accept it.

So reality came back. For her, reality had been the fighting against evil, the helping of boys, being there for them, doing her duty—doing what she really believed in. And now, suddenly, she was relegated to being a movie star. Well, my mother always said that with tremendous disgust. And I think, like a lot of the men, my mother suddenly had to go and get a job. And put on civilian clothes—it was a whole different world. Nobody was there to tell you where to be at a certain time, or where to go when you didn't have any travel papers. Now you had to make your own decisions about what to do. It was a very difficult time for her. I was much luckier. I came back and fell in love with my husband, which was wonderful. So, I had none of the same blues she had, caused by her separation from an organized duty to do something good and be lauded for it, you know. I just went from one duty to another with my husband, which I embraced for fifty-two years.

But for my mother, it was difficult. And from then on, all the work that she did in films was really what she used to call prostitution, which meant she did it for the salary that they were offering her. And then later, of course, she did films in which she played roles that she called real prostitution, which she only did because Billy Wilder asked her to—to play roles that were against her constitution, her beliefs.

My mother always said that only Billy Wilder could have persuaded her to do *A Foreign Affair.* I think that she was very good in it because if you think of some of the things that Billy asked her to do in this film, and knowing her, well, she really is acting [*she laughs*] for a change.

She did it, really, because she admired Billy Wilder, and loved him. And they went way back, you know, far back into the German days. And she knew what a great talent he was, and that he would not *really* put her too much over the coals. But on top of it, she always said to me, "The *only* reason I'm doing this film is because *you* had your first child, and from now on, you're going to need more money." So, I was blamed for this entire saga. And when she had to do the Nazi woman in that little insert in the film, I mean, it was one of those days where you wouldn't want to be near Dietrich at all! I mean, it was really glacial on the set. And again, she would glare at Billy and say, "Only you could make me do this. And Maria's child!" But they continued to do films together, even when it happened again in *Judgment at Nuremberg.* That film was, perhaps, one of the most difficult things for her to do. You know, looking at my mother's films, in retrospect, I must say that she was a far better actress than even I realized, and I was her greatest critic. I knew how great she was on the stage as a concert performer,

The most famous German actress in the world—who fought the Nazi regime—is asked to say "We did not know." Marlene works with her co-star Spencer Tracy to "get it right."

but as an actress I was never that enamored. I was too involved in the construction of it. But *Judgment at Nuremberg* took a great deal out of her. There was a scene that she had to do with Spencer Tracy, the scene where she has to say, "Well, you know, we never knew anything," and she has to represent the entire German way of thinking, and the exoneration of Germans who were involved and yet were not involved. Well, she really couldn't get it. For the first time, she rehearsed at home, and she came over to my house and she said, "How am I going to do this?" And I kept saying to her, "Just don't think about it. Don't think about what you're saying, the context of what you're saying." But she still had trouble. And then, finally, she had a talk with Spencer Tracy. It was the first time that Dietrich got close to Spencer Tracy, actor to actor, woman to man. My mother had a certain standoffish quality with Spence, mostly because of Katharine Hepburn. She felt that he belonged to Katharine Hepburn, so he shouldn't get too involved with Dietrich. It was partly honoring his talent, and partly honoring his position with Katharine. So for the first time she spoke to him, actor to actor, and he looked at her and he said, "You know, it is needed that *you* say it . . . because only from *you* will they believe it. We must close the wounds. It is necessary." And she did the scene, and I think they were right, how it turned out.

Of course, if anyone wants to know what Dietrich really thought about Hitler and the entire Second World War, just go and look and listen to her voice narrate *The Black Fox*. I think it is one of the most definitive documentaries ever done on the Second World War. We worked on it together, and it was really important to us both. She was so proud of what she did on this thing, that she gave her rights to it to me as a gift, "In perpetuity," she wrote on the script. And it's the real Marlene Dietrich—the one to be proud of—and as her daughter, I was exceedingly, and am exceedingly, proud of the work she did on that film.

People have always asked why Dietrich went to Las Vegas. And the very simple answer, which my mother would have given you if she could, and that is that she was broke. She was always broke. [*Laughs.*] She never had any money. She always spent a lot of money, but she never had any money, which drove my father crazy. But to do this concert in Vegas they offered her so much money that in a letter even to me, she said, "How could I refuse this?" But she was frightened of doing it. She said, "A movie star on a stage, in Las Vegas? I mean, they want people who can sing." And I said to her, "Do you remember the war years, Mass?" And there was a long silence on the telephone, and she said, "Oh, you mean like that?" I said, "*Exactly* like that." She, of course, sold out and then she began touring all over the world.

The tours that went through Germany, and Czechoslovakia, and Austria, and into Israel were extremely important for my mother, emotionally as well as professionally.

Professionally, as a single performer, it's a very frightening thing to be alone on the stage and have five thousand people look at you and say, "Okay, entertain us. Show us who you are," "So, you're the big Dietrich," et cetera, et cetera, but she did it magnificently. She did it very much like a soldier. But for her personally, this was also her return to Europe, and in many cases back to what had been occupied territory. My mother had never quite gotten over what she had seen in the war, and I don't think anyone who was in the war, or in any war, ever gets over it. And for those of us who were involved in the Second World War, the atrocities and the Holocaust live with you. Wherever you go and whatever happens in your life, you sort of relate to that. And for her, this was extremely important.

I went to Israel in the '50s to do the very first television program that was ever filmed in Israel. Unfortunately, the whole thing fell through, but I was there at that time. And what impressed me was that there was in Israel a real love of Germany as a country, the love of Germany as a language of great poets and great philosophers, and for the music of Germany, of great composers—that is something that those Jews who had escaped and were in Israel, the German Jews, and Berlin Jews particularly, uh, never left behind. They never lost that respect for it because *that* was not Hitler. And for them, that was the Germany that was their homeland.

When I came back from Israel, I said to my mother when she went on the tour, "Are you going to sing in German, in Israel?" And she said, "No." And I said, "You know, Mass, I think that you should because the German language is not what belonged to Hitler. The German language is the language of itself, of a great, great nation that once was great and once was clean. And I think that it is important that you do it." And she did, and it was a great success. In a way, the cool reception she got earlier when she toured in Germany was redeemed, I think.

You know, people think that Marlene Dietrich put herself to bed in an apartment on the Avenue Montaigne in Paris for so many, many years until her death because of her vanity—that she didn't want to destroy the imagery of the Dietrich face, the beauty of this magnificent icon. That wasn't at all what she wanted. She was *tired* of being a movie star. She was tired of putting on the makeup and putting on the wigs, and all that that entailed because, don't forget, she was already seventy-five when she did her last giant concert tour on television. So, she had had enough. She wanted to use her brain, which was still as sharp as a tack. She wrote articles, books, and wonderful things in newspapers, and gave interviews, et cetera, et cetera. But it was not out of vanity. But it was thought that that's what real movie stars do—they put themselves away or have facelifts and stuff, to preserve the image. Dietrich wasn't like that at all. You know, one of the reasons that my mother never saw anyone once she had finally put herself to bed was not because she didn't want them to see her but because she knew what they would expect to see.

When you're very, very beautiful, people have this image inside their heads, and no matter what happens, that's what they see. And she never wanted to disappoint anybody, you know. It was her decision to do it. It wasn't her vanity to do that.

My mother never really had a home. Every house that we ever lived in was rented. Every hotel had a suite. Every train, every boat—there was never a sense of home. And very often in the very last years of her life, she wanted to go back to Berlin. When the wall came down, that was the moment. And she said, "Maybe now." And then she would say, "Oh, no, of course, it's impossible," because she knew physically she couldn't do it. And certainly there would be so many reporters. But I said, "We can put on a wig." And she said, "No, no." So, I knew that deep down inside her there was something that wanted her to go back home.

For as long as I can remember, my mother always loved the Madeleine, the church in Paris. And she often said, "I'm going to be buried at the Madeleine," when she was telling her famous story about her funeral, which, really, she made up as a party piece.

So, when she died, I thought to myself, I'd love to give her that funeral. And still, at the same time, I wanted to bury her as the soldier that I always thought she was. She was a soldier in a real war. She was a soldier in her real life. And she was a soldier in her profession. And I thought, once she had had those burials and those ceremonies that I'd take her home, to the only home that she really ever knew, and to the one woman that, if she had loved her correctly, might have changed my mother's life entirely. But then, if she had, I suppose we wouldn't be talking about her still.

And so, we held her funeral at her beloved Madeleine, her coffin draped in a French flag in front of the altar. On top of the flag were all the medals that she had received for her war work: French, Belgian, as well as American. Then the coffin was carried out of the church, and was put on a plane. I wanted to make quite sure that people would know that she had been an American, not just a European, not just loving France, not just a German, but that she was basically an American who was proud of being an American during the war. So her coffin was draped in an American flag for the journey to Germany. And when we arrived in Germany, it was unloaded, and I refused to have the coffin then draped in a German flag. And that was rather a stumbling block. And then, finally, it was permitted that we could drape the coffin in a Berlin flag. And so, her coffin was draped in a Berlin flag. So, I took her home. And home was Berlin.

Something that our family did not know was that it was market day. On the way to Schöneberg Cemetery, it was flower market day. And as the open car, with her coffin draped with the flag of Berlin, went through the streets of this outskirt of Berlin, a suburb of Berlin, all these people rushed into the market and bought all the flowers that were there in the marketplace, and threw them onto the coffin. And I didn't know this. My family didn't know, because we were already at the cemetery waiting for the coffin to arrive. And as this coffin drove up to the cemetery, it was *covered* in all these cut flowers, and we didn't know where they had come from because they had been thrown! You know, there was just wild abandon. And so, she really had her welcome the way she would have loved it. And it was not staged, and it wasn't thought out for the photographers or the newsreels. It just happened.

But that's one of the things that I always loved about Dietrich. If you think of her as the icon, things always happened to her in just the right way and at just the right time. And as it happened, I am sure she would have been very pleased. She would have said, "That was well done." And that was the best you could hope for. To get a "well done" from Dietrich was the best you could ever get from anybody.

Marlene on touring through Europe and the German tour of 1960:

"I've been in Israel, twice now, I've been in Poland twice, and I've been in Russia. I always go back; I always go back to the places I like. Then again, I didn't go back to Germany. I was in Germany once in 1960. The audiences are wonderful; it's the press that is bad. And you know they put bombs in the theater and who wants to be bombed at this time? The German audiences are wonderful. It was just the press—they just didn't like me."

On "Where Have All the Flowers Gone" and its antiwar theme:

"It is a song against war, and I am very happy because at the moment this record is very successful, and I believe it is because there is no one in the world who likes war. So I think this song has a message for all of us: War is ridiculous, and it keeps on repeating itself. And my song asks, 'When will we ever learn?'"

BURT BACHARACH

One of the most significant performer/composers of the twentieth century, BURT BACHARACH has achieved top hits in each of the last four decades and has written for every medium. He is also unquestionably one of the greats of orchestration. In the late 1950s, he embarked with Marlene on her world tour, which included the most sensitive engagements of her career, including Berlin and Tel Aviv. In his Los Angeles sitting room, festooned with Academy Awards, Burt recalled his turbulent history with his close friend Marlene.

I'd been on my way to Los Angeles to maybe learn something about scoring for films.

I'd been under contract as a songwriter at Paramount Famous Music, and I thought if I got out to the studio, I could hang around and learn something about it, 'cause I wanted to score films.

And there was a girl out here in California I wanted to see, who was living out here—an actress. And we were gonna live together.

I got a call at the airport leaving New York from my friend, Peter Matz, who did the same thing I did. I conducted for acts. And he got me at the airport and he said, "I got a huge conflict. I'm supposed to conduct for Noël Coward *and* for Marlene Dietrich, at the same time in Las Vegas. Would you have any interest in, like, maybe taking my place in conducting for Dietrich? And I'll fulfill my engagement with Noël—that was my first commitment. And at least meet her?" And I said, "Well, sure. That really sounds interesting, Peter."

I got in, kind of moved into this little house with this girl, and called Marlene at the Beverly Hills Hotel. She expected the call. And I went over and met with her in one of the cottages.

Initially, it was very intimidating, seeing Marlene, because that's a very powerful presence—very huge, aura of a star, you know—very sweet, very nice, very giving, very kind, but I was still nervous, and I certainly wasn't comfortable with somebody of *that* star magnitude at the time.

But I came in, and we worked a little bit. She showed me the show music—she was going to open in about ten, twelve days in Las Vegas at the Sahara Hotel, and then perform again at either the Sahara or the Sands. And I worked with her every day. It got less intimidating.

It got so I could actually suggest things and say, "Relax here. Don't rush—don't rush the music there," or "You've got time, you don't need to go that fast." She was basically kind of okay with listening, and taking the advice, and getting comfortable with me.

And that's how we initially started this association, this friendship, this working relationship. The first time we worked in Vegas, I didn't stay in the hotel. I stayed at a place called the Bali Ha'i Motel. So I'm playing tennis with Ed Ames, of the Ames Brothers, and, wow, I look up from the tennis court, and there's Marlene with what looks like a big bag of groceries. I haven't known her very long at this point, you know. So she's getting the key from the front desk and she's going to let herself into my apartment—my bedroom–living room complex that I had at the Bali Ha'i Motel.

Well, she'd bought steaks. She knew I was playing tennis—but she wouldn't bother me, she just walked into my kitchen and when I came off the tennis court, she had condensed the juice from the steaks—six steaks—so I could just drink the broth.

Marlene in front of the Vegas Club, Las Vegas.

I didn't ask her for this. She just thought it would be good for me. I was kind of overwhelmed—wow! 'Cause as I say, I hardly knew her then, you know.

But I got out of my tennis clothes—I was sweating and I was going to take a shower, and it was summertime. And I just threw my tennis stuff on the floor, and she had made the steak juice. [*He laughs.*] I came out; she was washing my clothes. So, here there was this side of Marlene that was kind of incredible.

I always found it very interesting, the love and the kindness that Marlene would show to veterans, the guys who fought in the war, who were in the audience—particularly in Vegas. A lot of them would make that trip and come there to see her, to see the show.

And Marlene would have them backstage. Some of them were in wheelchairs; some were amputees; some just fought in the war and remembered her. She'd hang out with them all night. You know, this was one real side of Marlene. Maybe in another life she was a nurse, a doctor—big caregiver.

I always remember how she'd come back to L.A. and immediately go out to Rudy's house, her husband, and though they hadn't lived together for years and years, she would still clean the house—she just did. She was a maid, in a way. It's hard to explain, you know? And if you *don't* know Marlene initially, it's pretty strange.

It was a very exciting time, the prospect of going on tour. I had been stationed in Germany after the war, you know, in the '50s. So, for me, going back

Rioting crowd in front of Titania Palast, Berlin, 1960.

to Germany didn't matter. But for Marlene going back to Germany, to do a tour, was a very challenging, very exciting prospect. And it was quite something to see because it was full of unexpected stuff.

Berlin was okay. Berlin was good. I mean . . . there were a lot of people who were supportive of Marlene in Berlin, opposed to what happened when we got to the other areas. In Munich, too, there were a lot of people who were very supportive of her.

But there were other areas that were [*exhales audibly*]—it was almost like a silent boycott.

Norman Grands was the promoter, and he thought that there was, in a way, almost like a silent boycott because she fought . . . performed, entertained the American troops, so, therefore, she was the enemy in the last war.

Oh, give me a break. What is this, sixteen years after the war? To see a girl bust through a police cordon, coming out of the hotel—and I was right there with Marlene—and *spit* in Marlene's face and say in German, "Traitor."

And it wasn't just spit—it was something else, it was like a very foul substance. I thought it was acid, maybe. It felt like it was something to be concerned about on Marlene's face.

But it didn't turn out to be a real damaging thing or she couldn't have had it in her mouth. But this girl wasn't even born at the end of the war, and so she got this just handed down by what she heard in her house, what she was taught by her parents—that Marlene was a traitor. Marlene had fought with the enemy. There was a bomb scare in Düsseldorf, and who knows what else.

So, you know, there were times!

It was just the whole German trip, [*he laughs*] traveling with a French orchestra, with German strings that I was conducting, and then Marlene broke her shoulder somewhere on the Rhine. I mean she fell off the stage, and in the middle of a song! [*He laughs.*] "I got one for my baby / One more for—" then fell right off and landed right at von Sternberg's feet!

I mean, here's the man who . . . found her, who directed her, and came to see her perform, and she falls off the stage. And, like the brave, brave, brave person that Marlene was, she just kind of put her shoulder together, got up and made a makeshift sling, went up on stage, and finished the song! Hah!

So, we got out of there, and I tell you, the overall effect was less than comfortable, except in Munich, where they wouldn't let her off the stage, and that's the famous forty-three curtain calls and forty-three bows—that was great.

But I'd say overall, Norman Grands lost a ton of money. The tour was far from a success. Then we kind of regrouped and went from there to Israel, where there was a totally different picture of Marlene.

Marlene came into Israel within a week or a week and a half after what had happened in Germany. It was very strange what was happening in Israel then.

They were driving Volkswagens. They were making machine guns, I think, for the German armed forces, but yet *no* German was allowed—it could not be spoken on stage, and films in German were never shown.

They had cancelled a German performance of the Mahler Eighth or Ninth Symphony, where the chorus was going to sing in German. A public outcry before, the week before, was that, "Hey, you know, we're not going to permit this." And this is with Mahler, a Jew who lived before the Nazis!

Marlene was very outspoken. She hated the Nazis. And she worked her butt off with the USO shows and all.

So they welcomed her really big time in Israel.

But [*he laughs*] when the promoter met Marlene at the airport, he said, "You know, Marlene, you know, you can't sing in German here. No German is spoken on stage, in no films. We just had to cancel the Mahler Symphony. They're going to sing it in English. No German song can be sung here."

So, Marlene said, "No, I wouldn't sing one song in German. I will sing nine." [*He laughs.*] Nine songs. I thought the man was going to have a heart attack at the airport in Tel Aviv.

And she was . . . so brilliant, Marlene. She was so clever about, how she did it, because on that first night in Tel Aviv, she let the first two songs go by, in English—"My Blue Heaven," and "Cream in My Coffee."

And then she got to the third song, and she'd chosen a lullaby. And she said, "So, I'd like to do a song for you now. It's called, 'My Blondest Baby.'"

I mean, how brilliant she was, to take a mother's lullaby to her child instead of a heavy Richard Talbert song and make *that* the initial German song.

You could hear the ripple through the audience. I mean, the gasps: She was going to sing it in German. And as she sang, it was one of the most emotional things that I've ever seen, in this little concert hall in Tel Aviv, because it was sort of like the dam had broken, and people were crying. Nobody was upset . . . in a negative way. It was like a catharsis that freed them.

Then she got to the heavier Richard Talbert stuff last, and we were only going to sing the nine songs in all. But I remember that at the end of the show we sang all nine songs again. You know, it happened a long time ago, so is it totally accurate the way I remember, or has it become a little enlarged and bigger emotionally in my mind? Not much. It's pretty real. We did all nine songs again. Whew! It was a big moment.

She had a very strong passion especially about doing "Where Have All the Flowers Gone?" And I liked the song, and I could see the way she was approaching it, and what she wanted to convey.

You know, that song, it can be sung very understated all the way through. One verse follows another—Peter, Paul, and Mary or [Pete] Seeger, they never got too carried away much, you know. It stayed kind of one dimensional, and just with a guitar. It didn't get stronger orchestrally, or the drums start to play louder with other people's versions.

There's somewhere Marlene was going with it dramatically—the anger and the frustration by the third or fourth verse. And, you know, I sat down and wrote this orchestration, and I remember that she always referred to the pizzicato that I wrote for the violins as gunshots—"Yes, make them more like gunshots"—because it was so antiwar. And it was so powerful onstage. Every time we did it, every time Marlene did it, there was more comfortability with it, and it became a real signature moment in her concerts.

It was a very interesting time for me musically because working with Marlene—it's a very different kind of music than what was happening to me, and for me in the States.

I started to have all these R&B hits. Dionne [Warwick] had been discovered. I had been making a lot of urban, black records. And then, somehow winding up conducting "Go See What the Boys in the Backroom Will Have. . . ." [*He laughs.*] It was just another world—opposites, musically.

But I wouldn't have changed any of that for the world. I mean, I'd come back and then be working on my records and my songs, and go back and play this other kind of music with Marlene.

And, you know, I remember Quincy Jones coming backstage at the Olympia Theater and saying, after he saw me conducting for Marlene, "What are you doing, man? You should be back making records—what are you doing here?!"

And I said, "You know, I'm seeing the world, Quincy. Music is music. And, you know, I was classically trained, but I can do this, and I can also write for the urban market."

But I gotta say this about Marlene: the more successful that I became with the songwriting and record producing, the more of a champion she was. And . . . [*stumbles over words*] I'll never . . . never forget that.

The more successful I would become, you know that part of her would have to be saying, "I'm going to lose him because he's going to become impossible for me to count on to go to Warsaw, to go to Russia, or wherever; I'm going to have to get another conductor some of the time."

Dietrich and Bacharach on stage together in front of a sellout crowd, New York City. "There's only one Bacharach," she would say.

But she was a champion. I remember coming out a stage door in Edinburgh, and there were fifty, sixty fans. And they would shout, "Marlene! Marlene! May I have your autograph?" And she said, "You want his?" [*He laughs.*] They go, "Who is he?!" you know. And she said, "Oh, you don't know now, but you will." It was kind of great.

And when *Promises, Promises* opened, she clipped out fifty copies of the Clive Barnes review from the *New York Times,* sent them to all her friends in Europe and all over the world, and said, "See, I told you," "See, I told you." [*He laughs.*] It's really kind of . . . very sweet and very, very . . . endearing, you know? In some way, you could have had a person who would be rooting against you—"Oh, don't let him have a hit. Then I'll lose him," you know? "Then he won't be able to conduct for me." But not Marlene. Interesting.

There are some great things I learned from Marlene; I mean, about the drive to perfection, the drive to do it right.

I learned that if you want to get things done, you do it yourself. I mean, I could see that with Marlene. If she wanted something done, she would never delegate it to somebody else. Whatever it was, it got done more efficiently if she did it herself.

Another thing I learned from her was to go for a hundred percent on that stage, something she always did. I mean, did we over-rehearse? Absolutely. We had eight days of rehearsal with an orchestra.

When I look at it now, I mean, my God . . . to keep that band interested by the fifth day, whether we were in Madrid or wherever . . . and keep rehearsing the same material because they'd already peaked, [*he laughs*] you know?

No one's used to going in with a symphony orchestra on the day of performance and conducting the whole rehearsal for two and a half hours, and then do the concert that night!

But I understood her thing, that "go for the gold" attitude. Whether she stood there and isolated and adjusted one light on her, even if it meant standing there for an hour, two hours—not a stand-in, Marlene right there. But afterward that pin light was right on her, the way it had to be onstage.

She busted everybody's chops in a tough way. She expected the same from them. She's hard for people to work under, whether they were promoters, producers, or anyone—she was tough on them. I almost escaped. [*He laughs.*] I used to think it was because she needed me, so she didn't want to alienate me, antagonize me.

One year that I was up for another Oscar—I think it was for "The Look of Love"—they asked Marlene to present and give out the Best Song award. And [*he laughs*] she said, "I can do that, and I'll tell you why; if I open up the envelope and it's not Burt's song, I'm going to say it's Burt's song." [*He laughs.*] End of story. End of that presenter. No, they definitely got another presenter. [*He laughs.*]

I wish we could have made that one last record, like she wanted. In the last couple of years, when she would talk to me on the phone, and I understood her, you know, there were times that she wanted to be the maid and she didn't want to talk to anybody on the telephone, including me. And I'd say, "Marlene, it's me. It's Burt," when she was holed up in Paris and wasn't going anywhere, wasn't going out. But when I'd get her in the right frame of mind where she would say, "Ah, Burt," and she'd talk about the times, well, maybe I could have figured out how to make that record.

I'd say, "I'd like to do that, Marlene. How could we do that?" And she'd say, "I want to do 'Any Day Now,' that song of yours," a song I'd written.

And then she'd say, "I hear that timpani go, Ta ta ta ta ta," and I'd say, "That's good. I could make a track, Marlene. I could make a track . . . and we could somehow . . . get a situation where nobody had to come in and mike you or anything, slip the mike underneath [*he laughs*] the door, or something, and you could put your vocal on."

I'm sorry I didn't—we didn't get to . . . at least try it, you know?

ROSEMARY CLOONEY

ROSEMARY CLOONEY was a performer's performer. Sinatra and Dietrich both thought of her as the best friend a song could have, and the world certainly agreed. Born in Kentucky, she shared, in a strange way, the down-home attitude of Marlene, and together they made quite a team. Marlene and Rosy were friends from the very first time they met, although they weren't close until Marlene saw her talent, something peculiar to Marlene's selection process. Marlene could never befriend anyone—let alone talk to them—without respecting them first. They did radio together and over the years they stayed in touch and remained close. Rosemary was especially dedicated to Marlene when Rudy Sieber passed away. Even though she was on tour with Bing Crosby, Rosemary took the time to comfort Marlene via phone at all hours of the day and night. A large part of their friendship was also their shared history of war. Toward the end of her life, Rosy recorded a wonderful album of World War II songs called *For the Duration,* partly for which she drew inspiration from Marlene. Although much younger than my grandmother, Rosy became more like a doting aunt to us over the years, and she is sorely missed.

My first introduction, professionally, to Marlene was, naturally, her pictures. But I came from a very small town in Kentucky, so there weren't very many theaters—actually there were only two theaters—so, mostly, we listened to the radio.

And Marlene did very, very many radio shows as a guest, and she talked about the war. And she talked about her USO work, and how important it was to her. And so, these were my real beginnings with Marlene.

Radio was our window to the world, especially in a small town in Kentucky, on the Ohio River. My uncles went off to fight in the Pacific Theater and in Europe. But war for us was on the radio. And Marlene was a very big part of that.

We would sit around listening to the latest news. My grandfather was a great fan of any kind of news show, so I sort of got that from him. And I heard a lot about Marlene from my grandfather. Naturally, my grandfather also thought that she was the most beautiful thing that ever lived. He would kind of let me know that whether he was conscious of it or not.

I learned about the war. I learned about the outside world—everything came from the radio. It was very important, and she was very important—a very important part of it. And she sang a lot, too. And music at the time was so important to me because it was the time of the big band—the big bands, I should say: Tommy Dorsey, Jimmy Dorsey, Glenn Miller. And a guy by the name of Tony Pastor who I went on the road with, with my sister, Betty.

And it was a time when we were pretty young. My sister was thirteen, and so she had to have a legal guardian, and my Uncle George went on the road with us. Well, he was worse than having, you know, six duennas. He wouldn't let us go anywhere. We found ways, but it sure was difficult.

But the music was so wonderful, and every night we would be playing in a different little town. Everybody had a good time, and it was lovely. The music was wonderful, and you can hear that music today and still feel very, very good.

During the war, I know how important it was to the guys who were away, and Marlene loved it. She loved the music. Later, when I would record, I would let her hear the takes first.

Now, I saw Marlene for the first time at the Café

de Paris in London. I was married to José Ferrer, who loved Marlene—most of the time. [*She laughs.*] I say "most of the time" because when she came into our house, she would take over.

I mean, she was the one who fired the cook and—honestly—so José got a little upset about stuff like that. *But* he took me to the Café de Paris, and Noël Coward introduced her with this wonderful poem.

And then she came down a flight of stairs, with a Jean-Louis dress on. And at the very end of the show, she went back upstairs and made the quickest change that I've ever seen in my life, to be in white tie and tails. And a top hat to finish the show. And the way that she did it was a zipper all the way down the back. She stepped into it. And she was down in a moment. It was the most exciting show I'd ever seen in my life.

Yes, it still is the most important show that I ever saw in my life, and the most exciting. She was a killer.

I finally met Marlene around 1950. There was a show called "The Big Show," and it was the last gasp of big radio on NBC. Manny Sachs had come from Columbia Records and he was nice enough to give me a crack at it, even though I didn't have the credentials to do that kind of show. Tallulah Bankhead was the mistress of ceremonies, with Meredith Willson's orchestra, so it was a very, very big deal for me to be able to be on it.

Marlene Dietrich was also scheduled to be on it, and as I finished rehearsal and came down the steps, I saw this strange-looking person coming in the stage door.

It was raining outside, and this woman kind of backed in to the stage door. She had a very big raincoat, a babushka, and she was trying to put down the umbrella, and carry two bags.

And I said, "Can I help you?" And she said, "Ummmm [*negative*] . . ." And she put down the bags as she came in and kind of shook off the water.

And . . . then she started kind of unpeeling these clothes that she had on. She had on the babushka, as I said—that came off. And suddenly there was this kind of beige hair. And slowly . . . this blonde beauty came out of the huge raincoat, and suddenly the shoes matched, the stockings matched, the dress matched the hair—and there was Marlene Dietrich.

It was quite an introduction. And I said, "My name is Rosemary Clooney." And she said, "I know. Yeah. You're a good singer." I said, "Thank you—very much. I like the way you act." [*She laughs.*]

So that was the beginning of our friendship. Now, I don't think Tallulah was too thrilled that we became friends right away because we were gossiping from the moment we met until the last time I spoke to her, about everybody, everything. I bared my soul.

Mitch Miller, who was the head of Columbia Records then, decided it would be a good idea if Marlene and I recorded together, and found some songs that were based on kind of naughty stories because one of the titles was, "That's Nice, Don't-A Fight"—I can't tell you that story. And the other one was called, "Too Old to Cut the Mustard."

Marlene was *wonderful* because she's a wonderful actress. And she sang in tune, and her timing was right. And that's all that's necessary. And we had the best time in the world. I loved recording with her.

I was going to play the Palladium for the first time, and it was in 1955 because it was when my first son was born. And I was very excited about both.

I had sold an awful lot of records in England, and I had quite a few friends. But more than anything else, I knew that Marlene was coming to see me.

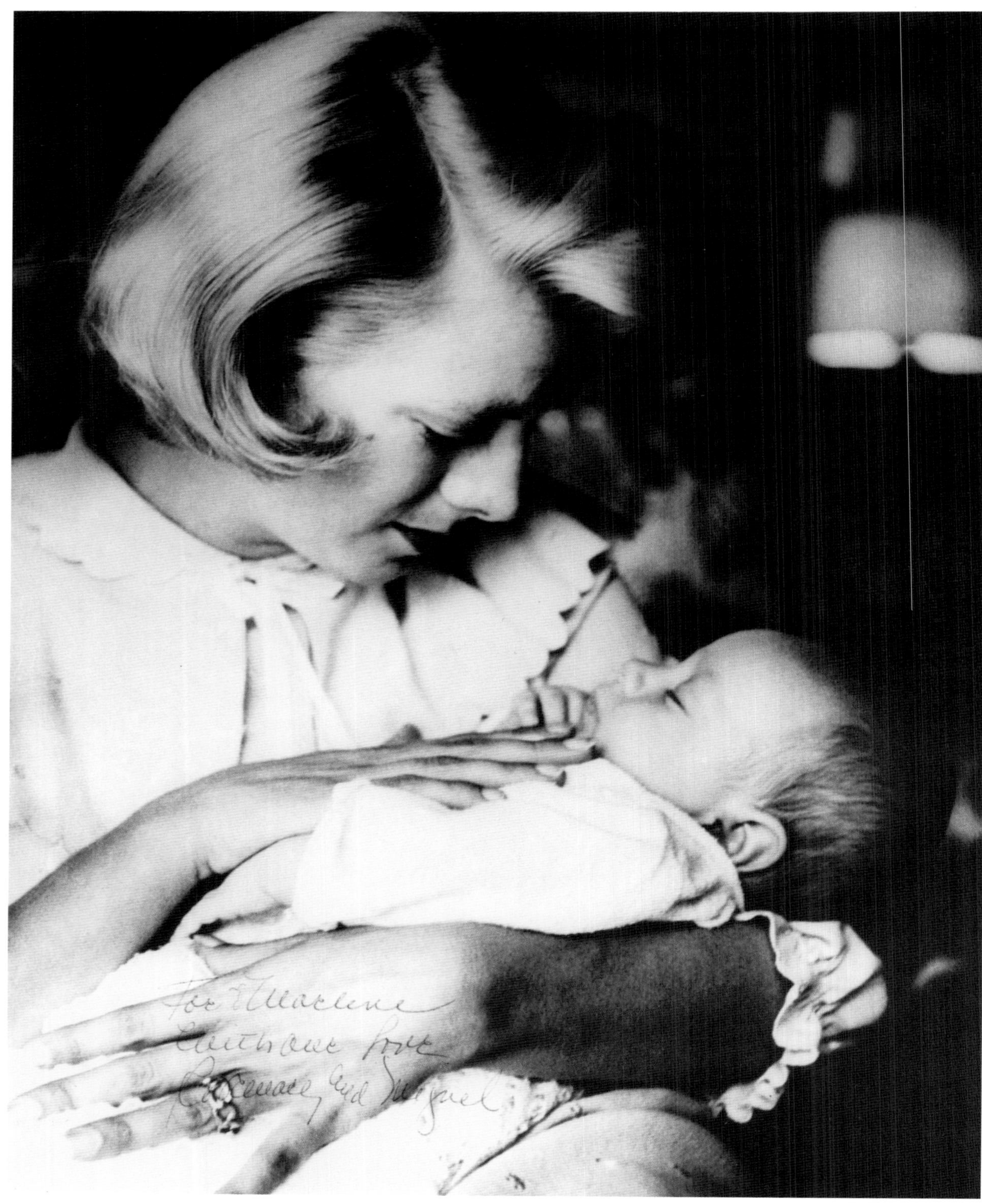

Rosemary Clooney cradles her son, Miguel Ferrer, in a photo carrying a dedication, "For Marlene with our love, Rosemary and Miguel."

And at that time they had a first house, and a second house. And the first house was at 6:00 in the evening, and then the second house was at 8:30. And so they were very close together.

The first house was mostly younger people, or people who were coming home from work, so it was a kind of a rowdy group. And so, I walked out on the stage, and there was a big, "Hurrah, hurrah, hurrah, hurrah."

The thing about the Palladium is that you can see the audience very well—it's a wonderful theater, a beautiful theater, a perfect theater. Except that I did not want to see Marlene Dietrich and Noël Coward in the third row, watching every move that I made. I did not want to see that. And there they were.

And suddenly, I forgot the words to "Come On-A My House," which aren't that difficult, you know. Every song that I ever knew went out of my head. Everything that I was about to say went. I think I got back into it, so it was okay. The audience liked it all right, I think. No, I know. I did okay.

But not really okay for my two friends, because they met me backstage *in between* shows. Now, they took turns telling me what I should do. Marlene, first of all, was telling me that I should not wear that particular dress that Edith Head had made for me. She said, "It doesn't move well when you walk from the piano."

I said, "Well . . . you know, how long does it take me to walk from the piano to the end of the stage—it's not that long, Marlene. I'm going into another song." "Well, it does—please, just listen to me."

And then Noël Coward said, "Why do you pay so much attention to your pianist?" I said, "I like him. I . . ." "No, no, no, no. You can't have anyone more important on the stage than you are. You just can't have your friends everywhere—this is not—this is not, uh, uh, Buddy Cole's show. This is your show."

And, honestly, it went on like that, until the 8:30 curtain, and then they left. And I was a shambles. I finally put it together and realized: they're not doing my show. I'm doing my show. And so, shut up, both of you! I didn't say that in front of them, or to them at all. I finally just did what I wanted to do.

Seeing Marlene and hearing Marlene in Las Vegas was always a thrill for me. One of the times was when she was seeing—or at least her boyfriend of the moment was—Frank Sinatra, and it was at a time when they were both working there.

It was quite an interesting time because it was fun to be around the two of them in between shows. I did recognize a cigarette case that she had given him [*she laughs*] because she had given it to another man, too. [*She laughs.*] I'm sorry, but that's the truth.

Anyway, I saw Marlene on the stage, and she just—she was a vision. She did dress fittings for hours. She walked with the dress on, she'd sit with the dress on, all so that she knew the way that it would look under any conditions—under all conditions.

She was the most, perfect—at least that's what she strived for. She really wanted to be perfect in any way that she could—every way that she could.

The song that she chose, "See What the Boys in the Back Room Will Have," was such an acting job for her, and it was so simple it was almost thrown away.

And I loved it because it reminded me of George Marshall who did *Destry Rides Again.* George Marshall directed me in a picture and Marlene came to see me. And she said, "You're doing me," because it was a picture called *Red Garters.* [*She laughs.*] And I said, "Well, I have the same director and he's telling me to do what you did."

She taught me the trick of how to roll a cigarette with one hand by putting a real cigarette inside, and you can do it with one hand. To listen to her sing, though, uh, always made me a little sad because there was a wistfulness about "Lili Marlene." And then there was "Where Have All the Flowers Gone"—not wistfulness there, but anger. There was an anger because of the words and the way that she interpreted it. It was—it was quite special.

I think that's where that camaraderie that she had at that point came from: Get the show on, get the dress on—is the dress on okay? Does that need sewing? Let's get it fixed—because the whole focus of her day and her time was the show. And I think that reminded her of the war, the happiest—seems strange to say "happiest," but "most fulfilling," perhaps, is a better term—time of her life. I guess I loved seeing her in Las Vegas because *she* loved to do it. She loved to work in front of people and do the two shows a night. She never complained. And I think that it brought back the days that she was

Sheet music for "Land, Sea and Air," which Clooney and Dietrich sang as a duet on the radio in 1952.

on the road for the servicemen that she sang for through the years.

There are some songs that instantly bring you to a place in your personal history, or everyone's history. And I made an album called *For the Duration.* The title came from my brother, who is a great buff of World War II, and he thought that that would be a good title for it. And he was absolutely right.

We had three uncles and one aunt in the war, three in the European Theater, and one in the Pacific. And, it was a time when we lived in this small town, and the word that we got back was very important, but all the songs were—you know, "I'll Be Home for Christmas"—all of them were tinged with the fact that we were separated from people that we loved.

The album, *For the Duration,* was important to me. It was sad for me. It brought back some memories that had been untouched by my own mentality. I just well, I didn't really want to think that deeply about it.

But it moved me, and it was important for me to do it. I loved the songs we did, but then I couldn't figure out what to put on the cover of the album.

And I had found this wonderful picture of my Uncle George, who was a bomber pilot. And he looked so young. And he was young. When he came back from the war, he was only twenty-five. So now there he is on the front of my album. I'm proud of it. I'm very proud of it. I thought Marlene would be, too. She would like it.

I remember I was working with Bing Crosby at the Palladium. It was the last year of his life, actually, 1977. And I was waiting in the wings to go on, and this man approached me. I always assumed that it was somebody who worked at the Palladium, but not backstage. It might not have been; it might have been somebody who just came in, you know, from some other place in the theater.

In any event, he came up to me and he said, "May I speak to you for a moment?" And I said, "Of course." And he said, "I have a coin that I'd like to give to you, to return to Marlene Dietrich. She gave me this coin at the beginning of the war. I was very young and very afraid. And she put this in my hand and said, 'As long as you have this, you'll be fine.' And she closed my hand around it, and I made it home. And this is the coin. Could you give this back to Ms. Dietrich? Please close her hand around it, and tell her as long as she has that, she'll be fine."

But there did come a time when Marlene had some difficulties. She was hurt. She was injured in a theater and broke her leg. And that was a difficult time for her.

And it was also a time when I was going through a divorce, and it seemed that so many . . . difficult things were keeping us apart from each other, even by phone. She moved to Paris, I had the children, I had to work, and I was not feeling in control very much myself. So, it was a difficult time. And we didn't see each other.

While I was at the Palladium, again with Bing, the phone rang in his dressing room. And he handed it to me. He said, "It's Dietrich, from Paris." And I took it and I said, "How are you?"

And the voice was there, and she said, "I hear you're singing wonderfully well." She said, "I've had some bad news," she said. "Rudy's gone."

Now, I knew what that meant because the first thing that she did when she came to California was go and cook for Rudy. That was what she did every single time that she came, no matter what she was doing later, that's what she did the first night. I know that. And I know what it meant for her when she lost him because somehow, somewhere, he was her rock. He was the one who made it possible. And there it was. And there it was. He was gone.

And she told me, and I could feel the loss. And I felt sad that I couldn't be with her and put my arms around her as many times as she had with me and helped me.

I had wonderful experiences with Marlene, and the best were when she would allow me to help her cook—usually it was chopping things, which she didn't want to do anyway. But at one point she turned to me and said, "You know, you're not a bad cook. And I know that because your Grandmother Cressence was German."

HILDEGARD KNEF

HILDEGARD KNEF was one of Marlene's closest friends. They shared a unique German heritage and with it a similar zest for life and the risqué. Twenty years her junior, Hildegard was Marlene's protégé, and Marlene did everything possible to guide her through the shark-infested waters of Hollywood and, later, Europe. Hildegard was perhaps Germany's most significant postwar actress, appearing in several controversial and wildly popular films including *The Murderers Are among Us,* the first film released in Germany after the war, and *The Sinner,* which included Germany's first nude scene. There was much in Hildegard that was reminiscent of Marlene. Both were liberated, self-confident women, and their friendship lasted for fifty years. Regrettably, Hildegard passed away a few months after our interview, but she will always remain unforgettable.

So, how it began—it will take some time to explain it. Marlene was probably, and is, and will remain until the end of my life my best and most wonderfully maternal friend that any person could want. She was, which sounds silly now that I'm old myself, from a generation *ahead* of me, and I have only now understood what it means to lose one's friends. I mean, because of age. You lose them; one dies just because she was ten years older, *he* dies because he is twenty years older, and suddenly one is on a plateau where one is left speechless. And I was twenty-one years younger, I think, than Marlene. She spoiled me, taught me so, so very much. She didn't manage to teach me cooking—I still can't boil an egg. But she brought me closer to what was the American culture back then, without me getting too lost in it. When it came to it, Marlene and I were not similar, not at all, *absolutely* in no way. I was never the beauty that Marlene was. I had in my youth a certain attraction, to some people I was even pretty, but the indescribable, unreproduceable beauty that Marlene had was unique. Nobody even got close, and no one should try. You can see it in all the films that are made about Marlene. And I don't know what all these new talents think they are doing in order to come close, closer to her. It's rubbish! You can't do it. She was one of a kind.

Marlene was an unparalleled woman with unparalleled talent, who also got unparalleled help back then, when she was young and came to America, after *The Blue Angel,* a protégé of Joseph von Sternberg. And she was indeed promoted by him and shaped by him. But he was not so successful at shaping her, or even at all, unless she decided it was to be. She was very much her own person.

How I met her is a whole different story. She had a friend whom I met with Marlene that first time. His name was Max Colpet. He wrote some of her songs, the lyrics at least. Max was living as an eternal immigrant with his friend Billy Wilder, a man I don't like to mention because I don't like him and we never agreed on anything. But Marlene got along with him, but that belongs to a friendship, too, that one person respects the other's likes and dislikes. And she did that with me. And I was always amazed at that, because in Germany everything was different, if someone was older, well then, one had to respect that one's point of view, damn it all. [*Laughs.*] Marlene didn't find that so necessary.

So Max called up one day. I had been in America maybe three months, scarcely understood English and was quite fearful. I had gotten myself into a contract with [David O.] Selznick, after I had made three wonderful films in Germany, and thought,

Hildegard meets her mentor Marlene on the tarmac at Tempelhof Airport, May 1960. This was Marlene's first visit since the war ended.

"My God, this is no piece of cake!" Absolutely nothing was opening up for me in America. And it was about at that peak of panic when Marlene had Max call, to say *she* would like to see me "this evening at the Beachcomber." Now the Beachcomber was an amazing restaurant, completely dark—you really needed a seeing-eye dog for that place. But she had ordered me to the Beachcomber, this place that was so incredibly chic, expensive, and out of my league. And so I *had* to go. And then I saw her—I described it in my book *Der geschenkte Gaul* [The Gift Horse], but of course not everyone has read my book. I saw this indescribably beautiful triangle, this face, this triangle that had such an unbelievably beautiful form that one couldn't pass it by; it took one's breath away. So now I am stumbling slowly into the vicinity of the chair, and she looks at me and says, "Come on, sit down." So I sat down across from her with wobbly knees, and she ordered for me. She noticed how nervous I was and that I even had no idea how I should behave. And then she said to Max Colpet, "Now I want to show you something. When were you born, Hilde?" I said, "The twenty-eighth of December." And she said, "So, there! You see? I'm on the twenty-seventh." We were both Capricorns. Since she very much believed in astrology, that is, in the astrologer Carol Righter, being a Capricorn like her was akin to winning a prize. And I found myself feeling better already, a little more at ease, and happier. But then, of course, she ordered one of those cursed meals that you have to eat with chopsticks, and I sat in front of those chopsticks and finally said out loud, "Well, if I have to eat with those, then I'll really starve to death." I fell right back into my Berlin accent. And she laughed so much that strands of her hair fell into the sauce. And in that moment all the spells were broken, almost everything that . . . well, my fascination of course wasn't gone, but the spell, this tension-filled terrible spell that *crippled* me, was broken. And from this second on she accompanied me through life. She looked after me like a mother, in fact like my mother [*laughs*] never did, I have to say—nothing against my mother, but she was never as maternal as Marlene. Marlene paid attention to what I ate, with whom I went out, whom I should fear, so unbelievable. Yes, that's it really. A lifelong friendship lasting until her death—which nevertheless did exclude me from her seclusion in Paris.

During those years she did telephone me all the time and I her. And she received a prize, which I accepted for her here in Berlin, but the hotel boy had to leave it in front of her door in Paris, and then I suppose she brought it in when no one was there. I told her once, "Hey, I am right across the street from your apartment in the Athene," or—well I don't know now what the hotel's name was, but it doesn't matter—I said, "I am *right* across the street from your apartment." And she said, "I see you," and she waved with the closed curtain. And I said, "Why don't you let me in? Our friendship is not based on appearances. It's clear that you haven't gotten any younger, but neither have I." And she said, "I don't want that." I said, "Okay, I will never ask again." And I never did. [*Takes deep breath.*]

COCO SCHUMANN

Jazz guitarist **COCO SCHUMANN** was born into a mixed Christian/Jewish family in Berlin as Heinz Jacob Schumann. Even as a child he became a devotee of swing music, which was outlawed by the Nazi regime. As a "half-Jew," he survived the concentration camps, including Theresienstadt (Terezien), where he became a member of the legendary "Ghetto Swingers." Also sent to the extermination camps of Auschwitz and Birkenau during the war years, he played music for the SS officers in order to survive. In 1945 he was deported to Kaufering, a subsidiary camp of Dachau. It was in this suburb of Munich where he was finally liberated by the advancing American army. After returning to Berlin, he performed once more as a jazz musician in numerous bars. In 1946 and 1947 he and Marlene appeared together in various USO shows for the American soldiers staged at the Titania Palast in Berlin. In the years that followed the war, Coco embarked on a successful career as an internationally known jazz guitarist. At the time I interviewed him, Coco was still making occasional appearances in Berlin.

Music had always been important to me, and like Marlene Dietrich, all of Germany's artists were very influenced by the '20s Berlin scene. Being a little too young, I can only say something about the end of the '30s personally, but as a child I perceived some of that atmosphere. Berlin was "roaring," as they say in America, a roaring town. And like today, it was very Americanized back then. People danced the Charleston. They liked jazz music. There were famous bands, like the Weintraub Syncopators. As well as I can remember, this time was hopping. Marlene Dietrich was a product of this time, like many world-renowned artists. They later went to America if they had the money—Bert Brecht, Kurt Weill, and Wachsmann, he made a lot of film scores. All of them were Berliners from that era, the famous ones. They settled into America right away, and became famous there, too. If Hitler hadn't come to power, I don't know if Hollywood would be what it is today, because it took in all these Europeans, or all these Berliners who were not allowed to work here. They probably exerted a lot of influence in America. Marlene was a child of her time, too. As I said, Berlin was back then already very Americanized, as it is again today—only there wasn't a McDonald's back then. [*Laughs.*]

Berlin was previously a "bubbling" city. There were very famous cabaret stars here and musicians. Often as a child I went with my parents to variety shows. There was all manner of activity there, and I knew all the names of the cabaret performers. Most of them were Jews; for example, Willy Rosen and many others. I met some of them again in the Theresienstadt concentration camp. I only knew their names, Kurt Gerron for example, and I met up with him later in Theresienstadt.

And then in 1933 there was the power takeover by Adolf Hitler. The Jews were prohibited from leaving, and a portion of them tried to emigrate. There were lots and lots of American films here. But the Germans here—not the Nazis, not all Germans who were Nazis—they were pretty Americanized as far as entertainment goes. Like it is today. Hitler wanted to stamp that out, but he never entirely succeeded. For example, the war broke out when I was fifteen. But I had already started to play music, and I sat at the Delphi Tanzpalast in Berlin outside on the wall and listened to the fantastic jazz bands. During the Olympics you were allowed to—since there were so many foreigners here, they wanted to show the world how enlightened they were. So I sat on the wall outside the Delphi and was fascinated by the big bands and all the music. Then there was always an underground here. We played forbidden music, for example in the Groschenkeller in the Kantstrasse. We tried to get around it. There was a Reichsmusik-Kammer, an Office for Music. As a musician you had to get permission from the Reich's Office for Music. We didn't have any. And in the Groschenkeller there was a student at the top of the stairs and a student at the bottom. When they came from the Office for Music, we could recognize them. They all had these slouch hats and leather coats. They must have had them issued. And if one of these types showed up, the guy at the top whistled down to that one, and he whistled over to the stage. If we happened to be playing Cab Calloway and scat, or Fats Waller or the like, then the entire band would switch over immediately to some "corny" German music, as they say in America. And then the whole crowd sang along and they came in and heard us sing "Rosamunde" or some kind of polka. They were satisfied and left again, and we laughed ourselves sick about it. Then we went right back to playing jazz.

Marlene had a natural distaste for National Socialism and Hitler. I value her for that as do all decent Germans—that she left this Germany where the Nazis were in power and where they had expelled her Jewish colleagues or had forbidden them

Marlene performing with a jazz band.

to work. She had a natural distaste for this regime, and all the decent Germans could understand that. But the Germans who were *not* the decent ones held it against her. Even today—I never believed when I came out of the camp in '45 that it would come again.

I, of course, had to stay in Germany, because my parents did not have enough money to emigrate. But I admired every person who could leave and did leave, especially Germans who didn't *have* to but who did not agree with this regime, with Hitler and his cohorts. I really admired them and as a result I admired Marlene more than before—I was her fan even as a child. But I admired her even more that she left and didn't play along with things here.

My father was a so-called Aryan. I had two lives here so to speak. My mother was a Jewess and my father an Aryan. I observed all the Christian holidays, but also the Jewish ones. There was no difference for me—that's why I was such a fat child [*laughs*]. Because I always ate so much on the holidays. [*Laughs.*] So in this regard, I was a sort of hybrid. Both of the families got along well together. I had counted on the fact that my father was an Aryan, but it didn't help at all. So then I played anyway, although it was forbidden. I had to wear the yellow star with "Jew" on it, and I always had it in my pocket. One day someone must have turned me in, because I was ordered to the Criminal Police—not the Gestapo—first to the Criminal Police at Alexander Square [Alexanderplatz]. And they accused me of playing music against the law and also "racial disgrace." It was a "racial disgrace" for Jews to be with Aryan girls, and I committed a lot of "racial disgrace" back then [*laughs*]. And they accused me of that, when I was up there. I wouldn't have gone if I had known that if you were up there once, they didn't let you go home again. So I was turned over to the Gestapo and came into the transport to the Greater Hamburg Street [Grosse Hamburger Strasse]. I was supposed to go directly to Auschwitz. I was already lined up to go, and my father went to Obersturmführer Tuberke and said, "Obersturmführer, my son and I are Germans. I was a fellow soldier. And I have always tried to raise him German." He was able to convince this ice-cold Tuberke and said, "At least send him to Theresienstadt." My grandparents were already there. Nobody knew exactly what was going on in the concentration camps, but rumors had gone around that Theresienstadt was not an extermination camp. And it wasn't. And he said, "Obersturmführer, at least send him to Theresienstadt." Then he was able to soften him up, this ice-cold Tuberke. I was already standing in the line for Auschwitz. And he said, "Schumann, step out. You're going to Theresienstadt." And that saved me.

Theresienstadt was a concentration camp for display. They had created a "pretend" world in there. If a commission came from Sweden, from Switzerland, or from the Red Cross, and they did come, then the concentration camp Theresienstadt was shown to them. But that was all castles in the air, and so it was not a genuine concentration camp. We had music there and cabaret in order to mislead the people. I played percussion in a big band called the Ghetto Kennel. Later Martin Rohmann came. He was a famous pianist. He played in Holland with Grunem and Horten, for example. He also did film music. He knew Kurt Gerold, who came from Westerburg to Theresienstadt and had to make a film there. It wasn't the correct title of this film, but the Jews who had to go along with everything had a cynical name for this film. They called it "The Führer Gives the Jews a City." Kurt Gerold was a very well-known director in Germany, and he also appeared with Marlene Dietrich in *The Blue An-*

gel. Nowadays there's a film called *Carousel,* and it contains a scene from *The Blue Angel* with Marlene Dietrich and Kurt Gerold in it.

Right after the war the Americans came in as occupying forces. Thank God I lived here with the Americans. They brought the American way of life here with them right away. I really liked it. And then a very famous violinist, Helmut Zacharias, came, and I played during the war with him. And he came to me and asked whether I wanted to play again with him. Of course I said yes. He was quite well known. He also played in the Armed Forces Radio, I think with Lala Andersen in "Lili Marlene." He was a famous violinist in the classics, but he fell into jazz like the rest of us. Then he got an engagement in an American club here in Tempelhof, and I know it was a cigarette gig. German money wasn't worth anything, and I remember as our pay, each of us got a carton of Lucky Strikes. That was a fortune to us. And then we started to play in the clubs. The Americans, they checked on us German players. They knew that I was in the concentration camps, in Auschwitz, probably; we never talked about it, but they were always especially nice to me.

So now, shortly after the war, when the Americans came here and began to set up some entertainment, I played in a lot of American clubs, NCO clubs, and at generals' parties, and the like. There were a lot of Germans who played. There were lots of clubs here, and they needed music. There were a good number of big bands and many American clubs. I don't know exactly how it happened; it is too long ago. But I know I was hired for the Titania Palast. Then in 1947, I think, Marlene Die-

Marlene enjoys her moment at the UNICEF gala performance "Musik der Welt" at the Kongresshalle in Düsseldorf, Germany, October 1962.

trich came to Berlin to do a show for the American troops in the Titania Palast. And she needed a band to accompany her, and I was hired as a guitarist to accompany her. It was one of the big bands, I think. I can't really remember who the other musicians were; it's too long ago. But Marlene appeared as an entertainer for the troops. And I was in the band. I accompanied her. We were to accompany Marlene Dietrich. That was an unbelievable situation for me. She came to me and told me what tempo she wanted, and where and what I was to play.

I'm back here for the first time since 1946 or '47. In my memory the stage was much bigger [*laughs*]. When I was a child or a little older, Marlene Dietrich was a superstar to me, comparable only to Greta Garbo somehow. And she was the most famous film star here in Germany. She made such wonderful films. *The Blue Angel* is a legend to this day. I saw a few excerpts recently. They were just wonderful. And so here I was playing for her. And I was very impressed by Marlene, I know that still. And above all I thought very highly of her, being a German and a star like she was, that she was against Hitler. Many, many actors went along with it and betrayed their Jewish colleagues. I really thought a lot of her for being so much against that. And I admired her for it.

I know that she had a concert here in 1960, and that many Germans were hostile toward her. But those were . . . what is the right expression? They were these souls stuck forever in the past, who never realized, or didn't want to understand, what the Nazis did. Maybe they were part of it. I didn't get the chance to see her personally, but I read in newspaper articles that many Germans rejected her. It was probably those Germans who were the evildoers and still had not learned anything from it. The others admired her for the strength she had to resist, not like so many of her film colleagues who stayed here and colluded with the Nazis. The decent people admired her for it, and me, too, by the way. But those who were stuck forever in yesterday never forgave her that she didn't stay here during the Nazi time.

There is a well-known journalist named Henryk M. Broder. He told me once, "Coco, they will never forgive us for what they did to us." And these were this scum who were against her.

The fact that she wanted to come back here to be buried—as a Berliner—I can understand that. I immigrated at one time to Australia, but I had my parents and my brother here and my roots, and after a while I came back. I think wherever you're born is where your roots are. So I can understand that she wanted to be buried here. She didn't want to live here probably, but she wanted to be here in death.

I can understand . . . to come back to this land of murderers? It must be inside of you, if you are born here in Berlin, and then you know the other side, then somehow you are homesick. The place of your birth is somehow "home." I have a little trouble with the word "home," but I can understand it, and I think she understood it too.

BEATE KLARSFELD

A journalist, author, and Nazi hunter, BEATE KLARSFELD collaborated with her husband, Serge Klarsfeld, in collecting documentary evidence about Nazi criminals and was thereby able to expose those who had escaped prosecution. Klaus Barbie, the notorious SS officer, was brought to justice because of their dedicated efforts, for which Beate was honored by the Nobel Committee. In 1960 she went to France as an au pair, and was hired as a secretary to the German-French youth council (Jugendwerk). On November 7, 1968, she boxed the ears of the then reigning German chancellor, Georg Kiesinger, during a party convention of the Christian Democratic Union, in order to call public attention to his Nazi past. For that incident she was sentenced to one year in prison. In 1974, the State of Israel bestowed upon her the Medal of Bravery for Ghetto Resistance Fighters. Her friendship with Marlene began during the Barbie trial and lasted until Marlene's death.

For many years I dedicated my life to finding and then exposing Nazi war criminals in order to bring about their deportation and trial. One such person was Klaus Barbie, the "butcher of Lyon," who had deported Jewish children from Lisieux. I had tracked him to Bolivia and after some time managed to get him deported to France for trial. In 1985, at the time of the trial, I got a phone call from Marlene Dietrich. She said, "My dear, I admire your work tracking down these Nazi war criminals." She was following the Barbie trial very closely. I was very honored that Marlene of all people honored my work, a person who was in my eyes not only a great actress, but like me an anti-Nazi activist. Like her, I, too, was a German-born woman who had decided one day to stand up against Nazi Germany, by facing a Nazi propagandist, a chancellor who had a hand in the "final solution" at the Wannsee conference. For a woman like Marlene to congratulate me, well, it was extraordinary.

Marlene was also a woman who was for us women a liberator in other things. She believed women were important, that they had a strong voice. Marlene was a woman who, by wearing her pants, liberated us in our personal lives. She had extraordinary male friends and lovers. But she was not passive. She brought a lot to us, from an artistic point of view but also from her beliefs. She stood for her convictions in many things and it was not because of her fame alone. There were other famous women like Leni Riefenstahl and the pilot Hanna Reich. They allowed themselves to be spoiled by the Nazis. Marlene didn't. She left Germany and proceeded to campaign against them. I think that a lot of Marlene's friends before the war were intellectuals and artists and, as we know, many of them were Jews. Those who left Germany (some later, with her help) and never went back. So Marlene's Germany wasn't the same anymore; it had become so she didn't have the same attachment as from before the war. When she decided to fight against the Nazis, well, the Germans never forgave her for that. I know that myself, because I, too, fight against war criminals.

Marlene had returned to Germany to see her mother and sister right after the war, but her symbolic return to Germany was the first real official event when she came to sing in Berlin. I think it disappointed her terribly. She saw during that tour that Germans were not ready to see in her the woman who had changed the image of Germany in the world. They were blind; they only looked at it from their narrow point of view. They never understood that a woman like Marlene saved Germany's honor, not really as an actress but by fighting against the Nazis, by singing to Allied soldiers and comforting them. It was she, the German, who had done those courageous things, and she felt that few understood her or what she had done. Yes, Germans were coming to her concerts and they were crying, but there were few of them. She knew the importance of her role. I think she was hurt she was the only one. Beyond her career as a star and a singer she had an incredible moral code and a political role worldwide. Marlene cast a bridge between the Germans and those who suffered. She has been honored in all countries, but Germans were not willing to recognize that, maybe until after her death. But while she lived in Paris, there were a thousand ways to lay down a red carpet to make her come back but I think that what was done didn't give her the desire to go back. I think it's the Germans' pettiness; I think she felt it.

The reception she got in Tel Aviv was different from Berlin. Israel was a nation made up of those who had suffered at the hands of the Nazis and they knew the role she had played.

Her concert in Israel, you have to realize, was in

German is sung for the first time in Israel by Marlene, Frederick Mann Auditorium, Tel Aviv, 1966.

front of the victims of Nazis, in front of the people who knew and saw her role in the fight against the Nazis, so when she asked, "Will you allow me to sing in German?" something never before allowed, it was a question asked by a German who had fought against the Nazis—the resistance fighter who was asking to sing to them, not just an extraordinary singer. So of course they were very emotional in front of this woman. And you may even ask just how many of them saw and knew of Marlene before the war, before she left Germany.

In the end I suppose you could say that Marlene had an admiration for my work. From that first day on we were in contact by mail and by phone. She talked to me about her worries. Life was not easy for her. One time she asked me, "Oh, you're going to Berlin? You know, my mother is buried in Berlin. I asked a young man to take care of the grave. Try to check if it's well taken care of." It was next to where I lived in Berlin, so I always went by her mother's grave, and told her it was well cared for. Like I told you, our contact was on the phone; unfortunately, I never saw her physically. During the holidays I had a caterer deliver to her and she would say, "No dessert, I only eat cheese and soup. It's enough to keep me alive!" Often, she had lows and highs, and you could feel it over the phone. It was a woman who always had a very strong voice, who was energetic and her professionalism always came back. I remember one day when Madonna was giving a concert in Paris, at Bercy. "Madonna," Marlene said, "now that's a real professional! She knows how to sing and dance!" So she was interested in everything. I think she read a lot and watched TV because she never left home but stayed connected. I don't think there was another woman like Marlene in Germany or anywhere else in the twentieth century, for that matter.

12. AVENUE MONTAIGNE. 8e

Chère, chère Madame — —
Je vous écris pour vous
dire que je vous admire
et que je vous aime
profondément et je suis
certaine que vous
savez pourquoi!
Comme je suis devenue
athéiste je ne peux pas
dire "Que Dieu vous bénisse"!
Marlene Dietrich

A note from Marlene expressing her profound admiration for Beate. She makes a tongue-in-cheek joke that "since I became an atheist, I can no longer say 'may God bless you.'"

CHER

During Marlene's lifetime there were few stars who she felt approached her style of tenacity and bravado. One of these was international superstar CHER. Although eons younger than my grandmother, Cher was a fashion icon at a young age, and hardly a single outfit of hers escaped Marlene's comment—she herself being a fan of Bob Mackie. Marlene watched Cher's career with interest and took great pride in having forged at least a small part of her path as a female performer, singer, and actress. Cher was able to make the notoriously difficult move from singing to acting seem effortless, and during the 1980s she was box-office dynamite with a run of commercial successes. She received nominations and won highly revered awards for her roles in *Silkwood* (Golden Globe Award, Best Supporting Actress), *Mask* (Cannes Film Festival, Best Actress), and *Moonstruck* (Academy Award, Best Actress). In 2002, Cher launched her worldwide Farewell Tour, which was, by any measure, a phenomen. Cher performed to more than three million fans in 325 concerts, including six sold-out shows at New York's Madison Square Garden. Having mastered virtually every entertainment medium, Cher continues to entertain and remains a pioneering force for the next generation of performers.

The first and only time I encountered Marlene, I was in a fitting at Bob Mackie's. I used to have to stand for hours being fitted for my costumes, and the door—which was five or six feet behind me—was open. I was used to people coming in and asking questions or walking up and down the hall, so I was not paying particularly close attention. But then I saw this woman walk by, and I heard kind of a murmur outside. Then later Bob was talking to me in the fitting and said, "That was Marlene." And I said, "What do you mean, that was Marlene? Why didn't you pinch me or push me in the hallway, make me trip or something like that? I wanted to see her!" And he said, "She just likes her privacy when she comes here." So I saw her, but it was an *instant*—just an instant! And this is the woman that I shaved my eyebrows off because of, you know? She had those teeny, penciled-up eyebrows, so I shaved mine and penciled them in for a whole season. And if you look at some reruns of *The Sonny and Cher Show,* my eyebrows were Marlene Dietrich eyebrows. Bob had given me a coffee table book for Christmas, and I had admired Marlene's photographs and thought, "I need to shave my eyebrows. That's what's missing—that's why I'm not Marlene."

Here's a woman who was not just an actress. I hate to sound cliché, but she was a *legendary* actress—a great, mythological actress as far as her beauty and her spirit. Isn't it fascinating that we're still intrigued by her and that I'm still talking about her? And how many years is this? Her first movies were in the '20s. We're talking eighty years.

Growing up I was *so* influenced by films. But it was my mother who made me appreciative of old black-and-white movies. I was crazy about Marlene from the first time I saw her on the screen. She wasn't necessarily the most beautiful or maybe the most talented, but she was the most charismatic. And actually she was quite a good actress for that time because acting was so stylized. And even though it *was* stylized, she was still quite a natural actress.

The thing that makes someone a star is that they command your attention—no matter who else is on screen. That's what she did, better than almost

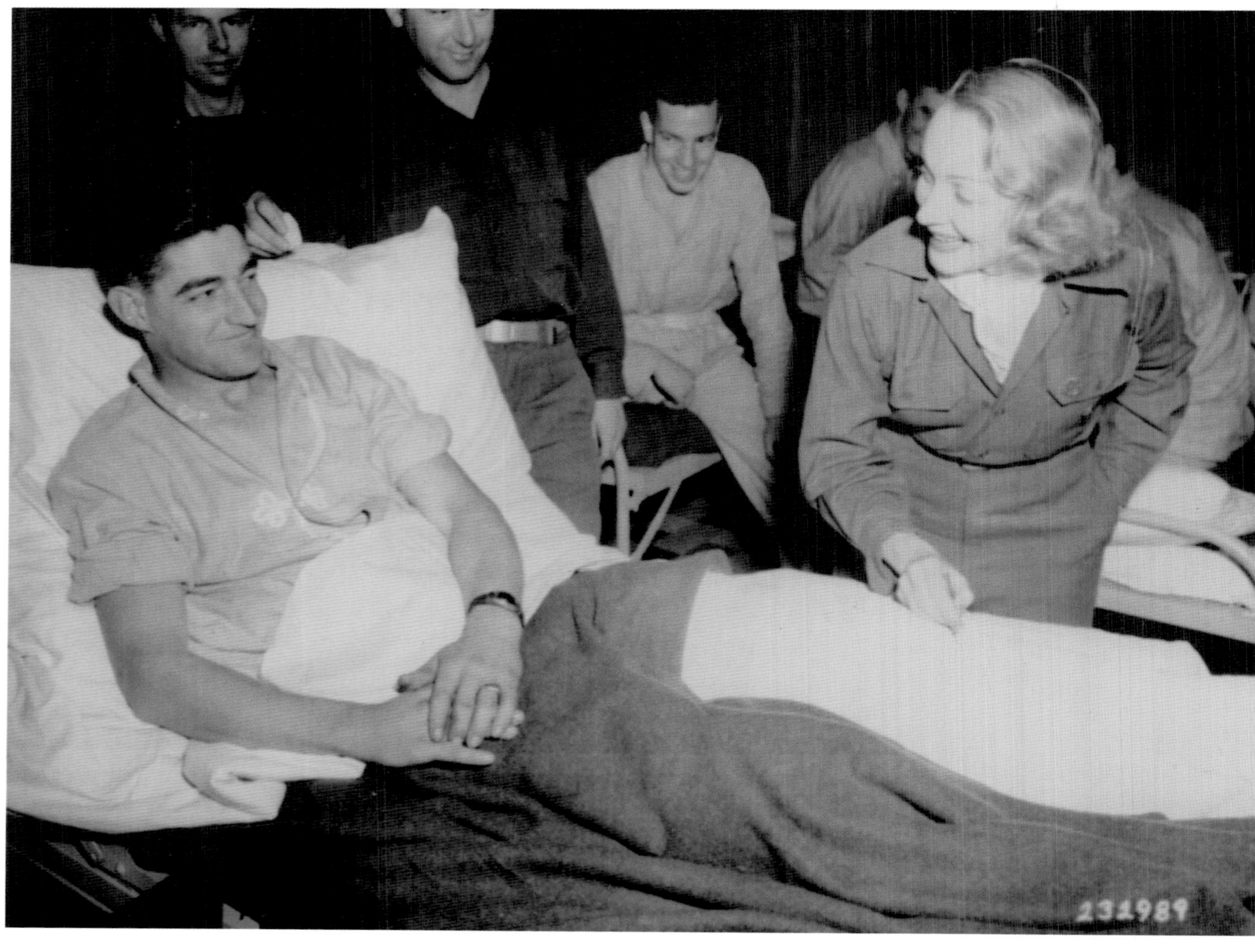

Signing the cast of an American soldier.

anyone. She just *made* you focus on her. She was usually the only woman in the film, even when she wasn't. Like in *A Foreign Affair,* the film she did with Jean Arthur. It's unfair! There's poor Jean Arthur next to Marlene Dietrich. Jean didn't have a chance because she was kind of a frump and certainly was in that movie! With Dietrich, no matter what part she's playing, you're always acutely aware that she's Marlene Dietrich—a huge star and all woman.

Her performance in *A Foreign Affair* always leads me again to think of her as an untapped source—she's funny, and there's a great comedic sense about her. She's raw and she's ironic. This movie and *Golden Earrings,* which seems forgotten now but was a big hit, showed her range. In *Golden Earrings* she's this filthy gypsy woman but wildly funny and still, of course, Dietrich! So that means sex and glamour, even as a crazy gypsy lady. She's poking out fish eyes and all sorts of gross behavior, but she's fantastic and sexy. And I loved her in *Destry Rides Again.* She was wonderful in that, her first big "comeback." She should have done more comedy because she had that light touch. But the end of *Destry* always makes me cry. It's so terrible when she wipes her face, wipes her lips, and looks up at James Stewart—she took the bullet for her man! That shows how good the performance is. She has involved you so much as this rowdy bar girl, you don't want to have that emotional sadness. It's surprising, that emotion. That's what happens. That's great performing.

Marlene's choice of roles was interesting because you could tell she was aware of the process. In earlier films like *The Scarlet Empress,* you see the influence of Joseph von Sternberg—the lighting, everything. He even told her where to look. And you see how adaptable she was. She was a lighting extravaganza in all of her early movies. She would stand there in that glowing halo of light and smoke and then move to another fabulous setup. I think a lot of actresses might have been content to just be a fabulous prop—a glorious puppet. But Marlene was interested in moving past that, and she made interesting choices as she grew as an actress. In *Seven Sinners,* with John Wayne, she plays this shady honky-tonk singer, a Sadie Thompson kind of character—funny, sexy but used up a bit, tough. After *Destry* they said, "Oh, Marlene is great now, she's the goddess pulled off her pedestal." But that honky-tonk type became her new goddess image, and then the war work was another image and her stage shows yet another. In mythology the goddess always changes to suit her whim and what the mortals expect. That was Marlene. She was never pushed off the pedestal, just moved to another one. She had chops and never really got her due as an actress because she had so much sex and glamour. In *Blonde Venus* she was totally convincing as a mother who'd do anything to keep her child. She becomes a hooker! This is a movie where she comes out of a gorilla suit to sing this loony song, "Hot Voodoo." Who else was doing this?! In *Witness for the Prosecution* she was *great* as the cool character, the wife. Then at one point she pretends to be a toothless Cockney hag, and she's fabulous. She took as many chances as her image safely allowed. But she knew the audience wanted Dietrich, and she never let them down. I like it also—maybe because I don't think much of my own voice—that she sang in almost all her movies and then had a huge concert career with no voice, no technical instrument. She was an actress, and she acted her songs, conveyed all the emotions. She was the Bob Dylan of her day. No voice at all!

Marlene was this warhorse too, balls to the wall, tough as they get, going out into the toughest areas of World War II. I always wondered how Marlene felt later, playing the parts she did in *A Foreign Af-*

Marlene's makeshift stage. She comments, "Two trucks and some boards—best stage ever! Even a dressing room!"

fair and *Judgment at Nuremberg,* because it was the absolute antithesis of who she was. I mean, in *A Foreign Affair* her character was a real Nazi! And Marlene was so staunchly pro-Allies and risked her life constantly during the war. She loved being with the soldiers. She would go and sit with people who were in varying degrees of pain or on the verge of death, and from what I understand, nobody did it better. Marlene went there, and she fought alongside these men. She sat with them, she cried with them, she listened to them, she entertained them. She was a German woman—and Prussian to the bone. But she hated Hitler, and she hated what her country had become. She believed in the United States, but she was a German. She must have suffered terribly, fighting her own people. She had that pain, and she made that pain work for her, like all great artists.

When I saw Marlene in some of the clips visiting soldiers in World War II, you could see she was only interested in the person she was talking to, and she was *genuinely* interested. She was committed to the conversation and committed to that person and their life. She visited with German POWs, too. Imagine what that was like for her—and them.

Her war work just proved she had giant, giant balls. I mean balls of steel that probably clanged in her slacks when she walked. Everyone could hear her coming—the sound of her coming into the room probably made a lot of people quake. I'll bet she could be a bitch, too. People want stars to be perfect, and they don't want to look at the part that can get ugly. Well, a lot of times the bigger your personality, the greater you can be and also the greater horse's ass you can be. To have the kind of guts that Marlene had costs something. That doesn't come without someone paying for it, and usually it's the people around you. If you judge her as a person, that's one thing, but if you're judging her for her life as Marlene Dietrich, in that way she was great.

Marlene was a definite precursor to the Women's Liberation Movement. She was a strong woman, had strong female friends, and led her own life and had a career. Men were important to her but not the only thing that made her life worthwhile. And that's the total committed career woman. It's a delicate balance where your career is very important and, yes, you love being a woman and you love having a husband or a boyfriend or a live-in companion. But that's not enough by itself, and being the extension of someone else is not enough. For Marlene, her career was primary, and she needed that career, needed that self-expression. This was paramount to who she was. You might say she lived like a man. But that's only in the context of her time. She lived without compromise. And like Katharine Hepburn, who also "lived like a man," that was an astonishing feat.

A lot of Marlene's craft sprung from her partnership with von Sternberg, and she was in her twenties when she started her career with him in Germany. He formed the initial and eternal image of Dietrich. I identify because I suppose I had a similar thing with Sonny. He completely shaped my early career. After our divorce I moved on, I achieved success apart from him, but the image had been formed. In a way it always went back to Sonny, just as Dietrich always went back to von Sternberg—the essence, the image, if not the person.

Marlene had her husband her whole life, but that was more of a friendship than anything. And I really relate to that, too! Famous women have more trouble finding suitable matches. Famous men can approach anyone, but if you're a famous woman, well, it's something strange. It takes a certain kind of man to be able to approach someone who they think is going to be scary or a little bit dangerous. So—and I love to say this!—like Marlene, I've had a series of fabulous relationships, but I always had to do what I wanted to do and wouldn't have had it any other way. A woman's fame is sometimes hard on relationships. Not sometimes—it always is.

But Marlene approached her life and her art with a real fearlessness! She would do whatever had to be done. Whatever she did, she went all the way. She did not complain, she did not explain—at least not publicly. She paved the way for women like me—she and Bette Davis and Katharine Hepburn. They were not timid, on or off the screen. They took what they wanted, and if they regretted their choices, it was not for public consumption. And she was so *not* timid on-screen—she was the sexiest sex goddess, as far as I'm concerned. She had so much humor, and God knows, sex is funny. But she stood aside from it a little. You didn't sense her screen women were sluts; they were just women involved in life, and sex was part of it. Her characters loved their men, more than the sex act. They were faithful, loyal, strong—very German! Maybe it was her androgynous quality that set her so much apart. Androgynous women, when they're really beautiful, have an amazing quality about them, and Marlene had that. She could go from completely feminine to completely masculine, and never for a second did you not see and feel that sex—and humor!—was right beneath the surface of the costume.

Playing the violin with an outdoor orchestra of soldiers.

Look at *Morocco,* where she was out there in pants and kissing a woman—really shocking for that time. That look changed a lot more than fashion. Just the trousers alone—wearing them made you able to sit and spread your legs. To have that ability gives you a whole different power; it changes the whole dynamic. Marlene could sit, put one elbow on a knee, raise her leg, and be equal to any man. It was an equalizer, and it changed everything. When you break down something, though it may seem like nothing, it's an important step. And if you do it with style or a laugh, it helps.

Marlene lived in a time when women didn't have as many choices, so her boldness presented women a glimpse at the possibilities. It gives hope when others break down barriers—even if they're just working, not getting married again, having younger lovers, wearing pants, or having as important a career as a man has.

But also I understand, in the deepest sense of the word, how hard it is. My sell-by date is so past due, and so was Marlene's. I keep going too, but it's very difficult. It's harder as time goes on—you know, the older you get, the harder it is. But it's also hard to give up something that you love to do. Even though the grind is killing, it's your life and your art. And Marlene's show went on for twenty years! She didn't stop until she was literally physically unable to go on.

Quite late in the game, Marlene was offered an Academy Award for lifetime achievement, but they wouldn't give it to her unless she showed up in person to receive it. And of course, she wouldn't show up. But when you've been the most beautiful woman in the world, how can you knowingly upset that image? Cary Grant had the same problem. He stopped making films because he couldn't be Cary Grant anymore. With a woman, however, it's so much more difficult. It's sad that she couldn't have enjoyed the end more—that her life force had to withdraw and start to dim because she was ashamed of letting people see something that she didn't want them to see. She wanted to preserve an earlier image of herself to keep her dignity in some sort of strange way. It's odd, the relationship the audience has with celebrities they attach to. The devotion of audience to image points out this sometimes superficial life that we have chosen.

But age has nothing to do with the legend. The legend defies time and even fact and flies into myth. The great thing to cherish about film and its preservation is that Marlene is always going to be the way she was in her movies—this incredible, talented figure of glamour and sex, and she was the best of all of them, truthfully. I liked Garbo, but she wasn't as sexy and I didn't think she was as interestingly beautiful. And she was *so* serious—always a suicide waiting to happen in her films. Marlene Dietrich was all stylized and artificial and yet very real and humorous and tender under the illusion. You had to pay attention, get past the feathers and beads, but her humanity was there. I started out saying I hated resorting to cliché, but I have to end with it too—there'll never be another like her. But a cliché is a cliché because it is true.

Talking about her is amazing and intimidating—just as she herself was! I feel like saying, "I'm not worthy," you know? It reminds me of the little role she did for Orson Welles as the fortune teller in *Touch of Evil.* Her last line is, "What does it matter, what you *say* about people?" I suppose it doesn't matter because people make up their own minds, but I'm proud to have gone on record. She made a difference, she made a sound, she made a statement. She made a little girl watching TV very happy, and she helped that little girl see the possibilities and dream the big dream.

She came out of that gorilla suit in *Blonde Venus* and went right into my head. She's still there.

MICHAEL NAUMANN

After earning his doctorate with a study about the Austrian satirist Karl Kraus, German journalist **MICHAEL NAUMANN** worked as an editor and foreign correspondent for two German weeklies, *Die Zeit* and *Spiegel.* He took over the Rowohlt-Verlag publishing house in 1985, and ten years later went to New York, where he became the publishing director for both Metropolitan Books and Henry Holt. In 1998 the chancellor of the German Federal Republic, Gerhard Schröder, appointed him minister of the newly created cabinet post for culture and media. He returned to *Die Zeit* in 2001 as the newspaper's publisher and became the editor-in-chief in 2004. We met during his tenure as Minister of Culture for Germany at a visit to the Filmmuseum Berlin, the repository of the world's largest collection of Dietrich memorabilia.

Of course, I remember many Marlene Dietrich films, especially *Witness for the Prosecution.* It was a film in which a great diva had the courage to look ugly, but beyond that, it showed the acting skill that she had. I thought it was a thrilling film. And then, of course, *The Blue Angel.*

Marlene Dietrich was probably the first self-created work of art in the history of film. That is, she knew the laws of media early on, which she drew upon and in part created. She styled herself into a media stereotype, as people like Cher have become to some degree nowadays. She was a woman who did not reconstruct her face with surgery but with a very gradual process of makeup changes, until she became a face of your dreams. She herself said that over time it was "photographed away," and "photographed to its death." That's why at the end of her life she had to go into seclusion, to hide. She no longer matched the myth of herself. But in Germany at least, she embodied the film industry like nobody else. On top of all this she remained a person who, above all, at the height of her career, destroyed the cliché of a Hollywood star. She was no bimbo, no sweet, dumb little blond. She was more egocentric, flaunted her erotic impulses, and had a high political sensibility. On top of that, she was moral—politically moral—quite a distinct person. To have all this embodied in an actress was her essence. It created something then that we Germans had bitter need of. But she wasn't there anymore, and she made the right decision at that time.

Marlene Dietrich was, as odd as it sounds, an ethical star. You wouldn't believe it, but there is such a thing. She was a highly political person, who made the right decision when other people were still in doubt about what National Socialism would bring. There are many reasons for this. One of the reasons was surely that as an actor, she was able to recognize the bad traits in other actors. She saw the cleverness, but also saw the completely vulgar exploitation of the new mass media of film and radio by actors who were political pawns. She knew who these people were, she noticed what roles they played, and thought, "This is an evil soul." That's why she didn't come back, why she made this political decision and moved to California. It was where many other representatives of this "other Germany" were living, like the Manns, Bertolt Brecht, and all the rest.

When she decided to come back with the American Army to attend to the troops, it was sickening to many Germans here who still idealized the old system. But for her, this "stupidity" that waged demonstrations against her was *never* confused with the Germany that *she* stood for. And her love of Berlin, her nostalgic, sentimental love of Ber-

In 1989 a square was named for Dietrich across from the site of the Berlin Film Festival and near the Filmmuseum Berlin, in Potsdamer Platz.

lin, is manifested in the fact that she decided to be buried here in the family grave. For that, I have an enormous respect for her. In her lifetime she was a torn person, even in her private life. But one thing was always clear for her. She stayed a Berliner, but she was a Berliner from the other, better city, which, thank God, with the help of the Allied troops, won out in the end, against its old ego, fascism.

Marlene Dietrich was misunderstood by German postwar politicians, to put it mildly. Like Willy Brandt and many other politicians, she contributed her part toward victory over National Socialism. But her public was not the political parties, but the masses. The masses had great difficulty in the '40s and '50s in admitting, first, that they were dumb, and second, that they were part of a criminal system. Marlene Dietrich knew that clearly. The question is, how was she treated in the '50s and '60s? She had triumphant tours in this country. Since then I think the dissension about her and her politics has been disinherited. A new generation of fans of this great actress has filled those shoes, together with those who *always* thought her decision was the right one. Admiration for her continues to grow, posthumously, and we in Berlin recognize her double role. She was an interesting politician, that is, a very politically involved actress, and she was one of Germany's greatest world stars. Now, in Berlin, we have dedicated this profound museum to her. She was an avid collector, who kept practically all her things throughout her life, and Berlin, with the help of the government and many others, saw to it that this collection came to Berlin. It is now part of the museum, which I find to be one of a kind. Items from international film history are gathered here, some of which are very moving, very touching. I believe that in the foreseeable future, our memories and notions of this woman will not ebb, but they will grow, as she deserves.

The Filmmuseum Berlin, Marlene Dietrich Collection, houses the largest collection of Marlene Dietrich memorabilia in the world.

AFTERWORD

After my brief encounter with Marlene Dietrich in Belgium during the winter of 1944–45, I did not think that I, in civilian life an upper-division undergraduate (and an itinerant waiter after classes), would ever see her again. And yet it turned out otherwise. As an instructor at Columbia some dozen years later I became a close friend of Lotte Lenya and George Davis, her second husband. In the summer of 1956, Lenya asked me to escort her to one of her performances at the City College of New York. En route from her apartment in Tudor City, I learned that I would be seated next to Dietrich. Dietrich had no personal recollection of Staff Sergeant Stern, but she remembered clearly, as we reminisced, many of the details of that memorable day in the vicinity of a provincial town in Belgium during that "winter of our despair." After Dietrich and I had clapped for Lenya in unison and left for intermission, she said, "There is no audience with whom I have been more in tune than you boys in the U.S. Army."

I have been an aficionado of Marlene Dietrich ever since and was thrilled when, years later, I was granted the opportunity to share the story of my encounter. I received a call from Dr. Heike Klapdor, an old friend and, incidentally, a trustee of Deutsche Kinemathek, Berlin's famous film museum and home to the largest collection of Dietrich's films, costumes, and props anywhere. "Guy," she said excitedly, "we had a call from David Riva, the grandson of Marlene. He asked for the use of our archive for his project about her. And he also requested names of U.S. soldiers who may have wartime recollections of her. We gave him your name."

The expected call from Los Angeles came several months later. "We heard of you through the Kinemathek in Berlin. Could we interview you?" I had known for months, ever since Heike's call, what my answer would be.

David was at work on a collected volume of essays and interviews with people who knew his grandmother, and he had thus far been disappointed with prospective publishers all wishing to sensationalize Marlene. I suggested this project to Wayne State University Press, which turned out to be more than appropriate. David's own father, William Riva, was an alumnus of Wayne State, and his mother, Maria, was thrilled to have her late husband's university involved in the project.

David later sent me a very flattering note, which gratified me as much as academic accolades: "You have added the kind of magic to our story which she would have appreciated." I am deeply honored to have been a part of this exciting collection of essays. Nothing pleases me more than to have been given the opportunity to participate in this thoughtful tribute to the legendary Marlene.

GUY STERN